California
HMH SCIENCE DIMENSIONS™
Volume 3

Grade 6
Units 5–6

Watch the cover come alive as you explore the body systems of a snail.

Download the HMH Science Dimensions AR app available on Android or iOS devices.

This Write-In Book belongs to

_____

Teacher/Room

_____

Houghton Mifflin Harcourt™

Consulting Authors

Michael A. DiSpezio

Global Educator
North Falmouth,
Massachusetts

Michael DiSpezio has authored many HMH instructional programs for Science and Mathematics. He has also authored numerous trade books and multimedia programs on various topics and hosted dozens of studio and location broadcasts for various organizations in the United States and worldwide. Most recently, he has been working with educators to provide strategies for implementing the Next Generation Science Standards, particularly the Science and Engineering Practices, Crosscutting Concepts, and the use of Evidence Notebooks. To all his projects, he brings his extensive background in science, his expertise in classroom teaching at the elementary, middle, and high school levels, and his deep experience in producing interactive and engaging instructional materials.

Marjorie Frank

Science Writer and Content-Area Reading Specialist
Brooklyn, New York

An educator and linguist by training, a writer and poet by nature, Marjorie Frank has authored and designed a generation of instructional materials in all subject areas, including past HMH Science programs. Her other credits include authoring science issues of an award-winning children's magazine, writing game-based digital assessments, developing blended learning materials for young children, and serving as instructional designer and coauthor of pioneering school-to-work software. In addition, she has served on the adjunct faculty of Hunter, Manhattan, and Brooklyn Colleges, teaching courses in science methods, literacy, and writing. For *California HMH Science Dimensions™*, she has guided the development of our K–2 strands and our approach to making connections between NGSS and Common Core ELA/literacy standards.

Acknowledgments

Cover credits: (garden snail) ©Johan Swanepoel/Alamy; (poison dart frog) ©Dirk Ercken/Alamy.

Section Header Master Art: (machinations) ©DNY59/E+/Getty Images; (rivers on top of Greenland ice sheet) ©Maria-José Viñas, NASA Earth Science News Team; (human cells, illustration) ©Sebastian Kaulitzki/Science Photo Library/Corbis; (waves) ©Alfred Pasieka/Science Source

Michael R. Heithaus, PhD

Dean, College of Arts, Sciences & Education Professor, Department of Biological Sciences
Florida International University
Miami, Florida

Mike Heithaus joined the FIU Biology Department in 2003 and has served as Director of the Marine Sciences Program and Executive Director of the School of Environment, Arts, and Society, which brings together the natural and social sciences and humanities to develop solutions to today's environmental challenges. He now serves as Dean of the College of Arts, Sciences & Education. His research focuses on predator-prey interactions and the ecological importance of large marine species. He has helped to guide the development of Life Science content in *California HMH Science Dimensions™*, with a focus on strategies for teaching challenging content as well as the science and engineering practices of analyzing data and using computational thinking.

Bernadine Okoro

Access and Equity Consultant

S.T.E.M. Learning Advocate & Consultant
Washington, DC

Bernadine Okoro is a chemical engineer by training and a playwright, novelist, director, and actress by nature. Okoro went from working with patents and biotechnology to teaching in K–12 classrooms. A 12-year science educator and Albert Einstein Distinguished Fellow, Okoro was one of the original authors of the Next Generation Science Standards. As a member of the Diversity and Equity Team, her focus on Alternative Education and Community Schools and on Integrating Social-Emotional Learning and Brain-Based Learning into NGSS is the vehicle she uses as a pathway to support underserved groups from elementary school to adult education. An article and book reviewer for NSTA and other educational publishing companies, Okoro currently works as a S.T.E.M. Learning Advocate & Consultant.

Cary I. Sneider, PhD

Associate Research Professor
Portland State University
Portland, Oregon

While studying astrophysics at Harvard, Cary Sneider volunteered to teach in an Upward Bound program and discovered his real calling as a science teacher. After teaching middle and high school science in Maine, California, Costa Rica, and Micronesia, he settled for nearly three decades at Lawrence Hall of Science in Berkeley, California, where he developed skills in curriculum development and teacher education. Over his career, Cary directed more than 20 federal, state, and foundation grant projects and was a writing team leader for the Next Generation Science Standards. He has been instrumental in ensuring *California HMH Science Dimensions™* meets the high expectations of the NGSS and provides an effective three-dimensional learning experience for all students.

Program Advisors

Paul D. Asimow, PhD
Eleanor and John R. McMillan
Professor of Geology and
Geochemistry
California Institute of Technology
Pasadena, California

Joanne Bourgeois
Professor Emerita
Earth & Space Sciences
University of Washington
Seattle, WA

Dr. Eileen Cashman
Professor
Humboldt State University
Arcata, California

Elizabeth A. De Stasio, PhD
Raymond J. Herzog Professor of
Science
Lawrence University
Appleton, Wisconsin

Perry Donham, PhD
Lecturer
Boston University
Boston, Massachusetts

Shila Garg, PhD
Professor Emerita of Physics
Former Dean of Faculty & Provost
The College of Wooster
Wooster, Ohio

Tatiana A. Krivosheev, PhD
Professor of Physics
Clayton State University
Morrow, Georgia

Mark B. Moldwin, PhD
Professor of Space Sciences and
Engineering
University of Michigan
Ann Arbor, Michigan

Ross H. Nehm
Stony Brook University (SUNY)
Stony Brook, NY

Kelly Y. Neiles, PhD
Assistant Professor of Chemistry
St. Mary's College of Maryland
St. Mary's City, Maryland

John Nielsen-Gammon, PhD
Regents Professor
Department of Atmospheric
Sciences
Texas A&M University
College Station, Texas

Dr. Sten Odenwald
Astronomer
NASA Goddard Spaceflight Center
Greenbelt, Maryland

Bruce W. Schafer
Executive Director
Oregon Robotics Tournament &
Outreach Program
Beaverton, Oregon

Barry A. Van Deman
President and CEO
Museum of Life and Science
Durham, North Carolina

Kim Withers, PhD
Assistant Professor
Texas A&M University-Corpus
Christi
Corpus Christi, Texas

Adam D. Woods, PhD
Professor
California State University,
Fullerton
Fullerton, California

English Development Advisors

Mercy D. Momary
Local District Northwest
Los Angeles, California

Michelle Sullivan
Balboa Elementary
San Diego, California

Lab Safety Reviewer

Kenneth R. Roy, Ph.D.
Senior Lab Safety Compliance Consultant
National Safety Consultants, LLC
Vernon, Connecticut

Classroom Reviewers & Hands-On Activities Advisors

Julie Arreola
Sun Valley Magnet School
Sun Valley, California

Pamela Bluestein
Sycamore Canyon School
Newbury Park, California

Andrea Brown
HLPUSD Science & STEAM TOSA
Hacienda Heights, California

Stephanie Greene
Science Department Chair
Sun Valley Magnet School
Sun Valley, California

Rana Mujtaba Khan
Will Rogers High School
Van Nuys, California

Suzanne Kirkhope
Willow Elementary and Round
Meadow Elementary
Agoura Hills, California

George Kwong
Schafer Park Elementary
Hayward, California

Imelda Madrid
Bassett St. Elementary School
Lake Balboa, California

Susana Martinez O'Brien
Diocese of San Diego
San Diego, California

Craig Moss
Mt. Gleason Middle School
Sunland, California

Isabel Souto
Schafer Park Elementary
Hayward, California

Emily R.C.G. Williams
South Pasadena Middle School
South Pasadena, California

© Houghton Mifflin Harcourt Publishing Company • Image Credits: ©Tyler Olson/Shutterstock

VOLUME 1

UNIT 1 Science and Engineering   1

Lesson 1 • Engineering, Science, and Society Are Related 4

   Hands-On Lab   Investigate a Technology Inspired by Nature 19

Lesson 2 • Engineer It: Defining Engineering Problems 26

   Hands-On Lab   Design a Model Car, Part 1 37

Lesson 3 • Engineer It: Developing and Testing Solutions 44

   Hands-On Lab   Design a Model Car, Part 2 54

Lesson 4 • Engineer It: Optimizing Solutions 62

   Hands-On Lab   Design a Model Car, Part 3 71

     People in Engineering   Ellen Ochoa, Electrical Engineer 73

Unit Review 79

ENGINEER IT   Unit Performance Task 83

UNIT 2 Systems in Organisms and Earth   85

Lesson 1 • Models Help Scientists Study Natural Systems 88

   Hands-On Lab   Model Tissue Structure and Function 94

Lesson 2 • Cells Are Living Systems 108

   Hands-On Lab   Observe Cells with a Microscope 113

   Hands-On Lab   Use Cell Models to Investigate Cell Size 120

     People in Science   Lynn Margulis, Biologist 123

Lesson 3 • Plants Are Living Systems 128

   Hands-On Lab   Observe Transport 135

Lesson 4 • Animals Are Living Systems 144

   Hands-On Lab   Measure System Response to Exercise 150

   Hands-On Lab   Measure Reaction Time 159

Unit Review 167

ENGINEER IT   Unit Performance Task 171

© Houghton Mifflin Harcourt Publishing Company • Image Credits: (t) ©Ryan McVay/ Stone/Getty Image; (b) ©Kotangens/Adobe Stock

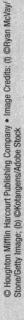

VOLUME 2

UNIT 3 The Flow of Energy in Systems

173

Lesson 1 • Energy Flows and Causes Change 176

 Hands-On Lab Investigate the Transfer of Energy 185

Lesson 2 • Heat Is a Flow of Energy 198

Hands-On Lab Compare Thermal Energy in Objects 204

Lesson 3 • Engineer It: Using Thermal Energy Transfer in Systems 216

Hands-On Lab Examine the Transfer of Thermal Energy through Radiation 222

Hands-On Lab Design and Test an Insulated Container 229

Careers in Engineering Energy Conservationist 231

Lesson 4 • Changes in Energy Drive the Water Cycle 236

Hands-On Lab Model the Formation of Clouds and Rain 243

Careers in Science Hydrologist 253

Unit Review 259

ENGINEER IT Unit Performance Task 263

© Houghton Mifflin Harcourt Publishing Company • Image Credits: ©Johnny Adolphson/Dreamstime

Flash floods can occur suddenly after a heavy rainfall. A lot of energy is released during a flash flood.

VOLUME 2

UNIT 4 Weather and Climate   265

Lesson 1 • Air Moves in Patterns in Earth's Atmosphere 268

Hands-On Lab Model the Formation of Wind 271

Lesson 2 • Water Moves in Patterns in Earth's Oceans 288

Hands-On Lab Explore Density Differences in Water 295

Careers in Science Physical Oceanographer 305

Lesson 3 • Interactions in Earth's Systems Cause Weather 310

Hands-On Lab Model an Air Mass Interaction 320

Lesson 4 • Weather Predictions Are Based on Patterns 332

Hands-On Lab Predict Costs Using a Model 337

People in Science J. Marshall Shepherd, Meteorologist and Climatologist 345

Lesson 5 • Earth Has Different Regional Climates 350

Hands-On Lab Model Your Climate 363

Unit Review 373

ENGINEER IT Unit Performance Task 377

Foggy summer mornings in San Francisco happen as water from the Pacific Ocean evaporates into the air and then condenses. Wind carries the foggy air over land.

VOLUME 3
UNIT 5 Environmental and Genetic Influence on Organisms 379

Lesson 1 • Organisms Are Adapted to Their Environment 382

Hands-On Lab Compare the Drought Tolerance of Plants 389

People in Science Dr. Gary Bañuelos, Soil Scientist..................................395

Lesson 2 • Organisms Inherit Traits from Their Parents 400

Hands-On Lab Model Genes and Traits...406

People in Science Genetic Engineers 411

Lesson 3 • Reproduction Affects Genetic Diversity 416

Hands-On Lab Model Asexual and Sexual Reproduction.............................426

Lesson 4 • The Environment and Genetics Affect Plant Survival 434

Hands-On Lab Investigate Flower Structures 443

Lesson 5 • The Environment and Genetics Affect Animal Survival 456

Hands-On Lab Model the Growth of an Animal 471

Unit Review 479

Unit Performance Task 483

This plumage display of a male bird of paradise attracts the female. With their needs met by the rich tropical rain forest, birds of paradise can spend extra time and energy on reproduction.

© Houghton Mifflin Harcourt Publishing Company • Image Credits: ©Tim Laman/National Geographic Magazines/Getty Images

VOLUME 3

UNIT 6 Human Impacts on the Environment

485

Lesson 1 • Human Activities Cause Changes in the Environment....................488

Hands-On Lab Model Ocean Pollution from Land 494

Lesson 2 • Human Activities Influence Climate Change 508

Hands-On Lab Model the Greenhouse Effect 512

People in Science Geeta G. Persad, Postdoctoral Research Scientist 527

Lesson 3 • Climate Change Affects the Survival of Organisms......................532

Hands-On Lab Map Monarch Migration 540

People in Science Shayle Matsuda, Marine Biologist 547

Lesson 4 • Engineer It: Reducing Human Impacts on the Environment.............552

Hands-On Lab Design a Method to Monitor Solid Waste from a School................561

Hands-On Lab Evaluate a Method to Reduce the Impact of Solid
Waste on the Environment...569

Unit Review..577

Unit Performance Task 581

© Houghton Mifflin Harcourt Publishing Company • Image Credits: ©WhitcombeRD/Adobe Stock

A lot of plastic trash ends up in the oceans, where it affects many organisms, such as plankton, corals, fish, and whales.

Claims, Evidence, and Reasoning

Constructing an Argument

Constructing a strong argument is useful in science and engineering and in everyday life. A strong argument has three parts: a claim, evidence, and reasoning. Scientists and engineers use claims-evidence-reasoning arguments to communicate their explanations and solutions to others and to challenge or debate the conclusions of other scientists and engineers. The words *argue* and *argument* do not mean that scientists or engineers are fighting about something. Instead, this is a way to support a claim using evidence. Argumentation is a calm and rational way for people to examine all the facts and come to the best conclusion.

A **claim** is a statement that answers the question "What do you know?" A claim is a statement of your understanding of a phenomenon, answer to a question, or solution to a problem. A claim states what you think is true based on the information you have.

Evidence is any data that are related to your claim and answer the question "How do you know that?" These data may be from your own experiments and observations, reports by scientists or engineers, or other reliable data. Arguments made in science and engineering should be supported by empirical evidence. Empirical evidence is evidence that comes from observation or experiment.

Evidence used to support a claim should also be relevant and sufficient. Relevant evidence is evidence that is about the claim, and not about something else. Evidence is sufficient when there is enough evidence to fully support the claim.

Reasoning is the use of logical, analytical thought to form conclusions or inferences. Reasoning answers the question "Why does your evidence support your claim?" So, reasoning explains the relationship between your evidence and your claim. Reasoning might include a scientific law or principle that helps explain the relationship between the evidence and the claim.

© Houghton Mifflin Harcourt Publishing Company • Image Credits: ©HMH

Here is an example of a claims-evidence-reasoning argument.

Claim	Ice melts faster in the sun than it does in the shade.
Evidence	Two ice cubes of the same size were each placed in a plastic dish. One dish was placed on a wooden bench in the sun and one was placed on a different part of the same bench in the shade. The ice cube in the sun melted in 14 minutes and 32 seconds. The ice cube in the shade melted in 18 minutes and 15 seconds.
Reasoning	This experiment was designed so that the only variable that was different in the set-up of the two ice cubes was whether they were in the shade or in the sun. Because the ice cube in the sun melted almost 4 minutes faster than the one in the shade, this is sufficient evidence to say that ice melts faster in the sun than it does in the shade.

To summarize, a strong argument:

- presents a claim that is clear, logical, and well-defended
- supports the claim with empirical evidence that is sufficient and relevant
- includes reasons that make sense and are presented in a logical order

Constructing Your Own Argument

Now construct your own argument by recording a claim, evidence, and reasoning. With your teacher's permission, you can do an investigation to answer a question you have about how the world works. Or you can construct your argument based on observations you have already made about the world.

Claim	
Evidence	
Reasoning	

 For more information on claims, evidence, and reasoning, see the online **English Language Arts Handbook.**

Whether you are in the lab or in the field, you are responsible for your own safety and the safety of others. To fulfill these responsibilities and avoid accidents, be aware of the safety of your classmates as well as your own safety at all times. Take your lab work and fieldwork seriously, and behave appropriately. Elements of safety to keep in mind are shown below and on the following pages.

Safety in the Lab

☐ Be sure you understand the materials, your procedure, and the safety rules before you start an investigation in the lab.

☐ Know where to find and how to use fire extinguishers, eyewash stations, shower stations, and emergency power shutoffs.

☐ Use proper safety equipment. Always wear personal protective equipment, such as eye protection and gloves, when setting up labs, during labs, and when cleaning up.

☐ Do not begin until your teacher has told you to start. Follow directions.

☐ Keep the lab neat and uncluttered. Clean up when you are finished. Report all spills to your teacher immediately. Watch for slip/fall and trip/fall hazards.

☐ If you or another student is injured in any way, tell your teacher immediately, even if the injury seems minor.

☐ Do not take any food or drink into the lab. Never take any chemicals out of the lab.

Safety in the Field

☐ Be sure you understand the goal of your fieldwork and the proper way to carry out the investigation before you begin fieldwork.

☐ Use proper safety equipment and personal protective equipment, such as eye protection, that suits the terrain and the weather.

☐ Follow directions, including appropriate safety procedures as provided by your teacher.

☐ Do not approach or touch wild animals. Do not touch plants unless instructed by your teacher to do so. Leave natural areas as you found them.

☐ Stay with your group.

☐ Use proper accident procedures, and let your teacher know about a hazard in the environment or an accident immediately, even if the hazard or accident seems minor.

Safety Symbols

To highlight specific types of precautions, the following symbols are used throughout the lab program. Remember that no matter what safety symbols you see within each lab, all safety rules should be followed at all times.

Dress Code

- Wear safety goggles (or safety glasses as appropriate for the activity) at all times in the lab as directed. If chemicals get into your eye, flush your eyes immediately for a minimum of 15 minutes.
- Do not wear contact lenses in the lab.
- Do not look directly at the sun or any intense light source or laser.
- Wear appropriate protective non-latex gloves as directed.
- Wear an apron or lab coat at all times in the lab as directed.
- Tie back long hair, secure loose clothing, and remove loose jewelry. Remove acrylic nails when working with active flames.
- Do not wear open-toed shoes, sandals, or canvas shoes in the lab.

Glassware and Sharp Object Safety

- Do not use chipped or cracked glassware.
- Use heat-resistant glassware for heating or storing hot materials.
- Notify your teacher immediately if a piece of glass breaks.
- Use extreme care when handling any sharp or pointed instruments.
- Do not cut an object while holding the object unsupported in your hands. Place the object on a suitable cutting surface, and always cut in a direction away from your body.

Chemical Safety

- If a chemical gets on your skin, on your clothing, or in your eyes, rinse it immediately for a minimum of 15 minutes (using the shower, faucet, or eyewash station), and alert your teacher.
- Do not clean up spilled chemicals unless your teacher directs you to do so.
- Do not inhale any gas or vapor unless directed to do so by your teacher. If you are instructed to note the odor of a substance, wave the fumes toward your nose with your hand. This is called wafting. Never put your nose close to the source of the odor.
- Handle materials that emit vapors or gases in a well-ventilated area.
- Keep your hands away from your face while you are working on any activity.

Safety Symbols, continued

Electrical Safety

- Do not use equipment with frayed electrical cords or loose plugs.
- Do not use electrical equipment near water or when clothing or hands are wet.
- Hold the plug housing when you plug in or unplug equipment. Do not pull on the cord.
- Use only GFI-protected electrical receptacles.

Heating and Fire Safety

- Be aware of any source of flames, sparks, or heat (such as flames, heating coils, or hot plates) before working with any flammable substances.
- Know the location of the lab's fire extinguisher and fire-safety blankets.
- Know your school's fire-evacuation routes.
- If your clothing catches on fire, walk to the lab shower to put out the fire. Do not run.
- Never leave a hot plate unattended while it is turned on or while it is cooling.
- Use tongs or appropriately insulated holders when handling heated objects.
- Allow all equipment to cool before storing it.

Plant and Animal Safety

- Do not eat any part of a plant.
- Do not pick any wild plant unless your teacher instructs you to do so.
- Handle animals only as your teacher directs.
- Treat animals carefully and respectfully.
- Wash your hands thoroughly with soap and water after handling any plant or animal.

Cleanup

- Clean all work surfaces and protective equipment as directed by your teacher.
- Dispose of hazardous materials or sharp objects only as directed by your teacher.
- Wash your hands thoroughly with soap and water before you leave the lab or after any activity.

© Houghton Mifflin Harcourt Publishing Company

Name: _____ **Date:** _____

Student Safety Quiz

Circle the letter of the BEST answer.

1. Before starting an investigation or lab procedure, you should
   A. try an experiment of your own
   B. open all containers and packages
   C. read all directions and make sure you understand them
   D. handle all the equipment to become familiar with it

2. At the end of any activity you should
   A. wash your hands thoroughly with soap and water before leaving the lab
   B. cover your face with your hands
   C. put on your safety goggles
   D. leave hot plates switched on

3. If you get hurt or injured in any way, you should
   A. tell your teacher immediately
   B. find bandages or a first aid kit
   C. go to your principal's office
   D. get help after you finish the lab

4. If your glassware is chipped or broken, you should
   A. use it only for solid materials
   B. give it to your teacher for recycling or disposal
   C. put it back into the storage cabinet
   D. increase the damage so that it is obvious

5. If you have unused chemicals after finishing a procedure, you should
   A. pour them down a sink or drain
   B. mix them all together in a bucket
   C. put them back into their original containers
   D. dispose of them as directed by your teacher

6. If electrical equipment has a frayed cord, you should
   A. unplug the equipment by pulling the cord
   B. let the cord hang over the side of a counter or table
   C. tell your teacher about the problem immediately
   D. wrap tape around the cord to repair it

7. If you need to determine the odor of a chemical or a solution, you should
   A. use your hand to bring fumes from the container to your nose
   B. bring the container under your nose and inhale deeply
   C. tell your teacher immediately
   D. use odor-sensing equipment

8. When working with materials that might fly into the air and hurt someone's eye, you should wear
   A. goggles
   B. an apron
   C. gloves
   D. a hat

9. Before doing experiments involving a heat source, you should know the location of the
   A. door
   B. window
   C. fire extinguisher
   D. overhead lights

10. If you get chemicals in your eye you should
    A. wash your hands immediately
    B. put the lid back on the chemical container
    C. wait to see if your eye becomes irritated
    D. use the eyewash station right away, for a minimum of 15 minutes

Go online to view the Lab Safety Handbook for additional information.

© Houghton Mifflin Harcourt Publishing Company

XV

Environmental and Genetic Influence on Organisms

How do the environment and genetics influence the traits of organisms?

Unit Project 380
Lesson 1   Organisms Are Adapted to Their Environment. 382
Lesson 2   Organisms Inherit Traits from Their Parents 400
Lesson 3   Reproduction Affects Genetic Diversity 416
Lesson 4   The Environment and Genetics Affect Plant Survival 434
Lesson 5   The Environment and Genetics Affect Animal Survival 456
Unit Review 479
Unit Performance Task 483

This plumage display of a male bird of paradise attracts the female. With their needs met by the rich tropical rain forest, birds of paradise can spend extra time and energy on reproduction.

You Solve It What Factors Affect Reproductive Success?

Analyze reproduction in a group of peacocks and peahens to see how genetic and environmental factors affect the number of offspring that survive.

Go online and complete the You Solve It to explore ways to solve a real-world problem.

Investigate Unique Reproductive Behaviors

A. Look at the photo. On a separate sheet of paper, write down as many different questions as you can about the photo.

B. Discuss With your class or a partner, share your questions. Record any additional questions generated in your discussion. Then choose the most important questions from the list that are related to how the unique reproductive behaviors of an animal are linked to the environment in which it lives. Write them below.

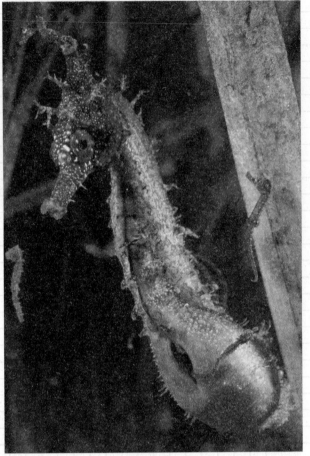

Male seahorses have a brood pouch on their fronts. The female deposits eggs in this pouch, and the male carries the eggs until the baby seahorses are born.

C. Choose an animal with a unique reproductive behavior to research. Here is a list of animals you can consider:

platypus	Monarch butterfly
desert spider	Emperor penguin
coral	Pacific salmon
alligator	brown-headed cowbird

D. Use the information above and your research to create a presentation that describes the unique reproductive behavior of your chosen animal and how that behavior is linked to the environment in which your animal lives.

 Discuss the next steps for your Unit Project with your teacher and go online to download the Unit Project Worksheet.

Language Development

Use the lessons in this unit to complete the network and expand your understanding of these key concepts.

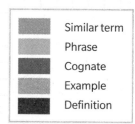

	Similar term
	Phrase
	Cognate
	Example
	Definition

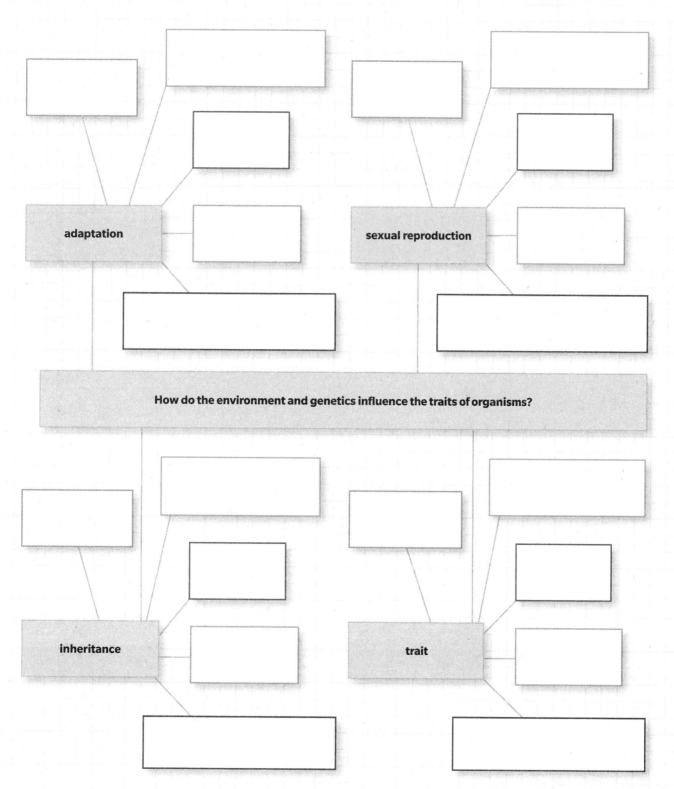

adaptation

sexual reproduction

How do the environment and genetics influence the traits of organisms?

inheritance

trait

© Houghton Mifflin Harcourt Publishing Company

Organisms Are Adapted to Their Environment

Ocotillos, such as this one from Anza-Borrego Desert State Park in California, are tall, thin plants that live in a dry desert environment. They grow small green leaves and bright red flowers after rainfall.

Explore First

Contrasting Plant Types Examine a succulent and a nonsucculent plant. List your observations about each plant. Which plant do you think would survive with less water? Why?

Go online to view the digital version of the Hands-On Lab for this lesson and to download additional lab resources.

CAN YOU EXPLAIN IT?

Why do Emperor penguins and roadrunners live in different areas of the world?

Emperor penguins

roadrunner

The Emperor penguin has many characteristics that allow it to live in Antarctica and survive some of the coldest temperatures on Earth. For example, the penguins have feathers and fat to conserve body heat. The greater roadrunner has characteristics that allow it to survive in the desert. For example, roadrunners get rid of excess salt through glands near their eyes. This allows them to conserve water and live in dry areas.

Explore Online

1. Describe the conditions where Emperor penguins and roadrunners live. Use the information from the descriptions and what you can observe from the pictures.

2. Describe the characteristics of plants or animals that would help them survive in the conditions you observed.

 EVIDENCE NOTEBOOK As you explore the lesson, gather evidence to help explain why Emperor penguins and roadrunners live in different areas of the world.

Analyzing Factors that Determine Climate

If you travel to a new place, you may experience a different climate. Alaska is known for its cold winters and snow. The Sahara Desert in Africa is known for its hot temperatures and lack of rain. Regions on Earth have different combinations of temperature, precipitation, wind patterns, and humidity that make up the climate. The climate of an area depends on where on Earth the area is located.

3. Label each photo with the number that matches the location on Earth where you think that climate occurs.

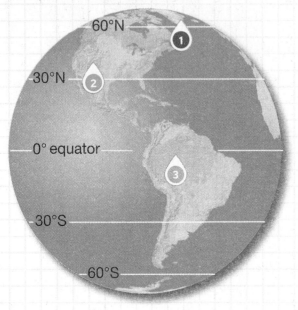

Primary Factors that Determine Climate

Weather refers to short-term conditions in the atmosphere. Climate refers to the long-term weather patterns of an area. Climate is influenced by interactions between sunlight, oceans, the atmosphere, ice, landforms, and living things. It is possible to predict the climate of a region if you know where on Earth it is located.

Latitude and Elevation

Latitude measures how far north or south of the equator a region is located. Locations at high latitudes (far from the equator) receive less sunlight than places at low latitudes (close to the equator) and are typically colder. Elevation is height above sea level. Places at high elevations are typically colder with more precipitation than places at low elevations.

Location of Mountains and Oceans

Mountains can cause different climates to form on each side of the mountain range. This is due to a rain shadow effect. Mountains typically have lower temperatures than nearby lowland areas. Oceans affect climate by absorbing energy from the sun, releasing it over time, and redistributing it across the globe through ocean currents. Water absorbs and releases energy more slowly than land does. This means that land near oceans experiences a smaller temperature range (less difference between temperature highs and lows) than land farther from oceans. Oceans and other large bodies of water also increase the amount of water in the air. This often leads to more precipitation in coastal areas.

© Houghton Mifflin Harcourt Publishing Company • Image Credits: (t) ©Image Source Trading Ltd/Shutterstock; (c) ©Computer Earth/Shutterstock; (b) ©Stefano Termanini/

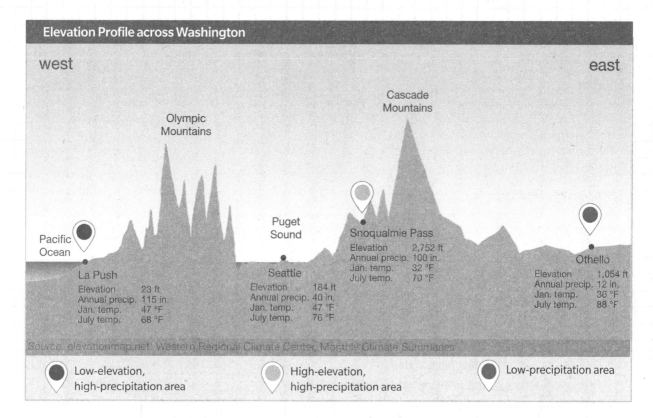

Elevation Profile across Washington

west   east

Olympic
Mountains

Cascade
Mountains

Puget
Sound

Snoqualmie Pass
Elevation   2,752 ft
Annual precip. 100 in.
Jan. temp.   32 °F
July temp.   70 °F

Pacific
Ocean

La Push
Elevation   23 ft
Annual precip. 115 in.
Jan. temp.   47 °F
July temp.   68 °F

Seattle
Elevation   184 ft
Annual precip. 40 in.
Jan. temp.   47 °F
July temp.   76 °F

Othello
Elevation   1,054 ft
Annual precip. 12 in.
Jan. temp.   36 °F
July temp.   88 °F

Source: elevationmap.net; Western Regional Climate Center Monthly Climate Summaries

Low-elevation,
high-precipitation area

High-elevation,
high-precipitation area

Low-precipitation area

4. Low-elevation, high-precipitation areas are close to / far from the
ocean, where moisture-filled air causes precipitation. Rain shadows occur
because the air is dry / moist after it crosses the mountains.

Climate Affects the Local Environment

Climate determines how hot or cold, sunny or
cloudy, windy or still, and dry or humid a particular
place is. This affects the amount of food, light, space,
and water in an area. Weather conditions that impact
local environments, such as fog, frost, or severe
storms, are also related to climate.

A temperate rain forest receives lots of sunlight and rain. This
allows trees to grow.

5. Match the climate listed on the left side
(the cause) with the environment described on
the right (the effect).

coastal climate	hot summers, limited water and plant life
high-latitude climate	cold, low amounts of sunlight and plant life
dry climate in rain shadow	plentiful plant life, water, and sunlight

Grasslands typically get enough rain for grasses and shrubs
to grow, but not large trees.

California Regional Climates

Arid and semiarid climates have hot, dry summers and cold winters with very low precipitation. These climates may form as part of a rain shadow.

Mediterranean climates have warm to hot, dry summers and mild, moderately wet winters.

Humid continental climates have large differences in seasonal temperatures, with hot summers and cold winters with snowfall.

Highland climates are cool to cold. Temperatures are typically colder at higher elevations.

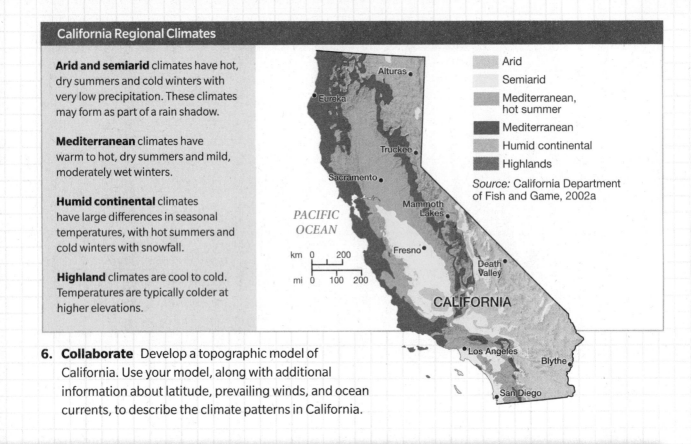

Legend:
- Arid
- Semiarid
- Mediterranean, hot summer
- Mediterranean
- Humid continental
- Highlands

Source: California Department of Fish and Game, 2002a

6. **Collaborate** Develop a topographic model of California. Use your model, along with additional information about latitude, prevailing winds, and ocean currents, to describe the climate patterns in California.

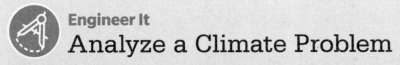

Engineer It
Analyze a Climate Problem

Desert climates can be very hot during the summer. That doesn't stop people from living in these areas, but most humans need help to live comfortably in hot climates. Use the decision matrix to help you evaluate the solutions for living in a hot climate.

7. The criteria are rated based on importance and the solutions have been evaluated for each criterion. Complete the totals by adding the numbers in each column. The highest total indicates the best solution for the stated problem.

Criteria	Criterion rating (1–5)	Solutions			
		Shade	Air conditioner	Swimming pool	Fan
Not expensive	3	2	1	1	3
Easy to maintain	2	2	2	1	2
Comfortable temps	5	2	5	2	2
Totals					

8. What is the best solution for this problem? What is the biggest trade-off for this solution? Provide evidence to support your answer.

_____

_____

_____

_____

Connecting Climate Patterns to Plant and Animal Life

If you mapped all of the world's tropical rain forests, they would exist in a band near the equator. You would see the same pattern if you mapped the location of humid, tropical climates on Earth. This relationship shows how environmental factors can affect where organisms live.

9. Look at the California Regional Climates Map and the California Land Cover Types Map. What questions do you have about how the two maps are related?

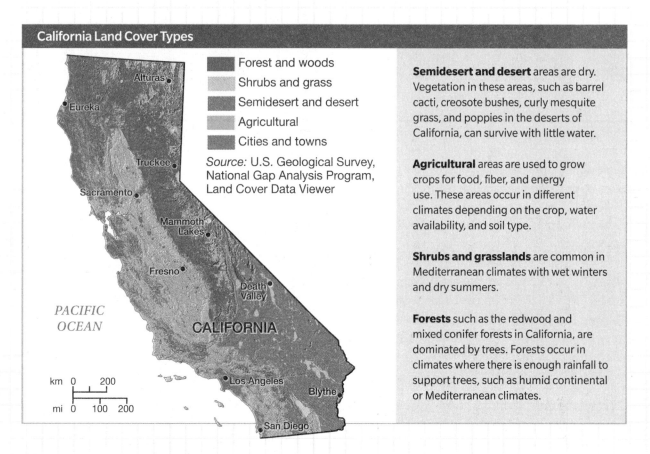

California Land Cover Types

- Forest and woods
- Shrubs and grass
- Semidesert and desert
- Agricultural
- Cities and towns

Altúras, Eureka, Truckee, Sacramento, Mammoth Lakes, Fresno, Death Valley, PACIFIC OCEAN, CALIFORNIA, Los Angeles, Blythe, San Diego

km 0   200
mi 0   100   200

Source: U.S. Geological Survey, National Gap Analysis Program, Land Cover Data Viewer

Semidesert and desert areas are dry. Vegetation in these areas, such as barrel cacti, creosote bushes, curly mesquite grass, and poppies in the deserts of California, can survive with little water.

Agricultural areas are used to grow crops for food, fiber, and energy use. These areas occur in different climates depending on the crop, water availability, and soil type.

Shrubs and grasslands are common in Mediterranean climates with wet winters and dry summers.

Forests such as the redwood and mixed conifer forests in California, are dominated by trees. Forests occur in climates where there is enough rainfall to support trees, such as humid continental or Mediterranean climates.

10. **Language SmArts | Discuss** Work with a partner. You should each select one of the land cover types that you are familiar with. Take turns asking each other questions that can be answered with yes, no, or a simple phrase in order to guess your partner's land cover type. What climate might occur in these areas?

Climate Helps Determine Where Plants and Animals Can Live

All living organisms require food, water, space, and suitable temperatures in which to grow and reproduce. The different climates around the world provide different temperatures and rainfall levels which support many different plant communities.

Plants Live in Specific Climates

Over many generations plants have developed specific characteristics that make them suited to grow and reproduce in specific climates. For example, some plants have adapted to extremely dry climates by developing long roots or the ability to store water in their leaves or cells. Some shrubs have adapted to the windy, salty environment of coastal areas by growing short, wind-resistant branches and leaves and the ability to filter out salt.

Plant Communities Influence Animal Communities

The number and kinds of plants that live in an area influence the number and kinds of animals that live in the same area. This is because plants make food and form the base of food chains on land. Different animals prefer different plants. Some animals need a specific type of plant to survive. For example, the koala depends on the eucalyptus tree. In the past, populations of koalas varied in their ability to break down eucalyptus leaves. Those koalas better able to digest the plants survived and reproduced, and the easy digestion of eucalyptus became more common in koalas. Koalas use the trees for shelter, food, and water. The eucalyptus trees in a region support the koalas. The koalas, in turn, are a food source for other animals, such as pythons and eagles. If eucalyptus trees disappeared from an area, it would negatively affect the koalas that feed on the eucalyptus trees, as well as the animals that feed on the koalas.

11. **Collaborate** There are tradeoffs when populations develop special traits to live in an environment. For example, redwood trees cannot be tall to reach sunlight in a crowded forest *and* be short to avoid strong winds. Select an organism with a partner. Present a poster that explains the tradeoffs that make the organism well-suited to its environment.

Pickleweed is a wetland plant native to California. Pickleweed is salt-tolerant and thrives in sunny conditions.

The redwood is a tree found mainly in the coastal forests of northern California.

The Joshua tree is the largest of the yuccas and thrives in the Mojave Desert.

Hands-On Lab
Compare the Drought Tolerance of Plants

Imagine you live in a dry climate and would like to add a plant to an outdoor garden. The garden is not often watered. Plan an investigation to determine which plant type is better suited to a dry environment.

MATERIALS

- graduated cylinder
- light source
- nonsucculent plant, small, potted
- succulent plant, small, potted
- water

Procedure

As you develop your investigation, consider these questions:

- How can your observations from the beginning of the lesson help you plan your procedure?
- What data should you measure and record?
- How can you determine the health of a plant?
- How will you handle having a control and more than one plant in a treatment group? (Hint: There may be an opportunity for team work.)

STEP 1 Plan and write your procedure to determine which plant is better suited to a dry environment. Your procedure should describe the independent and dependent variables.

STEP 2 Get your teacher's approval before you begin your investigation. Make any changes to your procedure requested by your teacher.

STEP 3 Predict the results of your experiment based on your prior observations.

STEP 4 Perform your investigation following the steps you have written. Record your observations on a separate sheet of paper.

Analysis

STEP 5 Write a short argument that identifies the drought-tolerant plant that you recommend for the garden. Use evidence from your investigation to support your answer and present your argument to the class.

STEP 6 Organisms are influenced by many environmental factors at once, such as the amount of water, nutrients, and sunlight available in an area. Why is it important to change only one variable in an experiment, even if there are many environmental factors that affect a plant in the natural world?

EVIDENCE NOTEBOOK

12. Emperor penguins eat fish, squid, and other animals they catch in the ocean. Roadrunners eat lizards, insects, and other animals they catch in the bushes and grass. How does the climate where these birds live affect the plant and animal life and what the birds eat? Record your evidence.

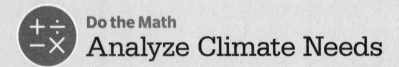

Do the Math
Analyze Climate Needs

Darwin's orchid (*Angraecum sesquipedale*) is an orchid species from the lowlands of Madagascar. This orchid often occurs in areas that get more than 203.2 cm (80 in.) of rain each year.

13. What information does the climate graph provide about the climate around Antananarivo, Madagascar? How much precipitation does this area receive annually? What is the average temperature in this area?

_____

_____

_____

_____

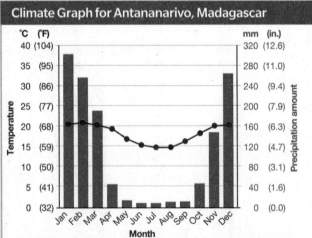

Climate Graph for Antananarivo, Madagascar

Credit: Adapted from Climate: Antananarivo by AM Online Projects. Copyright © by AM Online Projects. Adapted and reproduced by permission of Alexander Merkel, AM Online Projects, © Climate-Data.org.

14. Is the Darwin's orchid suited for the climate around Antananarivo? Use evidence to support your answer.

_____

_____

_____

Explaining How Adaptations Help Organisms Survive

Seals are as comfortable in water as humans are on land. Seals have flippers and a tail that help them swim and a thick layer of fat to keep them warm. Seals can hold their breath for a long time. This allows them to catch food and avoid predators.

15. Write Use the photo and your knowledge of seals to write a story about how this seal's traits help it survive in its environment.

Seals can live in very cold water. They are agile swimmers, which helps them to avoid predators and catch prey.

Adaptation

An **adaptation** is a trait that helps an organism survive and reproduce in its environment. Sometimes an adaptation helps an organism get food or water. For example, the long neck of a giraffe helps it reach leaves high in the trees. Sometimes an adaptation helps an organism protect itself or hide from predators. For example, stick insects developed traits that made them look like sticks. This makes it hard for other animals to see the insects. A trait that aids survival may become more common in the population as the trait is passed from parent to offspring during reproduction.

Explore Online

Giraffes' long necks allow them to graze on tall trees in the African savanna.

This insect is disguised as a stick. Camouflage is an adaptation that helps organisms avoid detection.

16. Leopards have spots that blend in with the patches of sunlight on the jungle floor. How might a trait like spots become more common in a population of leopards?

A. Leopards get their spots by rubbing against each other. Eventually all leopards in a population will have spots.

B. Blending in helps leopards successfully hunt for food. Leopards with more food are more likely to survive and pass on their spotted trait to offspring.

C. An adult leopard develops more spots during its lifetime in order to compete with other leopards.

Physical Adaptation

Physical adaptations are structures or physical characteristics that help animals survive and reproduce. For example, many animals have adaptations that serve as a disguise. The leaf katydid and the stick insect look like parts of a plant.

Behavioral Adaptation

Behavioral adaptations are actions that animals take in their environments in order to survive. Examples of behavioral adaptations that help animals survive cold weather are bears hibernating during long, cold winters and birds flying south for the winter in order to find more food. Bees store food during the summer to eat during the winter.

Explore Online

The desert beetle has long legs to raise its body up off the hot sand. This helps it to remain cool.

This carnivorous plant has evolved a physical adaptation that attracts and traps small insects for it to feed on.

Some bears hibernate during the winter. This behavior allows the bears to conserve energy when food is scarce and the weather is very cold.

17. Decide whether each adaptation is a physical or a behavioral adaptation.

Adaptation	Physical or Behavioral
Koalas have fur on their rumps which acts as a cushion for hard branches they sit on.	
The opossum "plays" dead for protection from its enemies.	
Coastal redwoods have shallow roots that extend far from the tree to provide support.	
Humpback whales migrate north from Antarctica to breed in warmer water.	

 EVIDENCE NOTEBOOK

18. What adaptations do Emperor penguins and roadrunners have? Record your evidence.

Banner Peak is part of the Ansel Adams Wilderness in the Sierra Nevada.

Sierra Nevada is a Spanish phrase that means "snow-covered mountain range." This region runs along the eastern side of California. The mid-latitude location and closeness to the Pacific Ocean means that the Sierra Nevada can have unusually mild mountain climates. Snowfall increases with elevation and latitude. Precipitation is heavy on the coastal side of the mountains from November to April.

American pikas have thick coats and small, round bodies to conserve heat in cold weather. They gather and store plants in a sheltered pile and eat the dried plants during the winter.

Sky pilot plants grow low to the ground where temperatures are warmer. Sky pilots bloom for a short time in the summer months. The flowers are showy to attract pollinators.

Bristlecone pines grow slowly in the poor soil and cold weather of the mountains. These trees keep their needles for many years instead of replacing them yearly. This is one way they save energy. Bristlecone pines occur in mountains just east of the Sierra Nevada.

Bighorn sheep have sharp eyesight to spot predators. Their padded hooves help them climb steep terrain. Males clash with their horns to compete for dominance and the chance to breed.

Some butterflies, such as this painted lady, can survive in the mountains. They depend on plants for food and a place to lay their eggs. Some plants depend on butterflies for pollination.

19. Pikas grow thick fur in winter, and their small bodies conserve heat. Kangaroo rats do not sweat, and oily fur helps them conserve moisture. They get water from seeds. Predict what would happen if a pika and a kangaroo rat switched environments.

Similar Adaptations Can Occur in Similar Environments

It is not uncommon for animals and plants that live in similar conditions to develop similar adaptations. For example, many desert-dwelling plants have similar adaptations to conserve water. Some plants have shallow, extensive root systems that allow them to absorb as much surface water as possible.

20. The rubber tree has smooth, thin bark and large, waxy leaves that allow rainwater to run off faster. Which organism is most likely to live in an environment similar to the rubber tree's environment?

   A. Kangaroo paw plants that have tiny hairs to hold on to water droplets.

   B. Giant water lilies with waxy leaves that float on water.

   C. Ocotillos that become dormant, or inactive, between rainfalls.

The *Sinopoda scurion* is an eyeless, cave-dwelling huntsman spider. There is little or no light where this spider lives.

The golden mole cannot see. Its eyes are covered with furred skin. These moles spend most of their time underground.

Identify Suitable Adaptations for Specific Environments

Deserts have extreme temperatures and little rainfall. Reptiles that can survive hot temperatures and cacti with shallow roots to capture water are common. Some animals pass through when the weather is more moderate. The tundra is cold with a short growing season. There is little rainfall and the tundra is snow-covered in the winter. Low-growing plants with shallow roots and migrating animals are common.

WORD BANK
- white winter coat
- migration
- active at night
- shallow roots
- thin fur
- spines, not leaves
- hibernation

21. Identify whether each adaptation is suitable for the desert, the tundra, or both areas. Then write each adaptation in the correct location in the Venn diagram.

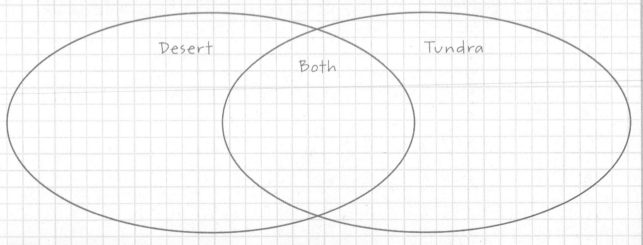

Desert   Both   Tundra

© Houghton Mifflin Harcourt Publishing Company • Image Credits: (t) ©Xinhua/Alamy; (b) ©Anthony Bannister/Gallo Images/Getty Images

Continue Your Exploration

Name: _____ Date: _____

Check out the path below or go online to choose one of the other paths shown.

People in Science

- Hibernation, Migration, or Staying Active
- Hands-On Labs ✋
- Propose Your Own Path

Go online to choose one of these other paths.

Dr. Gary Bañuelos, Soil Scientist

Gary Bañuelos grew up in Red Bluff, California. He studied German, crop science, and international agriculture before earning his PhD in plant nutrition from Hohenhiem University in Germany. During his studies in Germany, Dr. Bañuelos tested vegetables for radioactive contamination. This led to an interest in how some plants remove harmful substances from the environment. Dr. Bañuelos now studies the *phytoremediation* of soils—helping to improve soils through the use of plants—particularly in areas with high levels of selenium, boron, and salt in California.

Gary Bañuelos is a soil scientist at the US Department of Agriculture (USDA) Water Management Research Unit and teaches at several universities.

Selenium is an element that is harmful in large amounts. However, selenium is also a necessary micronutrient for humans and other animals. In other words, people need a little bit of selenium, but a lot of selenium can be harmful. Selenium occurs naturally in some soil. Selenium in farm fields dissolves in irrigation water. It may become part of water runoff from irrigated fields. This can lead to high, harmful levels of selenium in waterways and other ecosystems. As the human population has increased, more wildlands have been cleared for agriculture. This has caused more irrigation runoff and more selenium in waterways and natural areas. Selenium levels may become so high that they threaten aquatic and land-based wildlife. When irrigation runoff is more closely managed, selenium builds up in the soil of farm fields. Traditional crops may be unable to grow in soil with lots of selenium. To reduce threats to ecosystems and human populations, Dr. Bañuelos was asked to use phytoremediation techniques to manage selenium movement in ecosystems.

1. Plants are adapted to different conditions based on the environment in which the plant lives. What characteristics would you look for in a plant to be used in phytoremediation to improve soil with high levels of selenium and salt?

Continue Your Exploration

Dr. Bañuelos has studied many plants that are able to thrive in saline and selenium-rich soil. One of those plants is the prickly pear cactus (*Opuntia ficus-indica*). The prickly pear plant takes up selenium through its roots. The selenium is then stored in the prickly pear fruits and "paddles" of the plant, or the selenium is released into the air as a nontoxic gas. The amount of selenium stored in the cactus tissues is safe for humans and animals to eat. Prickly pear plants don't need a lot of water. This makes it an ideal plant for phytoremediation of selenium in dry areas of California.

2. What effect does phytoremediation with prickly pear cacti have on selenium-rich soil and the cacti? Select all that apply.

   A. more selenium in the soil

   B. less selenium in the soil

   C. more selenium in the prickly pear cacti

   D. less selenium in the prickly pear cacti

3. Develop a model that describes how selenium moves from the environment through the phytoremediation process.

Dr. Bañuelos (right) and collaborator John Diener (left) inspect a prickly pear cactus.

4. **Collaborate** With a partner, develop a multimedia presentation that describes how prickly pear cacti are used in the United States and other places in the world. Explain why farmers need an economic market for the prickly pear cactus in order for this crop to be planted. How does phytoremediation with prickly pear plants demonstrate the interdependence of science and society?

Can You Explain It?

Name: _____   Date: _____

Why do Emperor penguins and roadrunners live in different areas of the world?

Emperor penguins

roadrunner

EVIDENCE NOTEBOOK

Refer to the notes in your Evidence Notebook to help you construct an explanation for why Emperor penguins and roadrunners live in different areas of the world.

1. State your claim. Make sure your claim fully explains why Emperor penguins and roadrunners live in different areas of the world.

2. Summarize the evidence you have gathered to support your claim and explain your reasoning.

Checkpoints

Answer the following questions to check your understanding of the lesson.

Use the map to answer Questions 3–4.

3. In which places would you expect to find organisms with similar adaptations?

 A. 1 and 2

 B. 2 and 3

 C. 1 and 3

 D. 1, 2, and 3

4. Based on the relationship between plant life, climate, and latitude, which location is closest to the equator?

 A. 1

 B. 2

 C. 3

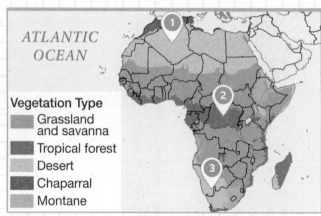

Vegetation Type
- Grassland and savanna
- Tropical forest
- Desert
- Chaparral
- Montane

Credit: Adapted from Population, Landscape and Climate Estimates, V3. Copyright © 2012 by Center for International Earth Science Information Network (CIESIN)/Columbia University, Palisades, NY. NASA Socioeconomic Data and Applications Center (SEDAC). Adapted and reproduced by permission of Center for International Earth Science Information Network.

Use the photo to answer Question 5.

5. Camels store fat in their humps, allowing them to go days without eating. What is a similar adaptation in a different animal?

 A. Cacti store water in their stems to help them live through dry periods.

 B. Bees store honey to feed the colony during the winter.

 C. Seals store fat to keep warm in cold water.

 D. Bears store fat to fuel their bodies during hibernation.

6. Adaptations help organisms to survive in specific environments. Match the adaptation with the most likely environment.

extreme heat	store water in stems
high winds	hibernation
extreme cold	active at night
lack of water	low-growing plants

Interactive Review

Complete this section to review the main concepts of the lesson.

Major factors that affect climate are latitude, elevation, closeness to oceans, and closeness to mountains.

A. How do mountain ranges affect regional climate?

The climate in an area helps determine the plants and animals that can survive in the region.

B. What patterns would you expect to see in a climate map and a vegetation map of the same area?

Adaptations help an organism survive and reproduce in its environment.

C. Use an example to illustrate the relationship between adaptations and environment.

Organisms Inherit Traits from Their Parents

These African cichlid fish all have a black stripe over their eyes. Do you think they could be related?

Explore First

Categorizing Traits List five traits that people may have. Then divide the traits into two categories: traits that don't come from parents and traits that do. How did you decide the category for each trait?

Go online to view the digital version of the Hands-On Lab for this lesson and to download additional lab resources.

CAN YOU EXPLAIN IT?

How did these kittens get their fur colors?

These kittens are all related because they have the same two parents. However, when you look at the fur colors of the kittens, you'll notice that they are not all the same.

1. Knowing the kittens' fur color, what would you predict the parents' fur looks like?

2. Why do you think these kittens look similar in some ways and different in other ways?

  EVIDENCE NOTEBOOK As you explore the lesson, gather evidence to help explain how the kittens got their fur color.

Investigating How Traits Are Passed from Parent to Offspring

More than 150 years ago, an Austrian monk named Gregor Mendel observed that pea plants in his garden had different forms of certain characteristics. Mendel studied the characteristics of pea plants, such as seed color and flower color. Each characteristic that Mendel studied had two different forms. For example, the color of a pea could be green or yellow. These different forms are called **traits**.

Mendel noticed that when the plants reproduced, the next generation of plants did not always share the same traits with their parents. He planned an experiment to investigate how the traits of the parent plants were passed on to the offspring.

3. **Discuss** What are some differences you notice in these pea plants?

Mendel used pea plants to study how traits are passed from parent to offspring.

Mendel's Pea Plant Investigation

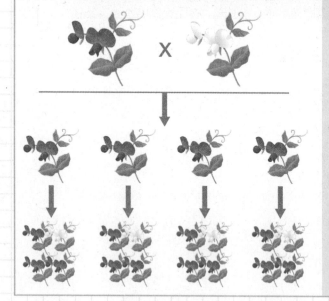

These two plants represent the parent generation. Usually, these pea plants self-pollinate. But instead, Mendel fertilized one parent plant with the pollen from the other parent plant.

These four plants represent the first generation of offspring (F1). In the F1 generation, all of the plants have purple flowers.

These plants represent the second generation of offspring (F2). Most of the F2 generation offspring have purple flowers, but some offspring have white flowers.

4. How does the presence of white flowers change from the parent generation, to the first generation of offspring, to the second generation of offspring?

Mendel's Investigation Methods

Mendel studied each pea plant trait separately, always starting with plants that were true breeding for that trait. A true-breeding plant is one that will always produce offspring with a certain trait when allowed to self-pollinate. The white-flowered and purple-flowered parent plants that Mendel studied were true-breeding plants for the flower color trait. Usually, pea plants self-pollinate, but Mendel *crossed* the two parent plants, meaning he fertilized one parent plant with pollen from the other parent plant. Then, he let the first generation self-pollinate. He used these same methods to study other pea plant traits.

Before Mendel became a monk, he attended a university and studied science and mathematics.

Dominant and Recessive Traits

When Mendel crossed the purple-flowered and white-flowered plants, all first-generation plants had purple flowers. Mendel called this trait the *dominant trait*. Because the white-flower trait seemed to recede, or fade away, he called it the *recessive trait*. For all traits that Mendel studied, a similar pattern occurred. One of the parents' traits would not show up in the first generation. These were all recessive traits. The other trait—that shows up in all first generation offspring—was the dominant trait.

But what about the second generation of offspring? About one-fourth of these plants had white flowers—the recessive trait. The rest had purple flowers. The trait that seemed to disappear in the first generation reappeared in the second generation. Again, for all of the traits that Mendel studied, this same pattern occurred.

Language SmArts
Construct an Explanation of Trait Inheritance

What could explain the mysterious disappearance and reappearance of the recessive traits? Mendel hypothesized that each plant must have two inherited "factors" for each trait, one from each parent. Some traits, such as white flower color, only occurred if a plant received two factors for white flower color. A plant with one white flower factor and one purple flower factor would have the dominant trait: purple flowers. However, this plant could still pass on the white flower factor to the next generation of plants.

5. Explain how Mendel's data supported his hypothesis. Support your answer by citing textual evidence from this lesson.

_____

_____

_____

_____

6. Mendel crossed a true-breeding plant with yellow peas with a true-breeding plant with green peas. All first generation offspring had yellow peas. Explain which trait is recessive.

_____

_____

Relating Genetic Structure to Traits

Mendel's experiments and conclusions were the beginnings of scientific thought about how traits are passed from parents to offspring. Mendel's observations can be further explained by our modern understanding of the molecule called DNA. DNA is short for deoxyribonucleic acid. DNA contains instructions that determine an organism's traits and coordinate the growth and development of an organism.

7. **Discuss** How is DNA similar to a recipe? What happens if a recipe is changed slightly?

Scientists can isolate DNA to investigate the relationship between the structure of DNA and traits in organisms.

Genes Influence Traits

DNA is organized into structures called **chromosomes**. An individual has paired sets of chromosomes. What Mendel called "factors" are now known as genes. A **gene** is a segment of the DNA that makes up a chromosome. Because an individual has pairs of chromosomes, an individual also has pairs of genes.

Each gene can have different forms, or variations. For example, Mendel's pea plants had two variations of the flower color gene, causing purple or white flowers. Each parent contributes one set of genes to its offspring. So, for a particular trait, one gene variation comes from each parent. The different gene forms are called **alleles**. Alleles carry the codes for producing various **proteins**, which are large molecules that do much of the work in a cell and also make up much of the cell's structure. Proteins are responsible for most aspects of how our bodies function, as well as for our physical appearance and behavior.

Mendel's pea plant traits were all controlled by just two alleles: a dominant one and a recessive one. For those pea plants, the allele for purple flowers is the dominant allele, and the allele for white flowers is the recessive allele. Some traits follow this inheritance pattern; however, most do not. Usually there are more than two alleles for a single gene within a population of organisms. Each organism, however, can carry only one or two alleles for one gene. Most traits, such as height and eye color, are determined by more than one gene.

The Structure of DNA

The chemical components that make up DNA are too small to be observed directly. However, experiments and imaging techniques have helped scientists to infer the shape of DNA and the arrangement of its parts. A molecule of DNA is shaped like a twisted ladder, a shape that is called a *double helix*. The rungs of the ladder are made of pairs of bases. A length of base pairs along a DNA molecule is what makes up a gene. The instructions of DNA are coded in specific sequences of base pairs.

8. **Collaborate** Build a model that illustrates the relationships among DNA, chromosomes, and genes. Present your model to the class.

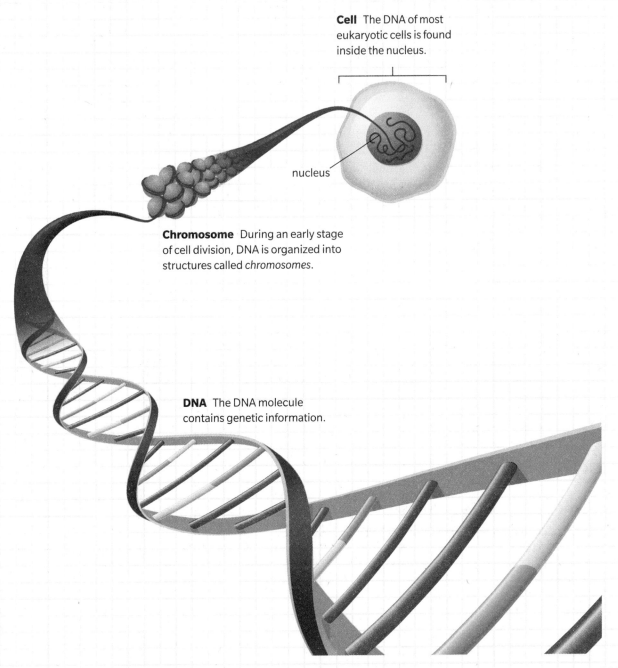

Cell The DNA of most eukaryotic cells is found inside the nucleus.

nucleus

Chromosome During an early stage of cell division, DNA is organized into structures called *chromosomes*.

DNA The DNA molecule contains genetic information.

Hands-On Lab
Model Genes and Traits

Use a model to describe genetic variation for the scale color of a hypothetical fish species. Use evidence to predict, over several generations, the proportions of dominant and recessive alleles in the population.

The combination of alleles that an organism receives from its parents is called the organism's *genotype*. The observable traits of an organism are its *phenotype*. Genotypes can be represented by letter symbols. Often, dominant alleles are shown with capital letters and recessive alleles are shown with lowercase letters. For example, *F* could represent the dominant allele of purple flower color and *f* could represent the recessive allele of white flower color in pea plants. You can write a genotype for a pea plant's flower color by using the letters to represent an individual's alleles. As an organism receives one allele from each parent, a pea plant might have the genotype *FF, Ff,* or *ff*.

MATERIALS
- cup
- red beads (12)
- yellow beads (10)

Procedure

STEP 1 The beads represent the alleles for a gene that determines the scale color of a hypothetical species of fish. All of the beads together represent all of the alleles in the population of fish. Red beads (*R*) are dominant alleles that code for the red-scale phenotype. Yellow beads (*r*) are recessive alleles that code for the yellow-scale phenotype.

STEP 2 Write the genotype(s) for each phenotype.

Red scales: _____

Yellow scales: _____

STEP 3 Without looking, choose pairs of beads until all the beads are gone. Set the pairs of beads on a table. Each pair represents the genotype of an individual fish in the population. Record the genotype and phenotype of each fish on a piece of paper. This is the first generation.

STEP 4 In the fish habitat, a type of algae is becoming more common. The algae is reddish in color. The red fish can hide from predators as they swim in the red algae, but the yellow fish are very visible. Model a predator eating three yellow fish by removing the alleles for three yellow "fish" from the population.

STEP 5 Replace the remaining alleles into the container and repeat Step 3, this time making a second generation of fish. Record the genotype and phenotype of each fish on a piece of paper.

Analysis

STEP 6 Compare the first- and second-generation phenotypes. Explain the reasons for any differences.

STEP 7 Use evidence from your simulation to explain what would happen after many generations if environmental conditions for these fish remained the same. Justify your response.

STEP 8 Suppose that yellow algae began to outcompete the red algae in the fish environment. Describe how you could model the next two generations of fish in this changed environment.

 EVIDENCE NOTEBOOK

9. Think about the different phenotypes of fish scale color in this lab and the phenotypes of fur color in the kittens at the beginning of this lesson. Explain why all of the kittens don't have the same fur color, even though they have the same parents. Record your evidence.

Predict Effects of Mutation

Changes in a section of DNA are known as *mutations*. How do mutations happen? One cause of mutations is random errors that occur when DNA is copied to make new cells.

A mutation in bacteria can make an individual bacterium resistant to antibiotics. Galactosemia in humans is caused by a mutation in one gene and prevents people from digesting a sugar found in dairy foods. This can lead to poor health or death. Mutations that cause a change in human eye or hair color do not affect the health of the individual. Some small changes in DNA do not change the protein that the DNA codes for.

10. Which mutation described in the paragraph is harmful, which is neutral, and which is beneficial? Explain your reasoning.

_____

_____

_____

_____

Modeling Inheritance of Traits

Not all traits are passed on from parent to offspring. Some traits are learned, such as the ability to ride a bicycle or write your name in cursive. Other traits are acquired, or taken on after birth. For example, a person might dye his hair blue, but that is not an inherited trait.

11. Engineer It The three processes below would allow a horticulturist to grow only purple-flowered pea plants for many generations. However, the horticulturist is constrained by time. Which of the following processes would allow the horticulturist to grow only purple-flowered plants in the shortest amount of time? Explain your reasoning below.

A. A horticulturist could start by crossing two plants with purple flowers. In each new generation, they should select plants with purple flowers to cross, until all of the plants for several generations have purple flowers.

B. A horticulturist could send plant specimens to a lab for genotype analysis, which usually takes 1–2 weeks.

C. A horticulturist could allow the purple plants to self-pollinate, then separate purple plants from the first generation and allow those plants to self-pollinate.

Flower color is an inherited trait.

Genes Are Passed from Parents to Offspring

Before anyone knew about DNA or genes, Mendel figured out that "factors"—what we now call genes—were passed from parent to offspring. **Inheritance** is the passing of genes from parents to offspring. In one form of reproduction, offspring inherit all of their genes from one parent, so that the offspring and the parent are genetically identical. For example, you can take a cutting of a houseplant and grow a new individual plant. The new plant is genetically identical to its parent unless mutations occur. In another form of reproduction, two parents contribute genetic material. The offspring of this type of reproduction are genetically different from each of the parents as well as from each other.

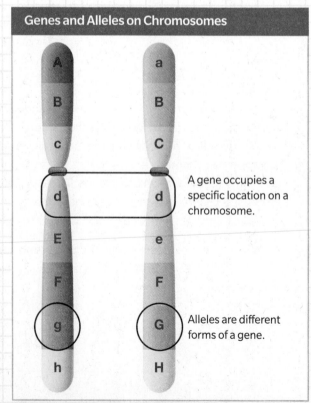

Genes and Alleles on Chromosomes

A gene occupies a specific location on a chromosome.

Alleles are different forms of a gene.

12. Mendel's peas had two phenotypes for pod color: yellow pods and green pods. The allele for yellow pod color is *Y* and the allele for green pod color is *y*. On the lines below, write the phenotype for each genotype. Then summarize how these alleles were passed from parent to offspring.

Genotype	Phenotype	Summary
Parent 1: *YY*	A. _____	
Parent 2: *yy*	B. _____	
All offspring: *Yy*	C. _____	

Inheritance Is Modeled with Punnett Squares

Mendel discovered the basic laws of inheritance through his studies of pea plants. His observations confirmed that each parent plant contributes one allele for each gene, offspring randomly receive one allele for each gene from each parent, and dominant alleles are always expressed in offspring.

One tool for understanding the basic patterns of heredity is a Punnett square. A *Punnett square* is a model used to predict the possible genotypes of offspring in a given cross. The example shows a cross between a pea plant with purple flowers (*FF*) and a pea plant with white flowers (*ff*). The top of the Punnett square shows the possible alleles for this trait from one parent (*F* and *F*). The left side shows the possible alleles from the other parent (*f* and *f*). Each square shows a possible allele combination for potential offspring.

Punnett Square for Flower Color

13. Fill in the missing genotype to complete the Punnett square.

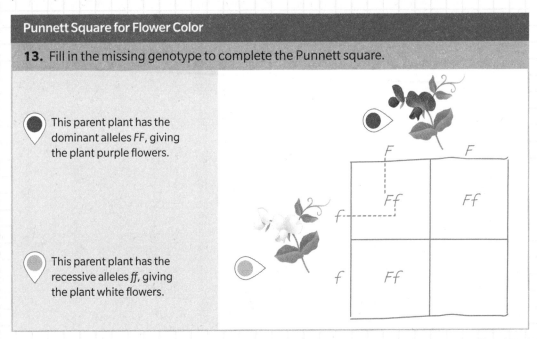

This parent plant has the dominant alleles *FF*, giving the plant purple flowers.

This parent plant has the recessive alleles *ff*, giving the plant white flowers.

14. Use the laws of inheritance and the predictions in the Punnett square to explain how genetic factors can influence the traits of organisms.

EVIDENCE NOTEBOOK

15. The pea plant traits studied by Mendel were determined by one gene. However, many traits, such as fur color, are determined by more than one gene. How might the influence of multiple genes affect the number of possible phenotypes for cat fur color? Record your evidence.

Do the Math
Calculate Genotype Probability

A Punnett square shows all possible genotypes for the offspring of a cross, not what the exact results of the cross will be. A Punnett square is used to predict the probability that an offspring will have a certain genotype. *Probability* is the mathematical chance of a specific outcome in relation to the total number of possible outcomes.

Probability can be expressed as a *ratio*, an expression that compares two quantities. A ratio written as 1:4 is read as "one to four." Punnett square ratios show the probability that any one offspring will get certain alleles. Probability can also be expressed as a percentage. A percentage compares a number to 100, stating the number of times a certain outcome might happen out of a hundred chances.

16. Complete the Punnett square. The allele for red feathers (*R*) is dominant and the allele for brown feathers (*r*) is recessive.

	R	r
R		
r		

17. Use probability to describe the likelihood that an offspring of this cross will have each genotype or phenotype:

Genotype or Phenotype	Probability	Percentage
RR genotype	1:4	$1 \div 4 = 0.25$ $0.25 \times 100 = 25\%$
Rr genotype		
rr genotype		
red feathers		
brown feathers		

Continue Your Exploration

Name: _____ **Date:** _____

Check out the path below or go online to choose one of the other paths shown.

People in Science

- **Genetic Engineering**
- **Hands-On Labs** 🖐
- **Propose Your Own Path**

Go online to choose one of these other paths.

In the mid-19th century, scientists knew that the DNA molecule existed, but they did not know what it looked like. Many scientists studied DNA's structure, and the combined work of four scientists in particular helped solve the mystery.

DNA is made up of chemical compounds called *nucleotides*. A nucleotide consists of a sugar, a phosphate, and a base: thymine, guanine, adenine, or cytosine. Erwin Chargaff found that in DNA, the amount of adenine equals the amount of thymine and the amount of guanine equals the amount of cytosine.

Rosalind Franklin used x-ray diffraction to make images of the DNA molecule; her research indicated DNA had a spiral shape. James Watson and Francis Crick used Chargaff's and Franklin's research to build a model of DNA. In their model, DNA is in the shape of a double helix, which looks like a twisted ladder. The sugars and phosphates make up the outsides of the ladder, while the "rungs" are made up of joined pairs of nucleotides. Adenine (A) pairs with thymine (T), and guanine (G) pairs with cytosine (C). These paired, or complementary, bases fit together like two pieces of a puzzle.

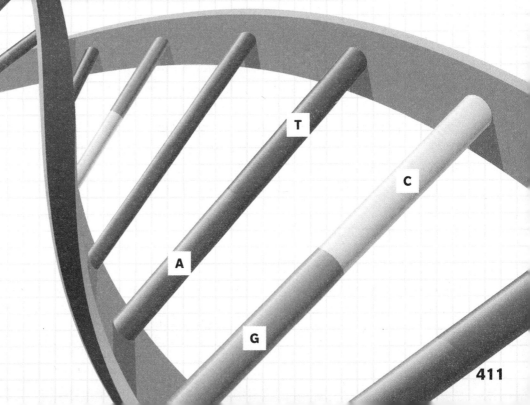

Continue Your Exploration

1. A scientist knows that a molecule of DNA is 27% cytosine. What else does the scientist know about the DNA molecule?

   A. The DNA molecule is 27% guanine.

   B. The DNA molecule is 27% adenine.

   C. The DNA molecule is 73% guanine.

   D. The DNA molecule is 27% thymine.

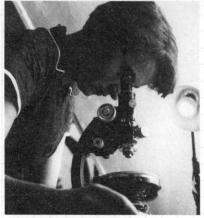

X-ray crystallographer Rosalind Franklin, circa 1942

Biochemist Erwin Chargaff, circa 1970

James Watson (left) and Francis Crick (right), in their laboratory, circa 1953

2. Describe how the contributions of Rosalind Franklin and Erwin Chargaff led to the discovery of the structure of DNA by James Watson and Francis Crick.

3. Suppose that the sequence of bases on one segment of DNA is ATCGGA. What is the sequence of bases on the complementary segment?

   A. ATCGGA

   B. CGATTC

   C. AGGCTA

   D. TAGCCT

4. **Collaborate** Work with classmates to research a recent discovery or advancement involving DNA. Write a paper that explains the discovery or advancement and present your findings to the class with a multimedia presentation.

Can You Explain It?

Name: _____   Date: _____

How did these kittens get their fur colors?

EVIDENCE NOTEBOOK

Refer to the notes in your Evidence Notebook to help you construct an explanation for how these kittens got their fur colors.

1. State your claim. Make sure your claim fully explains how the kittens got their fur colors.

2. Summarize the evidence you have gathered to support your claim and explain your reasoning.

Checkpoints

Answer the following questions to check your understanding of the lesson.

Use the diagram to answer Questions 3–4.

3. For which gene or genes will the recessive trait be expressed in this individual? Choose all that apply.

   A. the Q gene

   B. the S gene

   C. the T gene

   D. the U gene

4. What genotype(s) might the parents of this individual have for the Q gene? Select all that apply.

   A. *QQ*

   B. *Qq*

   C. *qq*

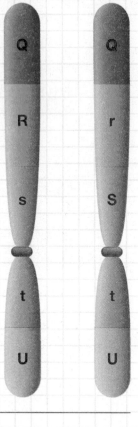

Use the diagram to answer Questions 5–6.

5. For Mendel's peas, seed shape was round (*R*) or wrinkled (*r*). Fill in all of the possible genotypes that could result from the cross shown in this Punnett square.

6. An offspring from this cross has a
   0% / 25% / 50% / 75% / 100%
   chance of having round peas and a
   0% / 25% / 50% / 75% / 100%
   chance of having wrinkled peas.

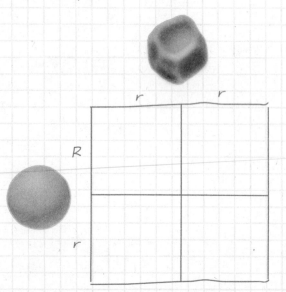

Interactive Review

415

Complete this section to review the main concepts of the lesson.

Mendel discovered a basic inheritance pattern by studying pea plants.

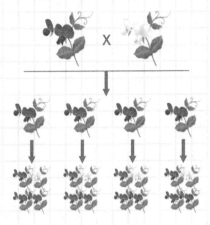

A. Mendel studied seven different features of pea plants, including flower color, seed shape, and seed color. Describe the evidence Mendel used to determine if a particular trait was dominant or recessive.

Genes, which are located on chromosomes, determine traits.

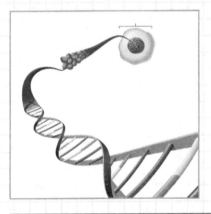

B. Explain how chromosomes, genes, and alleles are related.

The inheritance of some traits can be modeled using a Punnett square.

C. For Mendel's peas, yellow seed color (*G*) is dominant and green seed color (*g*) is recessive. Write and complete a Punnett square to model a cross between a *Gg* parent and a *GG* parent. Use evidence from the Punnett square to explain why the offspring may have different genotypes or phenotypes.

Reproduction Affects Genetic Diversity

Female grizzly bears have a litter of one to four cubs. The cubs will stay with their mother for two to three years.

Explore First

Modeling Variation Use marbles, beads, or other objects to model a population with high genetic diversity and a population with low genetic diversity. What environmental conditions would benefit a genetically diverse population and what environmental conditions would benefit a genetically similar population? Explain your reasoning.

Go online to view the digital version of the Hands-On Lab for this lesson and to download additional lab resources.

CAN YOU EXPLAIN IT?

Why is the Cavendish banana in danger of extinction?

Banana crops throughout the world are being devastated by a fungal infection commonly known as Panama disease.

Panama disease is caused by a soil fungus, which enters the plant through the roots. The fungus grows in the plant's transport tissue and blocks the flow of water and nutrients throughout the plant. The Cavendish banana is the variety of banana most commonly eaten by people in the United States. The Cavendish banana may become extinct, or no longer living on Earth, because of this widespread disease.

1. Why might this disease spread quickly in banana plantations?

 EVIDENCE NOTEBOOK As you explore the lesson, gather evidence to help you explain why the Cavendish banana is facing extinction.

Describing Types of Reproduction

Earth is home to millions of species of plants, animals, and other living things. In order for a species to survive, individual organisms of that species must make more organisms like themselves. Organisms produce **offspring**, or young organisms like themselves. Reproduction—the process by which organisms generate a new individual of the same species—is a characteristic of all living things. During the process of reproduction, organisms pass genetic material to their offspring.

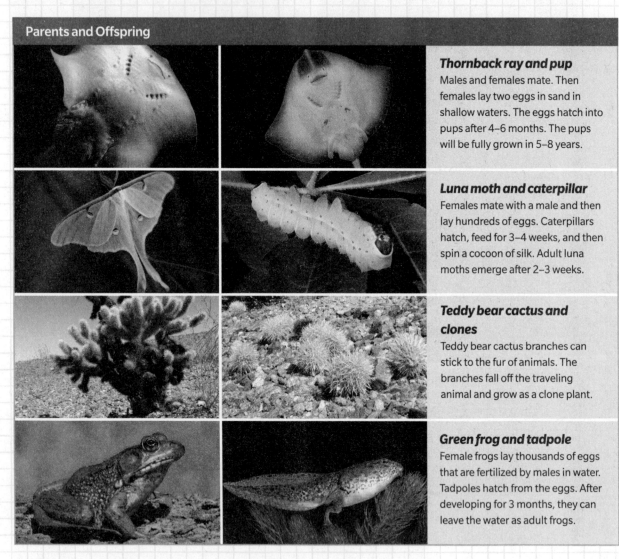

Parents and Offspring

Thornback ray and pup
Males and females mate. Then females lay two eggs in sand in shallow waters. The eggs hatch into pups after 4–6 months. The pups will be fully grown in 5–8 years.

Luna moth and caterpillar
Females mate with a male and then lay hundreds of eggs. Caterpillars hatch, feed for 3–4 weeks, and then spin a cocoon of silk. Adult luna moths emerge after 2–3 weeks.

Teddy bear cactus and clones
Teddy bear cactus branches can stick to the fur of animals. The branches fall off the traveling animal and grow as a clone plant.

Green frog and tadpole
Female frogs lay thousands of eggs that are fertilized by males in water. Tadpoles hatch from the eggs. After developing for 3 months, they can leave the water as adult frogs.

2. Compare and contrast the reproduction and growth of these organisms based on the information provided and your knowledge of reproduction.

Types of Reproduction

There are two types of reproduction: asexual reproduction and sexual reproduction. In **asexual reproduction**, a single individual is the parent. The parent passes copies of its genes to its offspring, so the offspring are genetically identical to the parent unless gene mutations occur. Most unicellular organisms reproduce asexually. Fungi, plants, and some animals can also reproduce asexually. Asexual reproduction allows an organism to reproduce quickly and can produce a large number of offspring in a short period of time.

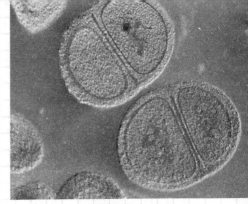

These bacteria reproduce by means of binary fission. During binary fission, an organism makes a copy of its DNA and then splits in two.

The New Mexico whiptail lizard is a unique, all-female population that reproduces asexually. These lizards have the ability to reproduce from unfertilized eggs. The offspring that have all of the mother's genetic material are called full clones. It is relatively rare for animals and other multicellular organisms to reproduce only asexually.

3. **Collaborate** With a partner, select an example of a clone from a biological system. Present your example to the class, explain why it is considered a clone, and add an illustration or image of your example to a class collage.

In **sexual reproduction**, there are two parents. Each parent contributes half of its genetic information to the offspring, so the offspring are genetically different from both parents. Most multicellular organisms reproduce sexually, including plants and animals. Sexual reproduction usually takes more time and produces fewer offspring than asexual reproduction. However, sexual reproduction increases genetic variation. This variation increases the chance that some offspring will have new traits that will help them survive in a changing environment.

4. A female elephant typically has one baby after mating and carrying the offspring in her womb for 18–22 months. Amoebas are microscopic aquatic organisms that can divide in half every two days. Which organism reproduces through sexual reproduction? Explain your reasoning.

This coral dahlia flower has male and female parts. The male parts make pollen, which contains male reproductive cells. Pollen from one flower can be transferred to the female part of another flower, beginning the process of reproduction.

EVIDENCE NOTEBOOK

5. Banana plants grown for food crops are the result of asexual reproduction. How many parents and how much genetic variation does each banana plant have? Record your evidence.

© Houghton Mifflin Harcourt Publishing Company • Image Credits: (t) ©CNRI/Science Source; (b) ©Dirk Herdramm/EyeEm/Getty Images

Some Organisms Can Use Both Types of Reproduction

Some organisms can reproduce both asexually and sexually, depending on environmental conditions and other factors. Organisms that can use both types of reproduction include fungi, many plants, some reptiles and fish, and a few types of insects.

Aphids reproduce asexually at the beginning of the season when the environment is favorable and there is plenty of space on the host plant. Aphids reproduce sexually at the end of the growing season, after they have dispersed from crowded host plants. Reproducing asexually during favorable conditions allows the aphids to pass along all beneficial genes. Reproducing sexually after dispersing provides a higher likelihood that some of the offspring will survive in the new environments.

6. Redwood trees can reproduce both sexually and asexually. Which type of reproduction might give offspring more of an advantage if a large clearing around the tree became available?

Identify Asexual and Sexual Reproduction

7. Read about the reproductive processes of the animals below. Then decide whether the process is an example of *asexual reproduction*, *sexual reproduction*, or *both*.

	Female bullheads lay their eggs under small overhangs or in a pit. The male bullheads fertilize the eggs with their sperm. Male bullheads guard the eggs until they hatch.	
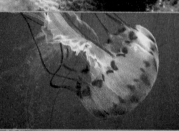	Male and female jellyfish release sperm and eggs into the water. A fertilized egg develops into a larva that will grow into a polyp. The polyp will release portions of its body into the water that will grow into adult jellyfish.	
	Corals can reproduce in a variety of ways. One way is by a process that can produce a new coral from a fragment. A portion of a coral may be broken off by a boat, a person, or an animal. The broken piece can grow into a new coral.	

Environmental Influence on Reproduction

Environmental factors influence the ability of organisms to reproduce and offspring to survive. The quality and availability of food, water, energy, and space are critical to successful reproduction. Many organisms time their reproduction to occur at the same time as favorable environmental conditions. This maximizes the chances of their offspring surviving.

Stable Conditions

Imagine an environment with stable conditions that remain the same year after year. In these environments, it can be beneficial for parents to pass along all of their traits to their offspring. This is because the parents are already well-adapted to the conditions. Because the conditions remain stable, there is less need for further diversity in the population. Organisms that reproduce asexually, such as the bacteria that live in hot springs, are particularly suited to stable environments. Their offspring take on all of the traits of the parent bacterium, which allows the offspring to survive in the extreme temperatures of thermal pools.

Hot springs and other thermal features are home to bacteria that can survive at very high temperatures.

8. Sexual / Asexual reproduction is more / less successful in a(n) stable / unstable environment as it passes on all of one parent's genetic traits that are suited to the environment.

Changing Conditions

In an unstable environment, such as one that is gradually warming, it is important for animals to be able to adapt to changing conditions. For example, sexual reproduction allows birds to develop different beak sizes over generations. Birds can use their beaks to release heat if they get too warm. A bigger beak is able to release more heat than a smaller beak. This can lead to different beak sizes between birds that live in a cooler coastal climate and inland birds of the same species that live in warmer climates.

Song sparrow populations in warm inland areas have larger beaks than populations in cooler coastal areas.

9. What are the most likely effects of human disturbance on stable environments? Select all that apply.

    A. Change the conditions from stable to variable.

    B. Change the conditions from variable to stable.

    C. Positively impact species that reproduce through asexual reproduction.

    D. Negatively impact species that reproduce through asexual reproduction.

Case Study: Joshua Trees

Joshua trees live in the Mojave Desert with hot summers, cold winters, and very little rainfall. Joshua trees reproduce sexually through the pollination of flowers, and asexually through vegetative reproduction from roots or branches. Asexual reproduction in Joshua trees is more common at higher elevations. The colder, windier conditions may make it more difficult for pollinators to successfully pollinate the trees. Joshua trees living at higher elevations may also benefit from asexual reproduction because they can pass along all of their beneficial genes to offspring.

Joshua trees live in harsh conditions that promote both sexual and asexual reproduction.

10. Decide whether asexual or sexual reproduction would be more beneficial in the following environments.

Environment	Asexual or Sexual
Same average temperature and rainfall for 50 years	
Rain shadow area of a mountain range with similar maximum and minimum temperatures for a century	
Apex predator has been hunted to near extinction	
Pollution is degrading the environment	
Humans are changing plant and animal life	

Engineer It
Develop a Hybrid

Farmers often breed two different varieties of a plant to produce offspring with desirable traits. These plants are called *hybrids*. The farmer selects parents with traits that are desired in the offspring, such as flower color, plant height, fruit yield, or pest resistance.

There are thousands of rose hybrids in nearly every color and variety of shapes.

11. A rose farmer needs to grow plants that produce orange flowers in the colder fall months to meet customer demand. Describe how the farmer might try to produce this hybrid.

_____

_____

_____

_____

_____

_____

Relating Reproduction to Genetic Variation

Reproduction is the process by which organisms inherit genes, which are segments of DNA on a chromosome. The genes inherited from the parent or parents determine the genetic traits of offspring. When an organism reproduces asexually, all the genetic material of the offspring is inherited from one parent. When an organism reproduces sexually, the offspring receives half of its genes from each parent.

Although hydras sometimes reproduce sexually, they reproduce mainly by *budding*, a type of asexual reproduction. A bud begins to grow on an adult's body. When it has developed a mouth and tentacles, the bud breaks off from the adult. Amphibians reproduce sexually. Female adult amphibians lay eggs that are fertilized by sperm from male adult amphibians.

12. **Discuss** Do you think the offspring of each organism are genetically identical to the parent or not genetically identical to the parent? Support your argument with evidence.

A hydra is an animal that lives in freshwater. Its body is shaped like a tube. It has tentacles around its mouth.

An amphibian is an animal that lives both on land and in water.

Inheritance and Asexual Reproduction

Prokaryotes, such as bacteria, are unicellular and reproduce by a type of cell division called *binary fission*. This process results in two unicellular organisms that are genetically identical to the parent. Asexual reproduction in multicellular organisms is more complicated but also usually involves a type of cell division that results in genetically identical cells.

Having offspring that are genetically identical to the parent ensures that any favorable traits that the parent has are passed on to the offspring. However, if the environment changes, a population with low genetic variation is less likely to have individuals with traits that allow them to survive.

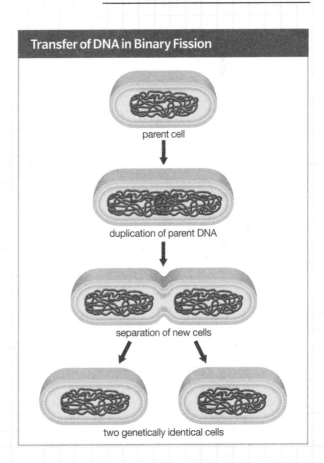

Transfer of DNA in Binary Fission

parent cell

duplication of parent DNA

separation of new cells

two genetically identical cells

Do the Math
Calculate the Rate of Asexual Reproduction

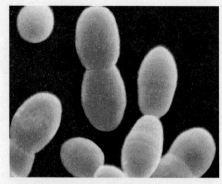

Lactococcus lactis is a bacteria used commonly in the production of cheese.

Generation time is the average time between two generations in a population. For example, if a certain type of bacteria reproduces every 20 minutes, then the generation time is 20 minutes. Since bacteria reproduce by dividing into two cells, a bacteria population doubles in a generation time.

13. Use the data from the table to create a line graph of the bacteria population over time. What can this model explain about bacteria populations? What information is not provided by this model?

Time (in minutes)	Number of *Lactococcus lactis* Cells
0	1
52	2
104	4
156	8
208	16
260	32
312	64

14. What is the independent variable? What is the dependent variable?

15. The generation time of most bacteria can be measured in minutes. What advantage might there be in being able to reproduce very rapidly?

16. If bacteria cells can reproduce so fast, then why don't bacteria take over the world?

Inheritance and Sexual Reproduction

Sexual reproduction requires two parents. Each parent makes **gametes**, or sex cells. In animals, many plants, algae, and fungi, female organisms produce egg cells, and male organisms produce sperm cells. Gametes have one copy of each chromosome, half the total number of chromosomes of a body cell. The parent gametes are all genetically different.

During sexual reproduction, a sperm cell and an egg cell join in a process called *fertilization*. When an egg cell is fertilized by a sperm cell, a new, genetically different cell is formed. This cell—called a *zygote*—has a complete set of genetic material because it has received half of its chromosomes from one parent and half from the other parent. Thus, the zygote has inherited two copies of each gene, one from each parent. The genes may be identical, or they may differ from one another. The zygote will go through many cell divisions to form an adult organism. The organism that forms is genetically different from both parents.

Transfer of DNA in Sexual Reproduction

17. What other genetic combinations might be possible from the parent organisms shown in the diagram? Circle the letter of all possibilities that apply.

A.
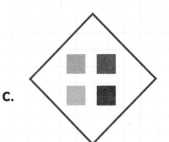

B.
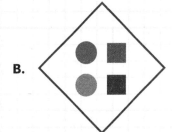

C.
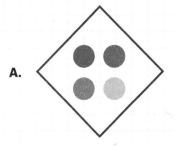

D.
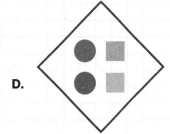

Advantages of Genetic Variation

Sexual reproduction increases genetic variation in a population of organisms. Offspring have different traits from their parents and from each other. This genetic variation improves the chance that at least some individuals will survive. If the environment changes, a population with greater genetic variation is more likely to have individuals with traits that will allow them to survive new conditions.

Hands-On Lab
Model Asexual and Sexual Reproduction

You will predict the genotypes and phenotypes resulting from the asexual and sexual reproduction of apple trees. You will then compare the effects that each type of reproduction has on genetic variation in the apple tree population.

Apple trees are one of the most valuable fruit crops in the United States, including nearly 100 different varieties, or *cultivars*. Apple trees produce flowers that are visited by animals, such as honeybees, that carry pollen from one tree to another tree. Apple trees can also be grown from stem cuttings grafted on roots. Aphids are common pests of the apple tree. They feed on the nutrients in leaves and can reduce tree growth if present in high numbers.

Procedure and Analysis

STEP 1 Examine the information in the table describing the genetics of several apple tree traits.

Trait	Dominant Allele (Symbol)	Recessive Allele (Symbol)
flower color	pink (F)	white (f)
fruit color	red (C)	green (c)
aphid resistance	not resistant (R)	resistant (r)

STEP 2 What are all the possible genotypes that can result in a tree with pink flowers, green fruit, and aphid resistance?

STEP 3 List all possible genotypes and phenotypes for each trait of the offspring that could result from the asexual reproduction of an apple tree with the genotype *FfCcRr*. Record the genotypes and phenotypes in the table below Step 4.

STEP 4 List all possible genotypes and phenotypes for each trait of the offspring that could result from the sexual reproduction of an apple tree with the parental genotypes *FfCcRr* × *FfCcRr*. Record the genotypes and phenotypes in the table.

Asexual Reproduction		Sexual Reproduction	
genotypes	phenotypes	genotypes	phenotypes

© Houghton Mifflin Harcourt Publishing Company

STEP 5 How do the genotypes and phenotypes of offspring for each type of reproduction compare to each other?

STEP 6 The probability of offspring receiving certain alleles as the result of sexual reproduction can be modeled using a coin toss. Use masking tape and a marker to make a set of three coins to represent the alleles of one parent (*FfCcRr*). For example, one coin should be labeled with *F* on one side and *f* on the other side.

STEP 7 Make another set of coins to represent the other parent (*FfCcRr*).

STEP 8 Toss all six coins to determine the genotype of one offspring. Record the offspring genotype and phenotype in the table.

STEP 9 Repeat the toss two more times. Record the offspring genotype and phenotypes in the table.

Round of Reproduction	Genotype	Phenotype
1		
2		
3		

STEP 10 How do the genotypes and phenotypes of the offspring compare to the parents and to each other?

STEP 11 Is it easier to predict the outcomes of sexual reproduction or asexual reproduction? Explain your answer and describe why it may be useful to predict the genotypes or phenotypes of offspring.

EVIDENCE NOTEBOOK

18. Genetic variation can result in differences in many traits, including resistance to diseases. Describe the genetic variation of the banana plants grown for food. How do you think this level of variation relates to the threat of Panama disease in banana crops? Record your evidence.

Language SmArts

Compare Asexual and Sexual Reproduction

19. Compare asexual reproduction and sexual reproduction by completing the Venn diagram with phrases from the word bank.

• one parent	• faster
• two parents	• slower
• produces offspring	• many offspring
• genetic variation	• few offspring

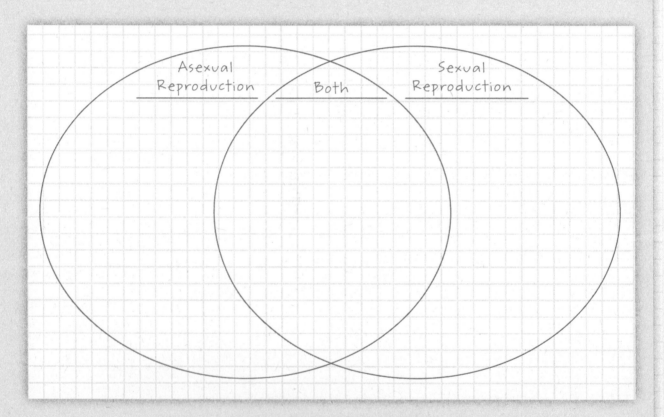

Asexual Reproduction Both Sexual Reproduction

20. Using your completed Venn diagram, write a summary detailing the advantages and disadvantages of each type of reproduction.

_____

_____

_____

_____

_____

_____

Continue Your Exploration

Name: _____   Date: _____

Check out the path below or go online to choose one of the other paths shown.

| Factors That Influence Reproduction | • Odd Reproduction
 • Hands-On Labs ✋
 • Propose Your Own Path | Go online to choose one of these other paths. |

Nearly every multicellular organism reproduces sexually, but some can also reproduce asexually. Environmental factors, such as light, temperature, and food supply, can influence the type of reproduction used by these organisms. Organisms that can use both types of reproduction are able to successfully reproduce when conditions are favorable and also when conditions become more challenging.

Honeybee reproduction occurs when a queen bee mates with a male bee, called a drone. The queen is the only female bee that mates. She uses the drone's sperm to fertilize eggs that will develop into female worker bees. An average colony has between 20,000 and 80,000 workers. The queen can also lay unfertilized eggs that will develop into drones. An average colony has between 300 and 800 drones.

1. How is this method of reproduction advantageous to the honeybee colony? Select all that apply.

   A. The queen bee is the only member of the hive that is the result of sexual reproduction.

   B. Sexually produced worker bees have genetic diversity, which could increase their overall fitness.

   C. Male bees can be produced only when needed for mating.

Continue Your Exploration

Fungi are multicellular organisms that can live anywhere there is decaying matter, but many species of fungi are associated with trees. Fungi often reproduce asexually by releasing spores, which are reproductive cells that can develop into a new individual without combining with another reproductive cell. Fungi can also reproduce asexually by budding. Fungi reproduce sexually when cells from two parents fuse.

2. Describe how environmental changes might affect the type of reproduction utilized by fungi. Relate the type of reproduction to genetic variation of offspring in your answer.

Strawberry plants can reproduce sexually by producing fruit or asexually by sending out runners. Runners are extensions of the central stem of the plant that spread out along the ground and grow into new strawberry plants.

3. What is the advantage of sending out many runners from the central stem? What is the disadvantage to the central plant?

4. **Collaborate** Select a scientific paper that investigates environmental factors that affect the reproduction or survival of an organism. Use the sources cited in the paper to explore how the author supported his or her claim with previous scientific studies. Then create a poster that explains the role that science as a body of knowledge plays in current and future scientific discoveries.

Can You Explain It?

Name: _____   Date: _____

Why is the Cavendish banana in danger of extinction?

EVIDENCE NOTEBOOK

Refer to the notes in your Evidence Notebook to help you construct an explanation for why the Cavendish banana is facing extinction.

1. State your claim. Make sure your claim fully explains why the Cavendish banana is in danger of extinction.

2. Summarize the evidence you have gathered to support your claim and explain your reasoning.

Checkpoints

Answer the following questions to check your understanding of the lesson.

Use the photo to answer Questions 3–4.

3. Marmosets usually give birth to fraternal twins, two offspring that grow from two different fertilized eggs. Marmoset twins are genetically identical / not identical.

4. What advantage does the white-faced marmoset gain by its method of reproduction?

   A. The marmoset population has genetic variation.

   B. The marmoset can reproduce without a mate.

   C. The marmoset can reproduce many offspring at a time.

   D. The marmoset can reproduce by budding.

A white-faced marmoset protects her fraternal twin pups.

Use the photo to answer Questions 5–6.

5. Dandelions can produce seeds by both asexual and sexual reproduction. How does this benefit the dandelion? Select all that apply.

   A. The sexually produced plants provide genetic diversity to the population.

   B. The asexually produced plants ensure that favorable traits are passed to the offspring.

   C. The sexually produced plants do not compete with the asexually produced plants.

   D. The asexually produced plants can rapidly colonize an area.

6. The dandelion seeds seen in the photo are a result of sexual reproduction. What events led to the development of the seeds?

   A. The seeds formed through binary fission.

   B. The seeds formed because of stable conditions.

   C. The fusion of gametes formed the seeds.

   D. Runners from the parent plant grew and formed the seeds.

A young dandelion flower (yellow florets) grows next to a mature flower with a full seed head.

Interactive Review

Complete this section to review the main concepts of the lesson.

Two types of reproduction are asexual reproduction, which involves one parent, and sexual reproduction, which involves two parents.

A. Compare the advantages of each type of reproduction.

Asexual reproduction results in offspring that are genetically identical to the parent. Sexual reproduction results in offspring that have a combination of genes from each parent.

B. Draw a diagram that compares inheritance that results from asexual reproduction to inheritance that results from sexual reproduction.

The Environment and Genetics Affect Plant Survival

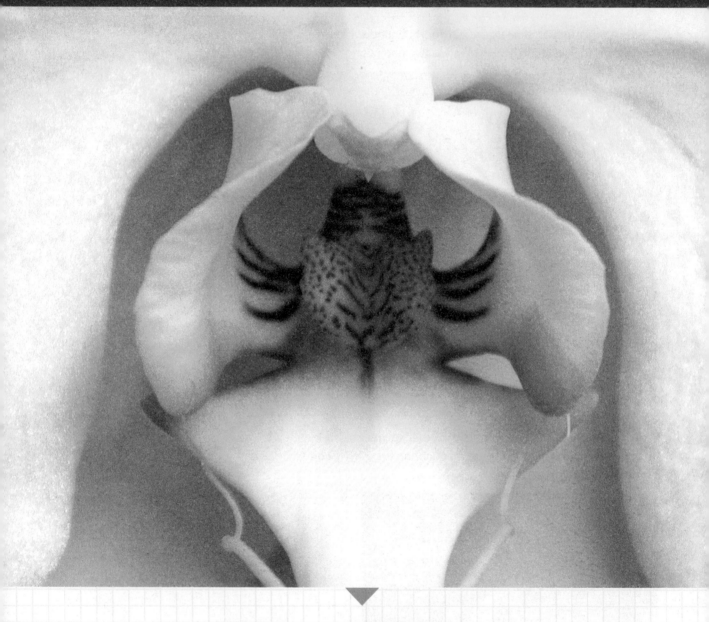

The moth orchid, which grows in Southeast Asia and Australia, has flowers that bloom for three months.

 Explore First

Modeling Seed Dispersal Use a cotton ball and a hook and loop fastener to model two seed types. Predict which is more likely to be dispersed by wind. Blow on the models to test your prediction. How might the other seed type be dispersed? What environmental factors might plants with these seed types depend upon for dispersal?

Go online to view the digital version of the Hands-On Lab for this lesson and to download additional lab resources.

CAN YOU EXPLAIN IT?

How do the characteristics of the sacred lotus flower relate to reproduction?

The sacred lotus grows in soil that is submerged in water. An individual plant can live for a thousand years, and the seeds can remain capable of reproducing for as long as 1,300 years.

Researchers have found that the sacred lotus plant has the ability to regulate the temperature of its flowers. As the air temperature cools, the flower maintains a steady temperature and gives off a fragrant scent.

1. What function do you think a flower that stays warm at night might have for a plant? What function do you think a sweet smelling flower might have for a plant?

EVIDENCE NOTEBOOK As you explore the lesson, gather evidence to help you explain the characteristics of the sacred lotus flower.

Investigating Reproductive Structures of Plants

Like all living organisms, plants produce offspring through reproduction. Different species have different ways of reproducing, but they all have specialized structures for reproduction. These structures come in a wide variety of colors, shapes, and sizes. They can be a source of nutrition for animals, and objects of beauty highly valued by people.

Analyze Plant Structures

2. Examine the plant structures below. Which functions do you think each structure plays in the plant's reproduction? Write the functions for each plant.

	attract animals	disperse seeds
	protect seeds	

	Willow trees have flower clusters, called catkins, that can be male or female. The female catkins contain seeds, and they are covered with long, fluffy hairs.	
	Cherry trees have distinctive flowers that range in color from white to pink. The flowers contain sugary nectar and protein-rich pollen.	
	Pomegranate trees grow in warm, dry climates. Their seeds are housed inside colorful, juicy fruits.	
	Blue spruce trees have male and female cones, both of which are covered with tough scales. The female cones contain lightweight seeds.	

Sexual Reproduction in Plants

Most plants can reproduce sexually. Plants produced by sexual reproduction are genetically different from both parents and from each other. This genetic variation increases the chance that some offspring will have traits that help them survive in a changing environment.

Reproduction of Seedless Plants

Seedless plants do not produce seeds for reproduction. Instead of seeds, the bodies of seedless plants grow from spores. A *spore* of a seedless plant is a tiny structure that is dispersed from the parent plant and can grow into a new plant body. To reproduce, sperm from one plant must swim through water to fertilize the egg of another plant. Because of this requirement for water, many seedless plants live in moist environments. The fertilized egg grows into a stalk-like structure that produces spores. Spores grow into new plants and the life cycle continues.

Reproductive Structures of Seedless Plants

Mosses are seedless plants that grow on rocks, soil, trees, and even between cracks in pavement.

 Release of Spores
Under the right conditions, spores are released from this part of the moss plant, called a *capsule*. Spores may land far away from the parent plant and grow into a new plant body.

 Fertilization
In this part of the plant, fertilization occurs when a sperm swims to an egg. A fertilized egg then grows into a stalk-like structure, on which spores are produced.

3. **Discuss** How might dry conditions affect the reproductive success of a seedless plant?

Reproduction of Seed Plants

In seed plants, sperm are carried in a microscopic structure called pollen. *Pollen* looks like fine dust and can be transported by wind, water, or animals. Eggs develop inside a structure called an *ovule*. The ovule has a small opening where transported pollen can get inside. When pollen reaches and fertilizes an egg, **pollination** occurs.

A fertilized egg develops into an embryo. The embryo will then grow into a new plant. The ovule becomes the **seed**, the structure that contains the embryo inside a protective coating. Seeds can be carried away from the parent plant by wind, water, or animals. After seed dispersal, the seeds grow into new plants if the conditions are right.

Seed plants can be classified as nonflowering or flowering. Nonflowering plants produce seeds that are not enclosed in a fruit. Most nonflowering seed plants produce seeds enclosed in a structure called a *cone*. Flowering plants produce flowers and fruit. Flowering plants are the largest group within the plant kingdom. They are also the largest group of plants that live on land.

Reproductive Structures of Nonflowering Seed Plants

Conifers are nonflowering plants that produce male and female cones.

 Male Cone Pollen sacs are located on the scales of the male cone. Pollen is produced here. Mature male cones release pollen into the air. Pollen often travels by wind.

 Female Cone The female cone has a pair of ovules on each scale. Pollination occurs when pollen reaches an egg inside an ovule. After they are pollinated, the fertilized eggs will develop into seeds. The seeds are dispersed when the cone breaks apart.

© Houghton Mifflin Harcourt Publishing Company • Image Credits: ©Kathy Merrifield/ Science Source

4. Based on the structure of the seeds below, decide if the method of dispersal is wind, water, or animals. Then describe your evidence. Write the answer in the space provided.

Seed Structure	Dispersal Method
milkweed seedlings	
dry burdock	
palm seed	

EVIDENCE NOTEBOOK

5. The sacred lotus plant has a large seedpod that eventually dries out and causes the flower to bend over. How do you think the sacred lotus flower's seeds are dispersed? Record your evidence.

Asexual Reproduction in Plants

Many plants are also able to reproduce asexually. For example, in some plants, a part of the parent plant, such as a root or a stem, can grow into a new plant. Tubers, such as potatoes, can sprout roots that take hold in the soil and produce a new plant. Other plants, such as spider plants, produce plantlets. *Plantlets* are tiny plants that grow along the edges of a plant's leaves or on special stalks. They eventually break off and develop into new plants. Asexual reproduction in plants results in offspring that are genetically identical to the parent.

Each "eye" on this potato is an asexual structure that can grow into a new plant.

6. Write asexual reproduction or sexual reproduction to indicate the type of reproduction that would be most advantageous in each environmental condition shown in the table below. Support your answers with reasoning.

Environmental Condition	Type of Reproduction	Reasoning
Sunlight and nutrient levels are stable.	asexual	Since there are plenty of resources, the plant can reproduce quickly and colonize the area.
Water becomes scarce.		
A pest species is introduced.		
A new space for growth becomes available with similar conditions.		

Language SmArts
Construct an Argument

7. The majority of plants on Earth are seed plants. Use reasoning and evidence from the text to construct an argument about why producing seeds might be advantageous to the reproductive success of a plant species.

_____

_____

_____

_____

_____

_____

Analyzing Reproductive Success of Flowering Plants

Plants cannot move around to find mates or to deposit their seeds in the perfect spot for growth. Wind and water can assist plant reproduction. However, many plants rely on insects, birds, or mammals to carry their pollen and seeds.

Explore Online

The hawk moth visits flowers at night.

8. Night-blooming plants are usually pollinated by animals that are active at night, such as some species of beetles, moths, and bats. What traits might a night-blooming flower have to attract nighttime feeders?

Pollination in Flowering Plants

The sperm of seed plants is carried in pollen. When pollen reaches an egg of the same kind of plant, it is called *pollination*. Some types of plants self-pollinate. This means that pollen is transferred to the egg of the same plant. Other types of plants cross-pollinate. In this case, the pollen from one plant is transferred to the egg of another plant. Animal pollinators play an important role in cross-pollination of plants.

Flowers contain nectar, a sugar-rich liquid that provides energy and nutrients to animals. Animals attracted to the flowers by their color or scent are rewarded with a tasty meal of nectar. The plant benefits because the animal carries away pollen that sticks to its body. The pollen is deposited on the next flower the animal visits.

9. **Discuss** Why might it be beneficial for a plant to be able to self-pollinate and to also have adaptations that attract animal pollinators?

Explore Reproduction in a Flowering Plant

The structures of the reproductive organs found in a flower relate to their function in pollination.

Pistil The pistil is the female reproductive structure of a flower. A pistil consists of the stigma, the style, and the ovary. The stigma is often sticky or covered in hairs. This makes it easier to collect pollen. The ovary contains the ovules, which produce eggs. After fertilization, the ovules develop into seeds. The ovary develops into a fruit.

Stamen The stamen is a flower's male reproductive structure. A stamen consists of an anther, the pollen-producing part of the flower. The anther sits on top of a thin stalk. The anther produces spores that develop into pollen.

Pollinator As pollinators feed on pollen and nectar, pollen from a flower's anther rubs off on their bodies. When they fly to a second flower, pollen from the first flower rubs off on the second flower's stigma. Meanwhile, pollen from the second flower's anther rubs off on the pollinators' bodies, ready to be delivered to another flower.

heliconia flower

Heliconia is found in the rain forests of Central America and southern Mexico.

10. Based on the structure of the heliconia flower, which animal do you think is its pollinator?

A.

long-nosed bat

B.

Hercules beetle

C.

green hermit hummingbird

Investigate Flower Structures

A flower contains the reproductive structures of a flowering plant. In addition, flowers have specialized leaves called *sepals* and *petals*. Sepals cover and protect the flower while it is budding. Petals are often colorful and can help attract animal pollinators. The pedicel is part of the stem that supports the flower. At the end of the pedicel is the receptacle, which forms the base of the flower.

You will dissect a flower and record drawings of the structures you discover.

MATERIALS
- flower
- hand lens
- lab gloves (as needed for allergies)
- scalpel
- surgical mask (as needed for allergies)

Procedure

STEP 1 Use the scalpel to carefully dissect the flower. Sort the structures.

STEP 2 **Draw** Use the hand lens to examine each structure. Draw and label one example of each structure. Depending on the type of flower you dissect, the structures of your flower might look different than the structures in the drawing.

Analysis and Conclusions

STEP 3 Describe patterns you observed in the arrangement of the flower parts.

STEP 4 **Collaborate** With a partner, model the body features you would expect of an animal that pollinates the type of flower you dissected. Present your model and explain how structure and function are important for plants and pollinators.

EVIDENCE NOTEBOOK

11. The sacred lotus plant is pollinated by bees and beetles. How do the traits of the sacred lotus flower help attract these pollinators? Record your evidence.

Seed Dispersal of Flowering Plants

Wind and water disperse the seeds of many plants. Animals also play a role in seed dispersal. Animals are attracted to the fruits of some flowering plants. When an animal eats a fruit, the seeds pass through the animal's digestive system. The seeds are then deposited away from the parent plant as the animal travels.

Other types of seeds can hitch a ride on the fur or feet of passing animals. The seeds have hooks, barbs, or sticky mucus that allows them to attach to animals.

Some animals bury the seeds of plants, planning to return and eat them later. If an animal does not retrieve the buried seeds, the seeds may germinate where they are buried. Squirrels that bury oak tree acorns are an example of this type of animal-assisted seed dispersal.

This bird will excrete the prickly pear seeds through its digestive system.

12. What are the benefits to the survival of offspring when seeds are dispersed far from the parent plant?

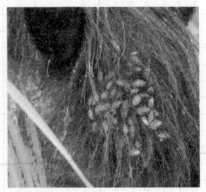

Burrs stick to the fur and feet of mammals, such as this horse.

13. What are the drawbacks to the survival of offspring when seeds are dispersed far from the parent plant?

© Houghton Mifflin Harcourt Publishing Company • Image Credits: (t) ©Paco Toscano/Shutterstock; (b) ©Lenz/blickwinkel/Alamy

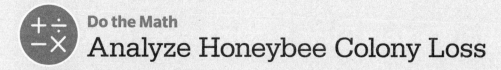

Do the Math
Analyze Honeybee Colony Loss

Bees are important pollinators for the global food supply. In the United States $15 billion of apples, berries, almonds, and cucumbers are pollinated by bees each year. However, since at least 2006, bees have been suffering from a phenomenon known as *colony collapse disorder* (CCD). Beekeepers have been experiencing higher than expected colony losses since CCD was first reported. Scientists are investigating various causes of CCD including bacteria, parasites, pesticide use, and habitat destruction. Other causes of colony loss include harsh temperatures, poor nutrition, and queen death.

U.S.-Managed Honeybee Colony Loss Estimates

The graph shows the honeybee colony losses reported over a ten-year period. Total annual loss estimates (summer and winter) were not reported between 2006 and 2009.

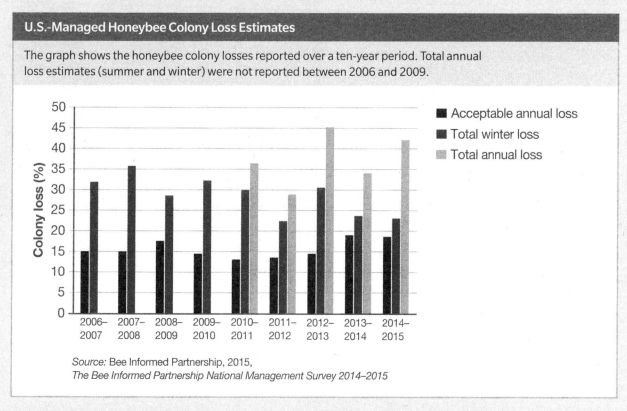

Source: Bee Informed Partnership, 2015,
The Bee Informed Partnership National Management Survey 2014–2015

14. What percentage of acceptable loss was estimated for 2006–2007 and 2007–2008 when CCD was first reported? How much did the total winter loss estimates for these years exceed this expectation? During which year was the difference between acceptable loss and total winter loss the greatest?

_____

_____

_____

15. What was the average total annual loss over the years for which these data were reported? What was the average total winter loss over this same period of time? Use evidence and reasoning to write an argument that supports or refutes the claim that summertime losses account for the majority of annual losses from 2010–2015.

_____

_____

_____

Describing Factors That Affect Plant Growth

Plants need air, sunlight, water, space, and nutrients for growth. Each plant species has its own specific requirements. For example, the seeds of different plants may have different requirements to *germinate*, or develop from a seed into a small plant. Processes controlled by genes inside the seed are triggered by temperature, moisture, and light. These environmental cues indicate that conditions are good for plant growth. Some seeds need extreme temperatures, such as freezing or fire, for germination. Extreme temperatures can help break down a hard seed coat so water and oxygen that an embryo needs to grow can enter the seed. Seeds can delay germination, or go *dormant*, until conditions are right for plant growth.

16. Explain how seed germination is caused by a combination of genetic and environmental factors. Cite evidence from the text to support your answer.

Dutch iris seeds need cold temperatures to germinate.

Genetic Factors Affect Plant Growth

Genes are passed from parent to offspring during reproduction. A plant's genes affect its traits. Therefore, different genes are responsible for the differences in the thousands of plant types, or species, that exist on Earth. For example, ferns grow well in the moist, low-light conditions of the forest floor, and cacti grow well in dry, full-light conditions. The ability of different types of plants to grow in such different conditions is due to genetic differences between plant species.

Individual plants of the same species can also have genetic differences. These differences exist because there can be different forms of the same gene. For example, different varieties of the same plant species may grow at different rates, even if they are planted in the same garden. Different forms of certain plant genes may affect drought tolerance or leaf size, both of which can affect the growth of plants.

Engineer It
Explore Plant Hybrids

Plant breeders cross-pollinate different types of plants in order to produce a desired trait or traits in the offspring. For instance, they might try to introduce resistance to disease, drought, or pests. Breeders also select for flower color, larger fruit, or a seedless variety. (Think seedless grapes and watermelon.) The resulting domesticated plants have genetic differences from the parent plants.

Heirloom tomatoes are valued for their taste, color, and unusual appearance.

Sun Gold tomatoes are very sweet and tolerant of cooler temperatures.

Grape tomatoes are sweet, small, and heat-tolerant.

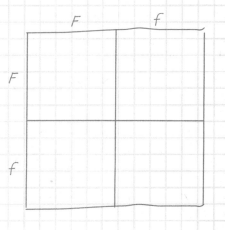

Juliet tomatoes are sweet, small, and resistant to disease.

17. How might a cross between the Sun Gold tomato and the Juliet tomato result in a desirable hybrid?

18. A tomato breeder has noticed that a hybrid is not attracting pollinators to its flowers. What genetic change may have occurred in this hybrid? What does that mean for the long-term survival of the hybrid?

19. Scientists have discovered a gene that affects how many tomatoes an individual plant produces. The gene controls a protein named *florigen*, which affects the number of fruit a plant develops. When a plant has a dominant (*F*) and recessive (*f*) allele for the gene, it produces a high tomato yield. Plants that have two dominant or two recessive alleles for the trait produce a lower tomato yield.
Fill out the Punnett square. Use evidence from this and other Punnett squares to support or refute a farmer's claim that this cross will result in the most offspring with high tomato yields when compared to other potential crosses.

	F	*f*
F		
f		

Environmental Factors Affect Plant Survival

The mosses and redwoods that inhabit California forests grow quite differently due to differences in their genes. Mosses are very short plants, while redwoods are very tall trees. Environmental conditions also play a role in plant growth. If a redwood seed was planted in soil that was contaminated by pollution, the tree may never reach its full potential height. Mosses thrive in cool, wet environments with plenty of shade. If the temperatures increase or the air becomes dry, moss may fail to grow.

Climate

The term climate refers to the predictable weather patterns of a region over a long period of time. If the climate of the region changes, it could affect a plant's ability to grow and survive. For example, California's dry climate makes the state prone to droughts, which are periods with lower-than-average rainfall. As average global temperatures increase, California may have more frequent droughts. Since plants need water to grow, extreme drought conditions could limit the growth of native California plants.

Local Conditions

Bigleaf hydrangeas produce different flower colors depending on the pH of the soil. The pH scale ranges from 0 to 14. Lower values are acidic, while higher values are alkaline, and 7.0 is neutral. If bigleaf hydrangeas are planted in neutral or alkaline soil, their flowers will be pink. If planted in very acidic soil, they will produce blue flowers. If the soil is only weakly acidic (pH = 5.5–6.5), the flowers will be purple or have a mix of blue and pink petals.

The color differences among these flowers are caused by pH differences in the soil.

20. A gardener wants to grow hydrangeas in his flowerbeds shown in the image. He has three different types of soil. Soil A has a pH of 5.0, Soil B has a pH of 6.0, and Soil C has a pH of 8.0. The gardener wants pink flowers in Bed #3, purple flowers in Bed #2, and blue flowers in Bed #1. Which soil should the gardener put in each flowerbed? Use evidence of environmental and genetic influence on hydrangeas to support your answer.

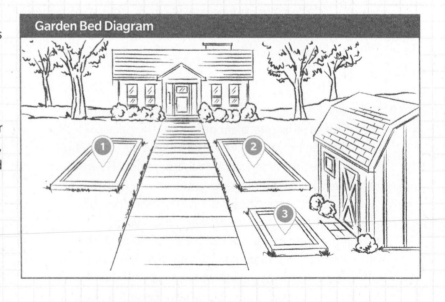

Garden Bed Diagram

Environmental Stimuli

Like all organisms, plants respond to environmental stimuli. Seasonal changes can stimulate a plant to grow, reproduce, or even become dormant until the conditions are more favorable. For example, many trees have green leaves during warmer seasons. In colder months, these leaves change color and fall off. Some seeds can stay dormant for months, or even years, until the conditions are right for growth.

Plants bend toward a light source because they need light to perform photosynthesis.

21. The diagram shows how a tree responds to changing seasons. Identify the environmental cues that cause the tree to change.

word bank
- change from cold to warm
- change from hot to cool
- ~~transition to longest days~~
- transition to shortest days

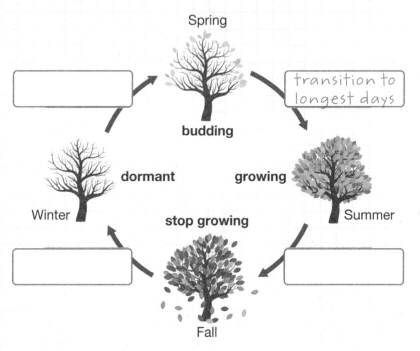

Spring

transition to longest days

budding

growing

dormant

Winter

stop growing

Summer

Fall

22. Read the environmental conditions. Decide whether the condition will result in *increased* or *decreased* growth of the parent plant.

   A. Nutrient-rich organic matter was added to the soil. _____

   B. The habitat experienced rainfall levels well below normal for the year. _____

   C. Tall trees grew around the plant. _____

   D. A plant that requires an alkaline soil is planted in soil that has a pH of 5.0. _____

Genetic and Environmental Influence on Plants

Many plants are sensitive to soil salinity, or the sodium content in soil. Saline soil occurs naturally in coastal areas that receive spray from the ocean. It is also caused by human activities, like irrigation and the de-icing of roadways.

Highly saline soil can limit a plant's ability to absorb water and restrict the plant's growth. In slightly saline soil, lettuce and other highly salt-sensitive food crops experience a 25 to 50% decrease in crop yield. Some crops, like sugar beets, carry salt-tolerant genes that allow them to grow even in highly saline soil.

Soil salinity is a problem in areas of California's Central Valley due to poor drainage, irrigation, and other factors. The region grows many profitable, salt-sensitive crops, like almonds and plums. In some areas, the soil salinity is now too high to grow food. Much of this land has been sold for other uses, like the construction of solar energy farms.

Analyze Aspen Growth

Aspen trees are a type of tree native to cold regions. Aspens are often a pioneer species, populating areas that have recently lost vegetation to erosion, fire, or disease. They provide cover for conifer seedlings, but they often die out as the conifers take over the area. Aspens can reproduce sexually but more often reproduce asexually by sending up multiple stems from a single root system.

aspen trees

23. Mountain aspens are often used to landscape homes in lower-elevation suburban or urban areas. What factors might affect the growth of the mountain aspen in the new habitat?

_____

_____

_____

_____

24. Would you expect an aspen tree to be able to tolerate shade? Why or why not?

_____

_____

_____

_____

25. Small groves of aspen trees that appear to be separate trees may be multiple stems attached to one extensive underground root system. Would you expect individuals in a grove to be able to adapt to a change in the environment? Explain.

_____

_____

_____

Continue Your Exploration

Name: _____   Date: _____

Check out the path below or go online to choose one of the other paths shown.

| Capsaicin Levels in Peppers | • Seed Vaults
• Hands-On Labs 🖐
• Propose Your Own Path | *Go online to choose one of these other paths.* |

The sensation of "heat" experienced when a person eats a hot pepper is not taste. Instead the pain receptors in the mouth are triggered when a person eats a hot pepper. The Scoville scale is a measurement scale that was created to measure the heat of a pepper, which is caused by a chemical compound called *capsaicin*.

The amount of capsaicin in a chili pepper is determined partially by its genetics and partially by the environmental conditions in which it grows. These conditions include factors, such as temperature, humidity, soil conditions, light, and the availability of water. When chili peppers are grown in less-than-ideal conditions, peppers that genetically should have low heat will become hotter, while peppers that genetically should have high heat will become less hot.

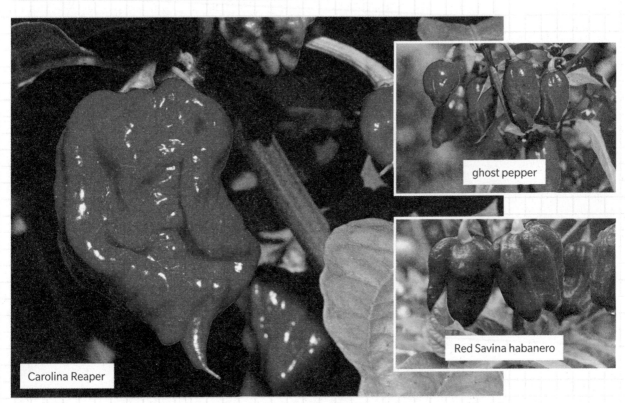

ghost pepper

Red Savina habanero

Carolina Reaper

The Carolina Reaper is currently the hottest chili pepper in the world, with an average measurement of 1,569,300 SHU (Scoville heat units). The Carolina Reaper is thought to be a hybrid of the ghost pepper and the Red Savina.

Continue Your Exploration

1. How could a farmer increase his or her chances of growing a pepper with a certain heat measurement on the Scoville scale?

2. A chili pepper plant that produces fruit with a low heat level is grown in an area that experiences a drought. What might the farmer expect will happen to the plant? Why?

3. A farmer wants to create a chili pepper that has a higher SHU measurement than the Carolina Reaper. What could he or she do to achieve this goal?

4. **Collaborate** Why do you think pepper fruits contain capsaicin? How might capsaicin affect the reproduction or growth of a pepper plant? Research hypotheses about the function of capsaicin. Use multiple, credible sources to collect your data. Write a short paper and present your findings in a multimedia presentation.

Can You Explain It?

Name: _____ **Date:** _____

How do the characteristics of the sacred lotus flower relate to reproduction?

 EVIDENCE NOTEBOOK
Refer to the notes in your Evidence Notebook to help you construct an explanation for how the characteristics of the sacred lotus flower contribute to the reproductive success of the plant.

1. State your claim. Make sure your claim fully explains the characteristics of the sacred lotus flower.

2. Summarize the evidence you have gathered to support your claim and explain your reasoning.

Checkpoints

Answer the following questions to check your understanding of the lesson.

Use the photo to answer Questions 3–4.

3. How might this flower contribute to the plant's reproductive success?

   A. The shape of the flower's petals attracts pollinators.

   B. The flower attracts bees that think they are meeting a mate.

   C. The flower scares away birds looking for a meal.

4. Number the statements in order to describe how an animal pollinator aids in the pollination of a flowering plant.

   _____ The ovules develop into seeds.

   _____ The pollinator flies to another flower where the pollen rubs off on the flower's stigma.

   _____ The sperm within the pollen fertilizes the eggs.

   _____ The animal pollinator feeds on nectar, and the flower's pollen attaches to its body.

Use the photo to answer Question 5.

5. Bonsai trees are kept small using the art of trimming and shaping. They can be grown from seeds or cuttings. Which statements are true about bonsai trees? Select all that apply.

   A. Bonsai trees do not need light, water, and nutrients to survive and reproduce.

   B. Bonsai trees need light, water, and nutrients just like the full-sized tree species.

   C. Bonsai trees can reproduce sexually and asexually.

   D. Bonsai trees can only reproduce sexually.

6. Can breeders always know the exact traits that a hybrid will have? Select all that apply.

   A. Yes. People create hybrid plants because they want to combine the desirable traits of one plant with the desirable traits of another plant.

   B. No. People cannot predict every trait that a hybrid will have.

   C. No. A breeder may succeed in breeding a hybrid that has the specific trait they find desirable, but the hybrid may also have another trait that is less desirable.

   D. Yes. The outcome of reproduction can be predicted with 100% certainty.

7. Eucalyptus plants grow in wildfire-prone areas. Their seeds have a thick coating that melts during a fire, releasing the seed into the ground. This coating allows the seed to stay dormant / grow tall until a wildfire occurs. This increases / decreases the chances that the seed will grow after the fire.

Interactive Review

Complete this section to review the main concepts of the lesson.

Most plants can reproduce sexually, producing genetically diverse offspring. Many can also reproduce asexually, producing genetically identical offspring.

A. How are non-flowering seed plants and flowering plants similar and different?

All plants have specialized reproductive structures. Plants can be pollinated by wind or water, and they can often self-pollinate. They may also rely on animal pollinators.

B. Describe how animals can contribute to the reproductive success of a plant.

Both environmental and genetic factors have an effect on plant growth.

C. Draw a cause-and-effect diagram with examples of how genetic and environmental factors can affect plant growth.

The Environment and Genetics Affect Animal Survival

An elephant calf develops inside its mother for 18–22 months, longer than any other mammal.

Explore First

Modeling Reproduction Develop a model that shows what might happen in a population if only the males with a certain trait reproduce. Can your model help you explain extravagant traits in males, such as the showy tail feathers of a peacock or the large antlers of a moose?

Go online to view the digital version of the Hands-On Lab for this lesson and to download additional lab resources.

CAN YOU EXPLAIN IT?

Why are these male zebras fighting?

These zebras live on the grassy plains in Etosha National Park in Namibia. Plains zebras live in family groups that include one male and several females with their offspring.

1. Think of three reasons why these zebras might be fighting with each other.

EVIDENCE NOTEBOOK As you explore the lesson, gather evidence to help you explain why male zebras fight with each other.

Describing Animal Reproduction

Scientists estimate that as many as eight or nine million species of animals may be living on Earth. Although some of these animals can reproduce asexually, sexual reproduction is the dominant form of reproduction in animals. Multiple factors influence the reproductive success of an animal. For example, genetic factors may result in a male bird that has a call that females prefer over the calls of other males. However, the survival of this male's offspring will depend on the available food supply, protection from predators, and weather conditions. Dragonflies are also influenced by multiple factors. Dragonflies reproduce sexually. Fertilized dragonfly eggs hatch into nymphs. The nymphs are aquatic. Therefore, dragonflies require an environment with water in order to reproduce successfully.

These mating dragonflies reproduce sexually.

2. Write *asexual reproduction*, *sexual reproduction*, or *both* in the table to describe the reproductive process of each animal.

Animal	Reproductive Process	Type of Reproduction
Eastern gray squirrel (mammal)	After a male and female squirrel mate, fertilization occurs inside the female's body. She gives birth to two or more offspring that she feeds with milk from her body.	sexual reproduction
Roseate spoonbill (bird)	After a male and female spoonbill mate, fertilization occurs inside the female's body. The female lays eggs that will hatch into chicks.	
New Zealand mud snail (mollusk)	Female mud snails are born with genetically identical embryos inside them. They can also mate with a male to produce young snails from fertilized eggs.	
Tree frog (amphibian)	In all of the many species of tree frogs, the female lays eggs, and then the male fertilizes them.	
Walking stick (insect)	Female stick insects can produce offspring from unfertilized eggs. They can also mate with a male to produce fertilized eggs.	
Pacific salmon (fish)	Salmon eggs are laid by a female and then fertilized by a male.	

Sexual Reproduction in Animals

Sexual reproduction is a type of reproduction that involves two parents. Offspring get one copy of their chromosomes from each parent. As a result, organisms produced by this type of reproduction are genetically different from both parents. This genetic variation increases the chance that some offspring will have traits that may help them survive in a changing environment. The ability of an organism to pass on its genes to healthy offspring is called *reproductive success.*

In sexual reproduction, fertilization can be internal or external. In some species, the male and female mate, and fertilization occurs inside the female's body. In other species, the female lays eggs, and the male fertilizes them outside the female's body. Some animals lay fertilized eggs, and others give birth to live offspring.

This male damselfish is protecting the eggs he fertilized outside the female's body.

This mother robin laid eggs that will develop into young birds that she and her mate will care for.

This mother kangaroo will carry her baby (joey) in her pouch until it is fully developed.

This mother seal gave birth to her pup. She will feed it with milk from her body until it can find its own food.

3. What behavior do all of these animal parents have in common? How do you think this behavior contributes to each animal's reproductive success?

JupiterImages/Getty Images; (bl) ©John White Photos/Moment Open/Getty Images

Asexual Reproduction in Animals

Asexual reproduction is a type of reproduction that involves only one parent. The parent passes a copy of its genes to its offspring. Unless there is a mutation, an organism produced by asexual reproduction is genetically identical to its parent and to other offspring produced asexually by the parent.

Environmental conditions can influence the type of reproduction used by an animal that can reproduce asexually or sexually. These animals might reproduce asexually when rapid reproduction is beneficial, such as the opportunity to colonize a large area. They might also reproduce asexually if conditions are unfavorable for sexual reproduction. For example, a shortage of mates or an unsuitable temperature for survival might favor asexual reproduction.

4. Which environmental stimulus might result in asexual reproduction in these animals? Use the terms in the word bank to complete the table.

> **WORD BANK**
> • lack of mates
> • injury
> • temperature change

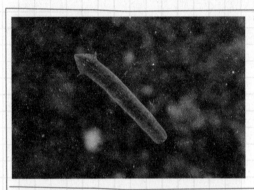	Planaria reproduce asexually by regeneration. If the animal is split or cut into pieces, the cut segments can grow into new animals.	
	Male and female sponges can reproduce asexually by producing structures that are able to survive harsh environmental conditions.	
	Female Komodo dragons can reproduce asexually through a process that does not require fertilization of their eggs by a male.	

 EVIDENCE NOTEBOOK

5. The zebra is a mammal like the eastern gray squirrel and the seal. How do you think a zebra reproduces and raises young? Record your evidence.

Language SmArts
Evaluate Reproductive Strategies

Aggregating anemones are animals that live in shallow ocean reefs. They are usually found in dense colonies that extend across a large, rocky area. *Aggregating* refers to forming a group or cluster. Each colony is a group of genetically identical animals that are hostile to members of other colonies that live on their borders.

Aggregating anemones can reproduce asexually by splitting into two pieces. They can also reproduce sexually by releasing sperm and eggs into the water. A fertilized egg develops into a larva that will eventually settle to the ocean floor and start a new colony of aggregating anemones.

aggregating anemone

6. How do both types of reproduction influence where aggregating anemone colonies establish and grow? Use reasoning and cite evidence from the text to support your claims.

_____

_____

_____

_____

_____

_____

Relating Animal Behaviors to Reproductive Success

Reproductive success is the ability to produce offspring that are healthy and that survive. Different species of animals use different strategies to increase their chance of reproductive success. These strategies include adult behaviors, such as courtship and parenting.

Strategies for reproductive success also include offspring behaviors. The offspring of some animal species imprint—or trust and follow—one or both parents. Young geese demonstrate this behavior. The offspring of other animals instinctively stop moving to avoid attracting the attention of predators.

These baby cardinals make loud calls and open their mouths wide when a parent is near.

7. How does the behavior of the bird's offspring contribute to reproductive success?

Courtship Behaviors

Courtship behaviors are attempts by animals to attract mates. Securing a healthy mate is one way to increase the odds of reproductive success. Courtship behaviors are exhibited mainly by males to convince females that they are valuable mates. In some species, females also engage in courtship behaviors.

Frogs, deer, bats, whales, and seals vocalize to attract a mate. Some animals, such as many species of birds, vocalize and perform dances. Males sometimes dance alone, although in some species the female joins in.

This male manakin moonwalks across a branch to impress a mate.

The males of many bird species display brightly colored feathers or other body parts in an attempt to attract females. Most females, by contrast, have feathers of neutral colors. They are the ones being courted by the colorful males.

Male animals of some species display their strength or fight with other males to court females or to establish dominance in a group. Male deer fight each other using their antlers. Male elephant seals slam their bodies into each other, while male damselflies ram each other's bodies.

The males of other animal species give presents to females or build structures for them. They do so to persuade the females to mate. Bowerbirds, for example, build intricate nests and show them to females, hoping to win their approval. Male kingfisher birds present females with fish.

8. What qualities do these males have that encourage females to accept them as mates? Use the Word Bank phrases to record your answers.

WORD BANK
- provides a meal
- protects offspring and females
- has good genetic fitness

Male elks' antlers can weigh up to 18 kilograms (40 pounds) and stand as tall as 1.2 meters (4 feet) above their heads. Elk use their antlers to fight with other males and chase off predators.

Male peacocks have long, beautiful tail feathers. The feathers are heavy, and the peacocks must be strong to carry them.

These are male and female spiders. The male, which is the smaller of the two, has a gift for the female––an insect wrapped in silk.

9. Discuss Birds sing for many reasons, but male birds produce particular songs to attract females. What other benefit might these loud vocalizations provide to the male? Talk about your ideas with a partner.

EVIDENCE NOTEBOOK

10. How could the fighting behavior of male zebras provide information to female zebras about reproductive success? Record your evidence.

Parenting Behaviors

Parenting behaviors are attempts by animals to ensure their offspring's survival. These behaviors are another way that animals increase their odds of reproductive success.

Many animal species build nests for their eggs and young. Males or females, or both, gather the materials and construct the nests. One or both parents might guard eggs and offspring in the nest.

Animals feed their young in a variety of ways. Female mammals nurse their young with milk from their bodies. Other species gather or hunt food for their offspring. For example, some birds eat food and then regurgitate it for their young. The offspring are better able to eat the food once it has been partially broken down by the parent bird's digestive system.

Animals care for their young for varying lengths of time. Many reptiles abandon their eggs before they hatch, so the young are on their own. Other species stay with their offspring for a few months (birds) or for years (elephants). Some animals also teach offspring how to fend for themselves. For example, lions teach their young to hunt.

Some animals sacrifice their health or their lives for their offspring. A male emperor penguin holds a single egg on the top of his feet, covered with a layer of skin to keep it warm. He does this for 60–68 days through extremely cold and windy conditions with no access to food. Another example of parent sacrifice is the female of many octopus species that guard and care for their eggs for months—even years—before they hatch. After the eggs hatch, the female dies. After the eggs of the killdeer bird hatch, both parents keep predators away from their offspring by pretending to be injured. A killdeer will drag its "broken wing" along the ground, luring the predators away from the young birds. Adult killdeers sometimes are caught and killed by predators while using this strategy.

> **WORD BANK**
> - building a nest
> - defending offspring
> - feeding offspring
> - teaching offspring

11. What parental behavior is shown by each of these animals?

red squirrel

Bengal tiger and cubs

penguins and caracara

brown bear and cubs

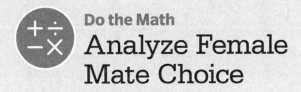

Do the Math
Analyze Female Mate Choice

Guppies are freshwater tropical fish native to South America. Males usually have brightly colored fins and tails. Researchers study the traits that female guppies prefer when choosing mates. The table show the results of experiments that tested female preference for three different tail sizes.

male guppy

12. Use the data from the table to describe the three experiments in your own words. How does female choice function in this system?

Experiment 1	
Male Tail Size	Female Choice (%)
Large-tailed male	78
Small-tailed male	22
Experiment 2	
Male Tail Size	Female Choice (%)
Large-tailed male	68
Medium-tailed male	32
Experiment 3	
Male Tail Size	Female Choice (%)
Medium-tailed male	65
Small-tailed male	35

Source: Bischoff et al., Behavioral Ecology and Sociobiology 17:3

13. Why might the percentage of female preference for medium-sized tails be greater in Experiment 3 than it was in Experiment 2?

14. In a population of guppies, there is an equal number of short-tailed, medium-tailed, and large-tailed males. Based on the data, which group of males would have the highest probability of reproductive success? Why?

Explaining Factors That Influence Animal Growth

Animals face many challenges to survive. Environments can be unpredictable, and many factors that affect health act on animals at the same time. For example, food supply, weather, and disease influence the growth of animals. Animals inherit traits that help them face these challenges. But, the growth and survival of an animal depends on complex interactions between genetic and environmental factors.

15. Do you think the bowl provides a healthy environment for the goldfish? Why or why not?

Common goldfish will eat as much food as they are given and produce large amounts of waste.

16. What factors might limit the growth of a goldfish living in a large pond?

Genetic Factors Affect Animal Survival

Sexual reproduction in animals results in genetic variation of traits in offspring. Differences in traits can give some individuals an advantage over other individuals. Some offspring might have better eyesight or hearing, stronger jaws or teeth, or thicker fur than other offspring. Some might not have inherited diseases that others have.

These genetic differences do not only affect individual offspring. They also affect entire populations. Due to differences in genetic traits, some individuals in an animal population might be able to survive changing environmental conditions better than other individuals. As a result, the population can continue to exist in the community.

Gray wolves have long legs and strong jaws that help them catch and kill prey.

© Houghton Mifflin Harcourt Publishing Company • Image Credits: (l) ©Jerry Shulman/ SuperStock/Alamy; (r) ©Capture Light/Shutterstock

Engineer It
Explain Trait Selection in Dog Breeds

At least 12,000 years ago, humans began to domesticate members of a wolf-like species. Scientists think that this animal is a common ancestor shared by the gray wolf and the dogs of today's world.

Each of the more than 300 different dog breeds was developed over a long period of time. Humans selected the dogs with the traits they wanted and then bred them. For example, the poodle is used during hunting to retrieve birds from the water for the hunter. Its keen intelligence, webbed feet, and curly coat that is almost waterproof make it well-suited to hunting in rivers and marshes. These traits are very different from the traits of the wolf-like ancestor of long ago.

In the past, dogs have been bred for many jobs, including hunting, guarding, herding, and being companions. Today, dogs are also bred and trained to help people who have visual impairments, mobility issues, and mental illnesses. Certain dogs help military and police personnel sniff out explosives and rescue people in distress.

The greyhound was bred as a hunting dog. It chases and captures fast prey, such as rabbits.

The dachshund was also bred as a hunting dog. It captures rats and other small animals that burrow in the ground.

17. Compare and contrast the traits that would be desirable in a dog that helps police locate explosives and a dog that provides companionship for the elderly.

18. Dog breeders choose mates in an effort to produce offspring with desired traits. How does this compare with the way that advantageous traits in wolves get passed on to offspring?

Environmental Factors Affect Animal Growth

Genetics is not the only factor that affects animal growth. The conditions of an animal's environment also affect growth and development. Beneficial environmental conditions include abundant food, water, air, and space. They also include a habitat free from pollution, as well as sufficient shelter from predators.

Harmful environmental conditions include weather, such as drought, that deprives animals of water or that negatively impacts the growth of the plants that the animals eat. Other harmful environmental conditions are overcrowding, pollution, and habitat destruction.

Multiple factors determine the growth of these grass-fed Angus cattle.

Adaptations to the Environment

All animals need the same basic resources to survive and reproduce: food and water, space, and a suitable temperature range. Climate and local conditions affect whether or not animals can find the basic resources they need to survive. Animals have adaptations that help them survive in a particular climate with specific local conditions.

Pronghorn antelope have adaptations that allow them to survive in their environment. Their hair is hollow which helps them control their body temperature in both hot and cold conditions. Pronghorns can survive for days without water in environments where water is scarce. Pronghorns are very fast, an adaptation to avoid predators. These animals also developed adaptations that allow them to take in large amounts of oxygen to fuel their fast runs. Finally, pronghorns have hair that pulls off easily, which allows them to elude the bite of many different predators.

Pronghorns are considered living fossils because the species has remained mostly unchanged for thousands of years.

19. **Collaborate** The Sonoran pronghorn is an endangered species that lives in the Sonoran desert. Work with a partner to identify environmental stressors that threaten the Sonoran pronghorn throughout its range. Organize your research into a graphic organizer that links causes (environmental stressors) with effects (impacts on pronghorns). Share your results with your class.

White-tailed ptarmigans are grayish-brown in the summer and white in the winter. Seasonal changes prompt the change in feather color.

The giant armadillo is nocturnal, or active at night. The sun going down cues these animals to start their day.

 EVIDENCE NOTEBOOK

20. Zebras live in groups of one male and several females or groups of young and weaker males. Why does the grouping of the zebras lead to males fighting? Record your evidence.

Case Study: The Pacific Flyway

Millions of birds migrate each year across the Pacific Flyway. Both genetic and environmental factors drive this migration. These birds travel to warmer climates because they lack physical adaptations to survive cold winters. Also, their food supply decreases as insects die off or burrow for the winter.

Some birds depend on the wetlands of California to be their winter nesting grounds, but over 95 percent of these wetlands have disappeared. Most of this land is now farmland. This is particularly true in California's Central Valley, the agricultural hub of California.

21. **Collaborate** Work with a partner to research solutions to the declining winter habitat in the Central Valley. Write and present an argument that could be used to convince others to accept this solution and put it into action. Support your argument with scientific reasoning and empirical evidence from reliable sources.

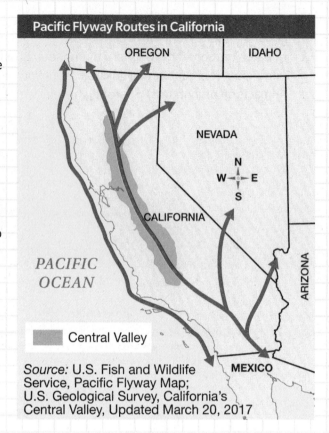

Pacific Flyway Routes in California

Central Valley

Source: U.S. Fish and Wildlife Service, Pacific Flyway Map; U.S. Geological Survey, California's Central Valley, Updated March 20, 2017

22. Decide if each change in animal growth is caused by a *genetic* or an *environmental* factor.

Causes	Effects
environmental	Bulls, calves, and cows grow weak when the grass is sparse due to drought.
	A cow grows better than other cows when the herd is moved to a colder climate.
	Young cattle do not grow well when a disease kills the grass.
	Calves are not growing well because of a parasite present in the herd.
	A bull grows better than other bulls during an unusually warm summer.

Model the Growth of an Animal

You will work with a group to design a board game that models how genetic and environmental factors affect animals. Then you will create the board game with provided materials. Finally, you will switch games with another group, play the other group's game, and give the group feedback about the game.

MATERIALS
- colored pencils, markers, or crayons
- objects that can be used as tokens
- paper
- poster board
- scissors

Procedure

STEP 1 With your group, brainstorm an idea for a board game that models the growth of an animal over time. The game must also meet the following conditions:

- Your game must incorporate five scenarios of genetic and environmental factors that have an effect on growth.

- Players will receive points or will move forward when there are positive effects on growth. For example, a player lands on a space or draws a card that reads, "Plenty of food this season! Move forward three spaces." Players will move backward or will lose a turn when there are negative effects on growth. For example, a player lands on a space or draws a card that reads, "Drought in progress! Lose a turn."

STEP 2 Once your group has finished brainstorming, discuss with group members the details of your game. Record your scenarios on a separate sheet of paper.

STEP 3 After your group has worked out all the details, create the game using the provided materials.

Analysis

STEP 4 Trade games with another group. Play the other group's game. As you play, write your comments and questions about the game: What did you like about the game? Is there anything the other group could do to improve its depiction of the genetic and environmental factors that influence the growth of animals?

STEP 5 Exchange your comments and questions with the other group.

STEP 6 Review the other group's comments and questions about your group's game. What could your group do to improve the game so that it better depicts how genetic and environmental factors influence the growth of animals?

Predict the Growth of Blackbuck Antelope

Blackbuck antelope live in groups on the hot, dry grasslands of India and Pakistan. They mostly eat grasses but will also eat leaves, fruits, and flowers. They are among the fastest animals on earth and have very sharp eyesight. Predators include leopards and wild dogs. Human populations use the blackbuck habitat for agriculture and hunt the antelope for their meat and horns.

The blackbuck antelope is an herbivore native to India and Pakistan.

Blackbuck antelope males compete with each other for territory and mates. They have long, spiraling horns that they use to fight and attract females. A female antelope gives birth to a single fawn that will stay hidden in grasses until it is ready to join the herd.

23. Use the facts about blackbuck antelopes to construct an explanation for how genetic and environmental factors influence the reproduction and growth of these animals. In your explanation be sure to include:

- factors that affect blackbuck reproduction, including the type of reproduction, as well as courtship, parenting, and offspring behaviors
- factors that affect blackbuck growth including weather conditions, predation, food supply, and genetic traits

_____

_____

_____

_____

_____

_____

_____

_____

Continue Your Exploration

Name: _____   Date: _____

Check out the path below or go online to choose one of the other paths shown.

| Teaching Offspring | • **Effect of Temperature on Gender**
• **Hands-On Labs** 🖐
• **Propose Your Own Path** | *Go online to choose one of these other paths.* |

Some animals teach their offspring skills that will help them survive when they are ready to live on their own. Parents teach their offspring in a variety of ways. Some parents directly teach skills or train offspring gradually over time. In other species of animals, offspring may simply observe adults and then use trial and error to learn.

Meerkats are prairie dog-like mammals that thrive in large packs. They use direct teaching of skills as a parenting behavior. Parents teach their offspring how to capture and kill dangerous prey, such as scorpions. They bring nearly dead animals to the offspring because the prey is too dangerous to start with for instructional purposes. They might render the prey animals harmless, for instance, by removing the stinger. This teaching behavior is not limited to the actual parents. Other adult meerkats, called helpers, will also teach offspring that are not theirs.

1. What benefit might adult meerkats gain by helping the offspring of others learn how to capture and kill dangerous prey?

meerkats

Continue Your Exploration

River otters are an example of a species in which offspring observe adults and then use trial and error to learn. River otters do not know how to swim at birth. The females teach their offspring by pushing them into the water when the offspring are about two months old. The females will carry the offspring on their backs if help is needed. The offspring learn by doing.

river otters

Orangutans are another species in which the offspring learn through observation. They participate in activities with adults and copy their behavior. Offspring remain with their mothers for eight years or more. They learn everything from swinging through trees to finding food to building a nest to sleep in at night.

orangutans

2. For adult animals, what are the advantages of making the investment of time and resources to teach offspring life skills?

3. For adult animals, what are the disadvantages of making the investment of time and resources to teach offspring life skills?

4. **Collaborate** Research another animal that invests in teaching of their offspring. Summarize your research in a multimedia presentation that describes details of the parenting behaviors. Cite multiple valid sources to support your research.

Can You Explain It?

Name: _____   **Date:** _____

Why are these male zebras fighting?

 EVIDENCE NOTEBOOK

Refer to the notes in your Evidence Notebook to help you construct an explanation for why the male zebras are fighting.

1. State your claim. Make sure your claim fully explains the function of the behavior.

2. Summarize the evidence you have gathered to support your claim and explain your reasoning.

Checkpoints

Answer the following questions to check your understanding of the lesson.

Use the photo to answer Questions 3–4.

3. The male midwife toad will carry the eggs he fertilized until they are ready to hatch. This male midwife toad most likely reproduces asexually / sexually.

4. The eggs will hatch into tadpoles that need water to grow and develop. Which statement includes a factor that might negatively affect the growth and development of the tadpoles?

   A. The tadpoles can grow in very shallow pools.

   B. The tadpoles' habitat is infected with a fungal disease.

   C. The tadpoles are prey for dragonflies.

   D. The tadpoles grow into adult toads in 3–5 weeks.

Use the photo to answer Questions 5–6.

5. The type of behavior shown by this pig-tailed macaque is best described as offspring / courtship / parenting behavior.

6. What is the possible benefit of this behavior to the macaques? Select all that apply.

   A. The reproductive success of the mother may increase.

   B. The offspring might grow and develop into a healthy adult.

   C. The offspring might learn this behavior from its mother.

   D. The reproductive success of the father may decrease.

7. The fishing industry typically captures fish larger than a minimum size. Due to decades of overfishing, the number of large fish in a river has decreased over time. Recently, scientists discovered that some fish in the river have started to reach maturity at a younger age when they are a smaller size. This early development decreases / increases / does not affect the fishes' chances for successful reproduction. This improves / reduces / does not affect the likelihood that the fish population will survive in this environment.

Interactive Review

Complete this section to review the main concepts of the lesson.

Sexual reproduction is the dominant type of reproduction among animals, although some also reproduce asexually.

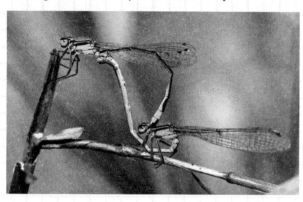

A. Explain the relationship between sexual reproduction and genetic variation in animals.

Courtship, parenting, and offspring behaviors contribute to the reproductive success of animals.

B. Describe one courtship behavior and one parenting behavior, including how each behavior contributes to the reproductive success of an animal.

Genetic and environmental factors influence the growth of animals.

C. Use a cause-and-effect diagram to illustrate how different factors can influence the growth of organisms.

Choose one of the activities to explore how this unit connects to other topics.

☐ People in Science

Phoebe Snetsinger, Birder Birding consists of viewing and identifying birds, often using binoculars or spotting scopes to see birds from longer distances. Phoebe Snetsinger was a renowned birder who saw over 8,000 different species of birds in her lifetime. Her birding adventures took her all over the world. Snetsinger used her knowledge of birds to help her accurately identify birds in the field. Birding can contribute to citizen science by helping scientists track changes in where bird species live.

Develop a map that shows the ranges of one bird on each continent that you would like to add to your "life list" of bird species. Explain how environmental conditions influence the range of each bird species.

Blackburnian warbler

☐ Earth Science Connection

Climate and Reproduction Patterns in reproduction and growth relate to patterns in biome distribution on Earth. While organisms at the equator may be able to reproduce all year, organisms living at the cold poles may focus more on basic survival needs, leaving little time or energy for growth and reproduction.

Research one organism and the climate from two different land biomes. Compare and contrast the biome climates and the patterns of reproduction and growth for the organisms. Use a multimedia presentation to share what you learn.

polar bear mother and cubs

☐ Art Connection

Landscape Architects Landscape architects use plant knowledge to make outdoor spaces beautiful and functional. They choose plants with a variety of reproductive strategies that can be successful during different seasons. For example, landscape architects for an amusement park might arrange plants according to flowering season to ensure blooms all year long.

Research different plants and design a landscape for an outdoor space in your community. Choose at least five climate-appropriate plants that use a variety of reproductive strategies. Explain the practical and artistic purposes for each plant in a landscape diagram you share with the class.

Butchart Gardens in British Columbia, Canada

Name: _____   Date: _____

Complete this review to check your understanding of the unit.

Use the table to answer Questions 1–3.

1. Blood type inheritance involves three alleles, which are shown in the table as A, B, and O. Study the genotypes and resulting blood types of Sam and Heidi's children. Based on this information, which statement about the alleles for blood type is correct?

   A. O is dominant over A and B.

   B. A and B are each dominant over O.

   C. Only A is dominant over O.

   D. A, B, and O alleles are equally dominant.

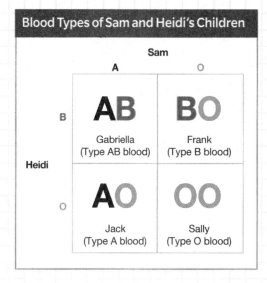

Blood Types of Sam and Heidi's Children

	Sam	
	A	O
B	**AB** Gabriella (Type AB blood)	**BO** Frank (Type B blood)
Heidi O	**AO** Jack (Type A blood)	**OO** Sally (Type O blood)

2. Which pieces of evidence from the chart help establish that humans reproduce sexually, not asexually? Select all that apply.

   A. Frank has the same genotype as his mother.

   B. Gabriella has a different blood type than each of her parents.

   C. Sally received one allele from each of her parents.

   D. Heidi had four children.

3. If Sam and Heidi were to have another child, the probability of that child having Type AB blood is 25 / 50 / 75 percent.

Use the photograph to answer Questions 4–6.

4. Male impala lock horns to compete for mates. The physical advantages that one male has over the other depend on:

   A. genetic factors

   B. environmental factors

   C. both genetic and environmental factors

5. Why is the winning male impala likely to have more reproductive success? Select all that apply.

   A. He is healthier and likely to produce healthy, viable gametes.

   B. He will attract more mates.

   C. He has only beneficial genes.

   D. He will defend the female and offspring more effectively than a weaker male.

6. Impalas may be more territorial during the wet season. Increasing precipitation amounts and the increase in vegetation that follows increases / decreases / has no effect on the number of altercations between impalas.

7. Think of an example related to each factor that affects the growth and survival of organisms. Describe the effect that each of your examples has on organisms.

Factors Affecting Survival	Cause	Effect
Climate	rain shadow	organisms adapted to minimal precipitation; plants grow relatively smaller compared to areas with more precipitation
Local conditions		
Genes		
Adaptations		

Use the diagram about reproduction in pine trees to answer Questions 8–11.

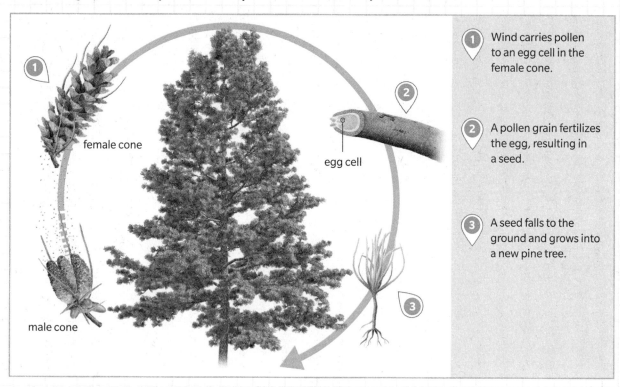

① Wind carries pollen to an egg cell in the female cone.

② A pollen grain fertilizes the egg, resulting in a seed.

③ A seed falls to the ground and grows into a new pine tree.

female cone

egg cell

male cone

8. Do pine trees reproduce sexually or asexually? Use evidence from the diagram to support your answer.

9. Male pine cones contain a large amount of pollen. Why?

10. Pine trees are *gymnosperms*, meaning "naked seeds." Their seeds are not enclosed in fruit, and they do not produce flowers that attract pollinators. How might the reproductive strategy of pine trees be partially responsible for their success in landscapes at high elevation and in cold climates?

11. Are all factors that affect the reproductive success of pine trees pictured in the diagram? Explain.

Use the photo to answer Questions 12–15.

12. The cardon cactus is native to the Sonoran desert in Baja California. It is not found further north because it does not tolerate freezing temperatures. Describe what might happen to the range of the cardon cactus if climate change causes areas north of Baja California to no longer have freezing temperatures.

13. Lesser long-nosed bats use nectar and pollen from the flowers of the cardon cactus as a food source. Bats often pollinate the cacti as they feed. What adaptations would you predict for the lesser long-nosed bat and the cardon cactus?

14. What ensures that the relationship between the cardon cactus and the lesser long-nosed bat will continue between generations?

15. What might happen to the lesser long-nosed bat population during a drought that causes the cardon cacti to produce very few flowers?

Name: _____   Date: _____

Save the Whitebark Pines!

The stately whitebark pines of Yellowstone National Park are in trouble! Normally, cold temperatures at the tree line keep away pine beetles, which infect the trees. However, the cold temperature band has shrunk with recent climate change. This leaves more trees at risk of pine-beetle infection. Climate change is influenced by human development, and in this way humans are impacting the range and viability of whitebark pines. A fungus also infects the trees, though scientists are encouraged to see that some pines have an inherited resistance to the fungus. The pines are important to many species in Yellowstone, including other coniferous trees, pine squirrels, birds, and grizzly bears.

As part of an Eco-Task Force, you will develop a plan to increase the number of healthy whitebark pines in Yellowstone. You should consider genetic solutions, as well as actions that might improve reproductive success and enhance sapling growth. Save the whitebark pines!

Clark's nutcracker on a healthy whitebark pine

whitebark pine infected with fungus that causes blister rust

The steps below will help guide your research and develop your recommendation.

1. **Define the Problem** Write a statement defining the problem you have been asked to solve. What factors limit the success of the pines?

2. **Conduct Research** Using library or Internet resources, learn more about how environmental scientists help threatened populations. What can your Eco-Task Force do to improve the genetic variation, growth, and reproduction of the whitebark pines in Yellowstone?

3. **Develop a Model** Genetic solutions often require breeding programs. Use Punnett squares to show how you could increase fungus resistance in whitebark populations, depending on whether the allele for resistance is recessive or dominant. Show what crosses would be ideal in each situation. What process will the Eco-Task Force need to use to breed fungus-resistant offspring?

4. **Recommend a Solution** Make a recommendation based on your research. How will you protect adult trees from pine beetles and fungus, as well as ensure successful growth of new saplings?

5. **Communicate** How will you convince officials that your plan will work? Create a multimedia presentation to present your plan to save the whitebark pines in Yellowstone. Use evidence and reasoning to support your claims.

✓ **Self-Check**

	I listed all factors (genetic, reproductive, and environmental) that limit the number of whitebark pines in Yellowstone.
	I researched how environmental scientists help threatened populations.
	I used a model to consider genetic solutions that could help the whitebark pines.
	My solutions are based on research and a correct understanding of the whitebark pine's pattern of growth and reproduction.
	My presentation used effective scientific argumentation to defend the Eco-Task Force proposal.

Human Impacts on the Environment

How do human activities affect climate change, ecosystems, and living things?

Unit Project 486

Lesson 1   Human Activities Cause Changes in the Environment 488

Lesson 2   Human Activities Influence Climate Change 508

Lesson 3   Climate Change Affects the Survival of Organisms 532

Lesson 4   Engineer It: Reducing Human Impacts on the Environment . . . 552

Unit Review 577

Unit Performance Task 581

A lot of plastic trash ends up in the oceans, where it affects many organisms, such as plankton, corals, fish, and whales.

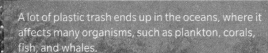

You Solve It How Can You Grow a Crop Using Water Efficiently?

Design a method for irrigating a melon crop that uses the least amount of water possible while still growing a successful crop.

Go online and complete the You Solve It to explore ways to solve a real-world problem.

Minimize Community Effects on Climate Change

Community projects, such as litter pick-ups, can bring together people of various ages and backgrounds to help protect the environment.

A. Look at the photo. On a separate sheet of paper, write down as many different questions as you can about the photo.

B. **Discuss** With your class or partner, share your questions. Record any additional questions generated in your discussion. Then choose the most important questions from the list that are related to how communities can work together to reduce climate change. Write them below.

C. Choose a human activity that emits greenhouse gases and that your community or school could focus on to reduce its impact on climate change. What activity will you design a solution to address?

D. Use the information above, along with your research, to plan a multimedia presentation to explain your solution and to convince others to participate in your program.

Discuss the next steps for your Unit Project with your teacher and go online to download the Unit Project Worksheet.

Language Development

Use the lessons in this unit to complete the network and expand your understanding of these key concepts.

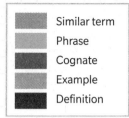

- Similar term
- Phrase
- Cognate
- Example
- Definition

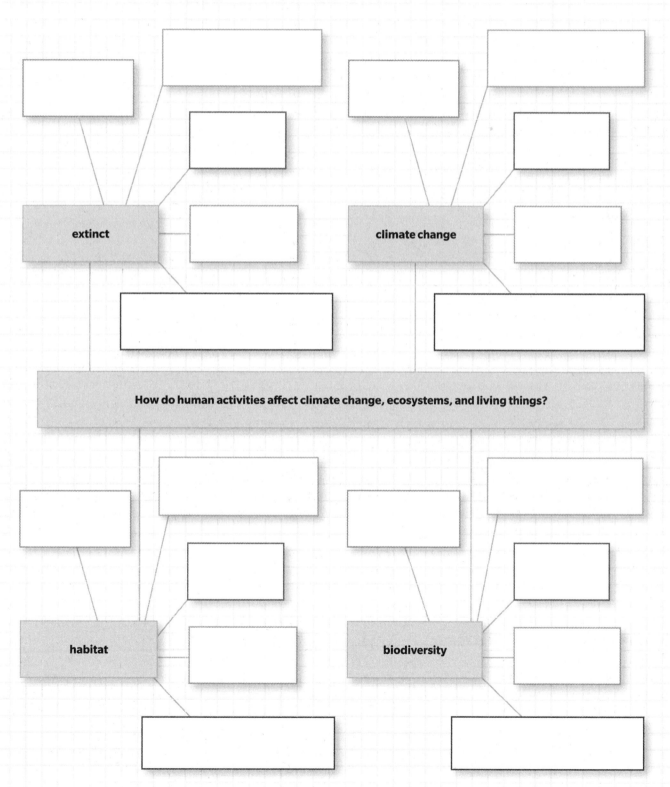

extinct

climate change

How do human activities affect climate change, ecosystems, and living things?

habitat

biodiversity

Human Activities Cause Changes in the Environment

The grass for this golf course in Arizona does not naturally grow in this area. It was brought here by humans.

Explore First

Identifying Human Impacts Choose an area, such as your school campus, your neighborhood, or your town. Make a map that shows which parts of your area are natural and which areas have been altered by humans. How did you determine which areas had been changed by humans and which areas were unaltered?

Go online to view the digital version of the Hands-On Lab for this lesson and to download additional lab resources.

CAN YOU EXPLAIN IT?

How can farming on land contribute to the growth of algal blooms in the ocean?

Algae vary in color. When large amounts of algae are in a body of water, the color of the water may appear to change.

Algae are plant-like organisms that live in fresh water and salt water. Algae get the nutrients they need from the water they live in, and they use the energy from sunlight to make sugars. An algal bloom happens when the population of algae in a body of water increases rapidly. As the algae population grows, more algae also die and decompose. Bacteria that decompose the dead algae use more oxygen, which depletes the amount of dissolved oxygen in the water. Fish and other organisms that need oxygen may die as a result of the algal bloom.

1. Describe how land and oceans are connected.

2. What do you think might cause algae to start growing very rapidly?

EVIDENCE NOTEBOOK As you explore this lesson, gather evidence to help explain how farming on land relates to the growth of algal blooms in the ocean.

Exploring the Environment

All living things need certain materials to stay healthy. Organisms depend on their environment to provide those materials. A **habitat** is the place where an organism lives. It includes the living and nonliving factors that affect the organism, or the *environment* around the organism. The living and nonliving parts of the environment interact. Humans and other organisms rely on the environment for natural resources, such as water and soil. Natural systems also provide ecosystem services, such as the filtering of pollutants from water. These products and services are essential to human life. They are also important to the functioning of human cultures and economies.

3. Identify each factor in the beaver's habitat as *living* or *nonliving*.

air: _____

mountain: _____

grasses: _____

trees: _____

water: _____

A beaver uses sticks and branches from nearby trees to build a dam in a river.

4. How might the beaver use or depend on at least three of the environmental factors labeled in the photo?

© Houghton Mifflin Harcourt Publishing Company • Image Credits: (c) ©Richard Hamilton Smith/Corbis Documentary/Getty Images; (inset) ©Robert McGouey/All Canada Photos/

EVIDENCE NOTEBOOK

5. Describe the environment of the algae shown at the beginning of the lesson. How are algae connected to their environment? Record your evidence.

Changes in the Environment

Changes in Earth systems happen all the time. Natural events cause some changes. For example, a flood caused by a severe rainstorm might destroy trees or remove topsoil. Humans can also cause change by actions such as damming a river or removing trees. Natural events and human activities can both disturb the environment. These disturbances can alter resources that living things, including humans, need.

The path of a tornado can easily be seen in this forest. Tornadoes are natural events that disrupt the environment.

Deforestation is the removal of trees and other plants from an area. Humans cut down forests to use the wood or the land.

6. **Discuss** With a partner, look at the images and compare the changes to a forest from a tornado and from deforestation.

Changes Caused by Natural Events

Some natural changes in the environment involve patterns. For example, in some places ocean tides change from high to low twice a day. Weather changes seasonally in many parts of Earth. It can become cooler and then warmer throughout a year. Because these events happen in a repeating pattern, many species have ways to deal with these changes. For example, fur color in Arctic hares changes from brown to white in the winter, an advantage when hiding from predators in the snow. Other natural changes happen suddenly or without a pattern. A forest fire caused by a lightning strike is a sudden natural event that can cause large changes to the environment.

Changes Caused by Human Activity

Human activities can have many different effects on Earth systems. For example, humans can change the shape of the land to meet their needs. Humans may use resources at a faster rate than they can be replaced. This use causes resources to become scarce in the environment and is called *resource depletion*. Humans also affect the environment when they pollute resources. *Pollution* is an undesirable change in a natural environment that is caused by adding substances that are harmful to living organisms.

7. Decide whether each example is caused by human actions or by natural events. Write H for human actions and N for natural events.

   A. asteroid impact flattens a forest _____

   B. flooding from a concrete dam _____

   C. flooding from a severe storm _____

   D. oil spill in the ocean _____

   E. deforestation to clear land for crops _____

© Houghton Mifflin Harcourt Publishing Company • Image Credits: (l) ©DariuszPa/iStock/Getty Images Plus/Getty Images; (r) ©Getty Images

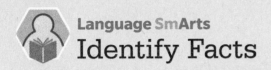

Language SmArts
Identify Facts

A *fact* is a statement that can be proven. An *opinion* is what someone believes about something. The following is an excerpt from a newspaper article about a dam and its impact on the environment. While you read the article, watch for statements that present facts and statements that present opinions.

The Three Gorges Dam

In 2003, the Three Gorges Dam opened across China's Yangtze River. The dam provides China with a sustainable source of electrical energy for a fast-growing population. It also helps decrease the risk of flooding in the river basin. In 2014, the dam produced 98.8 billion kilowatt-hours of electricity. The dam uses flowing water instead of fossil fuels to produce electrical energy. This process reduced the environmental impact of China's power plants by lowering the amount of carbon dioxide produced by about 120 million tons per year.

Although these results help the Chinese people, the construction of the dam is not as fantastic as it first appears. Building the dam required large amounts of concrete and released harmful chemicals and carbon dioxide into the air. Scientists think that earthquakes may result from water pressure in ground cracks near the dam's reservoir. The worst effect was that people were moved from their villages, and the villages were flooded. Sadly, many natural ecosystems were destroyed, and more than 500 species of rare plants and 300 species of fish were negatively affected. Many living things died because their ecosystems were lost. Building the dam helped the people. However, its effects on certain ecosystems were devastating.

---

8. Identify each statement as a fact or an opinion.

   A. The dam provides China with a sustainable energy source for producing electrical energy. _____

   B. The dam is not as fantastic as it first appears. _____

   C. It also helps decrease the risk of flooding in the river basin. _____

   D. The worst effect was that people were moved from their villages. _____

9. Using evidence provided in the article, identify two different cause-effect relationships involving the construction of the Three Gorges Dam and the environment.

   _____

   _____

   _____

   _____

   _____

   _____

   _____

   _____

   _____

Relating Human Activity to the Environment

Human Activity in Earth Systems

Did you ever see someone throw a plastic cup on the ground and walk away? Some people might say, "Well, it is just one cup." People may not think about how pollution adds up when many people do the same thing.

The Earth system is sometimes divided into four parts, or subsystems. These interconnected subsystems are the hydrosphere, atmosphere, geosphere, and biosphere. The health of each subsystem affects the resources and ecosystem services that individuals and society get from that part of the Earth system. A human activity that directly affects one subsystem may indirectly affect the others. These interconnected changes may affect the quality, quantity, and availability of resources and services that people need.

10. What are three human actions that affect the environment?

Recycling cell phones, which contain metals and plastics, reduces environmental pollution.

Human Impact on the Hydrosphere

All water on Earth is part of the *hydrosphere*, including polar ice caps, snow, groundwater, and surface water. Humans rely on surface water to drink, swim, fish, and transport goods. Farmers might divert water from rivers to give to crops or livestock. Humans also dig wells to pump groundwater to areas where surface water is unavailable. Human use of these water resources can lead to a scarcity of fresh and clean water in the environment.

Water pollution may result from human activities on or near water sources. Water pollution affects organisms that depend on the water supply. **Point-source pollution** occurs when harmful materials enter Earth's hydrosphere from a single, identifiable source such as a factory. **Nonpoint-source pollution** comes from many sources, including rainwater that picks up pollutants as it moves across land.

When wastes are dumped into Earth's hydrosphere, pollutants can travel to different parts of the environment.

Hands-On Lab
Model Ocean Pollution from Land

You will make a model to explore how land and ocean pollution are connected.

Procedure and Analysis

STEP 1 Make a prediction about how point-source pollution and nonpoint-source pollution on land may affect water pollution.

MATERIALS
- camera (optional)
- food coloring, blue
- food coloring, red
- metric ruler
- sand, coarse, wet (1/3 volume of washtub)
- spray bottle
- washtub, plastic
- water

STEP 2 Use the materials provided to create a model of either point-source or nonpoint-source pollution on land near an ocean shore.

STEP 3 Explain how your model represents either point-source or nonpoint-source pollution.

STEP 4 Design a method to simulate precipitation with your model. Explore how precipitation affects the land pollution and ocean pollution. Record your observations.

STEP 5 Compare your observations with those of other groups. Is there a difference in how point-source pollution and nonpoint-source pollution on land affect ocean pollution? Explain your reasoning.

STEP 6 **Draw** On a separate sheet of paper, draw a cartoon with three or four frames. Illustrate a human activity that could contribute to the process of pollution that you modeled in this activity. In your cartoon, show at least two effects on the environment of the human activity shown.

 EVIDENCE NOTEBOOK

11. Identify the different materials that may enter a body of water by the same process explored in this lab. Record your evidence.

Human Impact on the Atmosphere

The *atmosphere* is the layer of gases that surrounds Earth. If you stand outside and look up, you might see blue sky and some clouds. You may not see air pollution because many air pollutants are colorless gases. Other pollutants may be in liquid or solid form, such as tiny particles suspended in the atmosphere. Air pollution may cause problems for humans and other species alike. Respiratory problems such as asthma can be made worse by air pollution. Many pollutants enter the atmosphere as the result of burning fossil fuels. Other pollutants such as dust may come from construction sites or agriculture as dry soil is carried by the wind.

Burning fossil fuels releases potentially harmful particles and gases into the atmosphere.

Human Impact on the Geosphere

The mostly solid, rocky part of Earth is called the *geosphere*. Humans change the geosphere when they reshape the land to meet their needs. Humans level land to build homes and offices. Humans may also change the land to mine for resources or to farm. Some farming and mining practices can degrade the soil. Degraded soil cannot support plants or crops, leaving the soil exposed. The exposed soil may then be swept away by wind or water, further changing the shape of the land. Humans may change the land to reduce the chance of erosion by planting different types of crops or by terracing sloped lands.

Mining provides people with materials they need, but it also changes the geosphere.

Human Impact on the Biosphere

The *biosphere* is all living things on Earth, including you. Humans affect the biosphere when they hunt, fish, or harvest plants. A species may become extinct if humans remove more organisms than can be replenished. A species is **extinct** when no more individuals remain on Earth. Human activity may also positively impact the biosphere. In many areas, deer populations no longer have natural predators. These deer populations may grow so large that their grazing negatively affects their ecosystem. Hunting deer in these areas can reduce the deer population to protect the forest ecosystem.

Commercial fishing can deplete the food for other species living in the area and add pollution to the water.

Changes to other Earth systems may indirectly affect the biosphere. For example, changes to land or water might degrade or destroy habitats. When an organism's habitat is degraded, the habitat may no longer be able to support the organism. Imagine that a lake is polluted or its water is removed for human use. In this example, organisms that depend on the water in the lake to survive either move to other sources, or, if they cannot move, they may not survive.

Connected Effects of Human Activity

Human activity may affect multiple parts of the Earth system. Burning fossil fuels releases particles and several different gases into the air. Some of these gases pollute the air. For example, gases such as nitrogen oxides and sulfur dioxide, react with water in the air to form acid rain. Acid rain may kill trees or crops and cause surface water to become more acidic. These effects can harm living organisms in the biosphere.

A mine in West Virginia, where the top of a mountain was removed to reach the coal in the ground.

12. Complete the paragraph with the words geosphere, hydrosphere, atmosphere, and biosphere.

Surface mining changes the shape of the land, which affects the _____. These land changes may fragment or destroy habitats in the area, which affects the _____. Mining exposes new materials to the surface. Rain may carry these materials into rivers and streams, which affects the _____. The process of mining can also cause small particles to enter the _____.

Human Impact on the Florida Panther

In the 1500s, the Florida panther roamed most of what is now the southeastern United States. The Florida panther lives in forested areas, wetlands, and swamps.

13. How might a growing human population have affected the Florida panther population?

Florida panther

As European settlers arrived in the 1600s, they clear-cut the land so they could grow crops. Today much of the area has been urbanized. The cutting of trees and building of roads and cities fragmented the panther's habitat. It reduced large, connected habitats to smaller, less connected areas. The panther was also hunted to protect livestock.

In 1967, the Florida panther was listed as an endangered species by the United States government and conservation efforts began. Conservation efforts included protecting and connecting panther habitats and making it illegal to hunt these large cats. In the early 1970s, there were approximately 20 adult wild panthers in southern Florida. Conservation efforts resulted in there being almost 200 in the same area in 2014. Despite the increase in numbers, Florida panthers still face many dangers. For example, 24 panthers were killed by cars while trying to cross roadways in 2014.

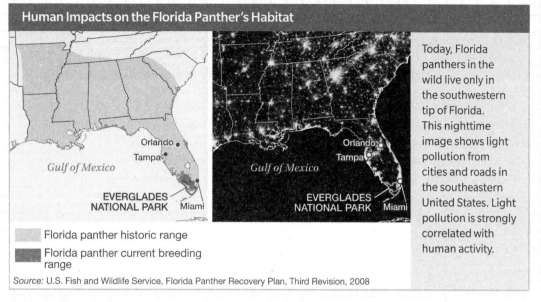

Human Impacts on the Florida Panther's Habitat

Today, Florida panthers in the wild live only in the southwestern tip of Florida. This nighttime image shows light pollution from cities and roads in the southeastern United States. Light pollution is strongly correlated with human activity.

Florida panther historic range

Florida panther current breeding range

Source: U.S. Fish and Wildlife Service, Florida Panther Recovery Plan, Third Revision, 2008

14. Look at the maps. How do the data in the maps support the claim that human activity has negatively affected the population of Florida panthers?

Engineer It
Evaluate Tradeoffs

Suppose you are an engineer who is designing a new drive system for an automobile. Two criteria for the product are that the design must keep the emission of carbon dioxide (CO_2) low, and that the cost of owning the product must be low. Use the graph to compare ownership costs with yearly CO_2 emissions for three drive system designs.

15. Which design has the greatest release of CO_2 per year in comparison to the others?

16. Based on the design criteria, describe the tradeoff that must be made when choosing one of the three designs. Use the graph to support your argument.

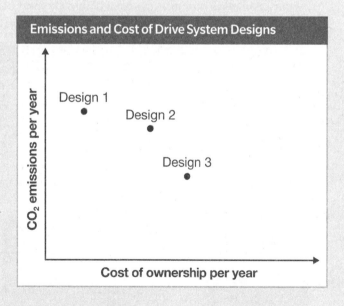

Emissions and Cost of Drive System Designs

Design 1

Design 2

Design 3

CO_2 emissions per year

Cost of ownership per year

Analyzing the Scale of Human Impacts on the Environment

Human effects on the environment can vary in scale over time and space. Some effects are more noticeable in the long term, such as the increase in the acidity of oceans. Some effects can happen more quickly. For example, developers may fill in a wetland to build a neighborhood, which can impact the environment in the area in a short amount of time. A person cutting down a single tree affects a small area, but when large areas of trees are cut down, a larger area of the environment will be affected. The scale of a human impact on the environment affects the ability of the environment to recover or stabilize.

17. **Discuss** How might a human activity that impacts a small area affect a larger area over time?

Case Study: The Mississippi River

The Mississippi River is one of the largest rivers in the world. The river is an important shipping route and freshwater source for the central United States. Human activity that affects the Mississippi River can have widespread effects due to the size of the river.

Rivers naturally change course over time and occasionally flood due to natural events. The *mouth* of a river is where it empties into a larger body of water. Rivers naturally slow down near their mouths and deposit sediment in a fan-shaped area. This fan-shaped landform is called the *delta* of the river. To protect cities near the river from floodwaters and to help maintain the course of the river, humans built levees along the river. A *levee* is a raised part of land either naturally occurring or human-built to contain rising river waters. Levees prevent the river waters from spreading out, slowing down, and depositing sediment. Instead, sediment is carried beyond the river's mouth.

The shape of the Mississippi River Delta has changed greatly during the twentieth century. A change this great over a geologically short period of time indicates that human activity has had a role in changing the shape of the delta.

The Changing Mississippi River Delta

The images show the landmass and coastline of the Mississippi River Delta in 1932 and 2011. The main path of the river is shown in orange. Rising sea level and other factors have contributed to a large loss of land in the Mississippi River Delta over 79 years.

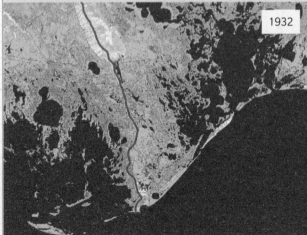
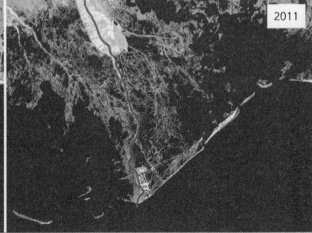

1932 2011

Human-Built Structures to Control the Mississippi River

Humans built several lock-and-dam systems so that larger boats could travel farther upstream on the Mississippi River. The lock portion allows boats passage, and the dam increases the depth of the water. The building of a dam can affect the environment in several ways.

Flow of a River Upstream of a Dam

River water carries sediment downstream. The sediment is suspended in the flowing water and makes the water cloudy or *turbid*. The flow of water slows down as it approaches a dam, and much of the sediment is deposited upstream of the dam.

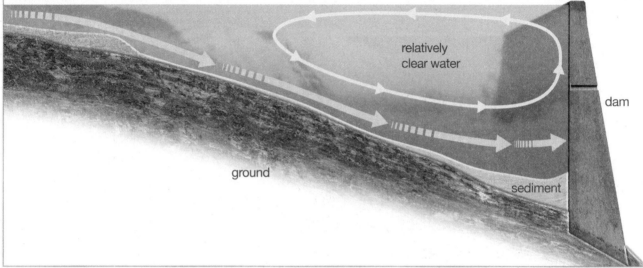

18. The following are effects of lock-and-dam systems in a river. Which effect will most likely impact the formation of land in the delta?

    A. They prevent the flow of sediments downstream.

    B. They can interfere with fish migration.

    C. They make navigation possible in places.

    D. They can affect water temperature.

For the cities in the Mississippi River Delta, it is important that the path of the Mississippi River does not change, as it would without human intervention. Many levees and other structures have been built to keep most of the flow of the Mississippi River along the same path it followed when cities in the area were established.

19. How might the building of levees have affected the shape of the Mississippi River Delta?

Levees are ridges along riverbanks that prevent rising river waters from overflowing the banks and causing floods.

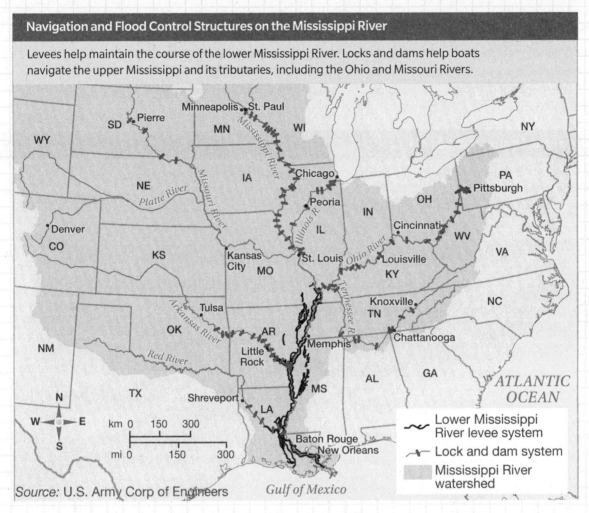

Navigation and Flood Control Structures on the Mississippi River

Levees help maintain the course of the lower Mississippi River. Locks and dams help boats navigate the upper Mississippi and its tributaries, including the Ohio and Missouri Rivers.

Legend:
- Lower Mississippi River levee system
- Lock and dam system
- Mississippi River watershed

Source: U.S. Army Corp of Engineers

20. How does the number of levees and dams on the Mississippi River affect the scale of human impact on the river and the organisms that depend on it?

Dead Zone at the Mouth of the Mississippi River

In 1972, humans first noticed that a large area in the ocean near the mouth of the Mississippi River appeared "dead." The normally rich community of fish, crustaceans, shellfish, and other animals had disappeared. At first, this happened every few years, but later happened every year. This dead zone appears in the summer when the algae population in the Gulf of Mexico's warm water suddenly increases. The increase in algae reduces the amount of oxygen dissolved in the water. Organisms sensitive to oxygen levels in the water either die or leave the area. More oxygen is removed from the water as dead organisms decay. The result is a *dead zone*, an area where organisms cannot live. Fish leave the area to find waters with more oxygen. Fish-dependent species such as some kinds of birds must look elsewhere for food. The size of the dead zone varies each year. For the last several years, the average size of the dead zone has been almost 6,000 square miles. It is one of the largest dead zones in the world.

Mississippi River Watershed

A *watershed* is an area of land drained by a river system. Forty-one percent of the continental United States is part of the Mississippi River watershed, which drains into the Gulf of Mexico.

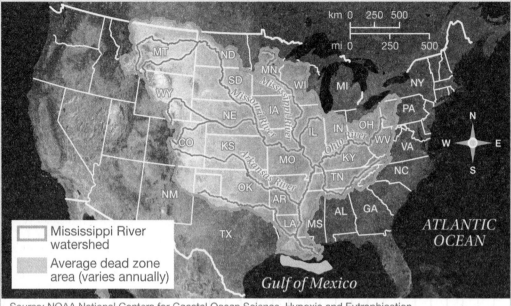

Mississippi River watershed

Average dead zone area (varies annually)

Source: NOAA National Centers for Coastal Ocean Science, Hypoxia and Eutrophication

The Mississippi River watershed includes many cities and farms. Human activities in the watershed contribute to pollution in the water. Some pollutants are directly added to the waterways. Other pollutants are picked up from cities and farms by the rain that runs into streams and rivers. The pollutants include contaminants from roadways and fertilizers that farmers apply to crops to help them grow.

21. Explain how wastewater from a manufacturing plant in southern Ohio could affect fish in the Mississippi River. Use the watershed map to support your answer.

22. Farmers often apply extra nutrients to their crops in the form of fertilizer. Describe how these extra nutrients might affect the Mississippi River.

EVIDENCE NOTEBOOK

23. What materials might runoff in the Mississippi watershed contain that could contribute to algae growth in waterways? Record your evidence.

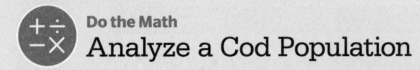

Do the Math
Analyze a Cod Population

Renewable resources must be used carefully to maintain the availability of the resource. For centuries, humans fished for cod off the coast of Newfoundland, Canada. Then, in the mid-twentieth century, new technologies allowed cod to be harvested in much greater numbers than in previous years. Soon after, the cod population declined rapidly. In 1992, Canada introduced a ban on cod fishing in the area. Even after the ban started, the cod population failed to recover as quickly as expected.

Northern Cod Landings

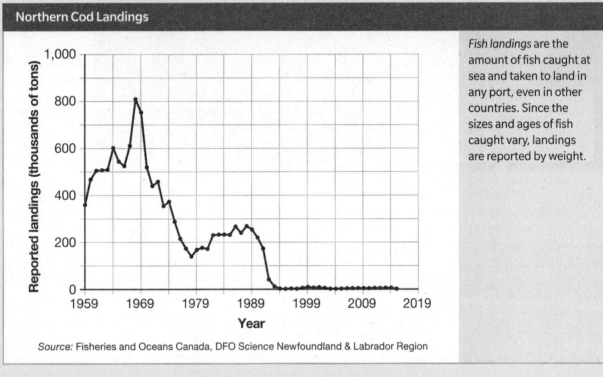

Source: Fisheries and Oceans Canada, DFO Science Newfoundland & Labrador Region

Fish landings are the amount of fish caught at sea and taken to land in any port, even in other countries. Since the sizes and ages of fish caught vary, landings are reported by weight.

24. Use the graph to answer the following questions.

   A. What is the average weight of fish caught per year from 1959–1969, to the nearest 20,000 tons? _____

   B. What is the average weight of fish caught per year from 1979–1989, to the nearest 20,000 tons? _____

   C. About what percentage of the average in part A is the average in part B, to the nearest 5%? _____

25. Why do you think the fishing industry was unable to continue catching the same amount of fish in the decades after the 1960s as had been caught in the 1960s?

_____

_____

_____

_____

_____

_____

Continue Your Exploration

Name: _____ Date: _____

Check out the path below or go online to choose one of the other paths shown.

| Chernobyl Nuclear Disaster | • Impact of *Deepwater Horizon* Oil Well Accident
• Hands-On Labs 🖐
• Propose Your Own Path | *Go online to choose one of these other paths.* |

Under normal operating conditions, nuclear power generation is safe and releases minimal pollutants into the atmosphere. But in 1986, an accident at the Chernobyl Nuclear Power Plant in Ukraine released huge amounts of radioactive material into the environment. Soon after the incident, the government closed the area within 30 kilometers of the plant and evacuated about 115,000 people. In the following years, 220,000 more people were evacuated to reduce their risk of radiation exposure.

The effects of radiation sickness on people and other organisms vary with the type of radiation, and the level and duration of exposure. Minor exposure may lead to nausea, hair loss, vomiting, headaches, and fevers. More severe exposure may reduce an organism's life span. Within four months after the incident, 28 people had died from severe radiation exposure and thermal burns. About 6,000 cases of thyroid cancer in children have been linked to the accident. Radioactive material is hard to clean up. It continues to be dangerous as it breaks down slowly over time—sometimes over centuries. As of 2017, the Chernobyl area is still closed to the general population.

Human Exposure to Radiation

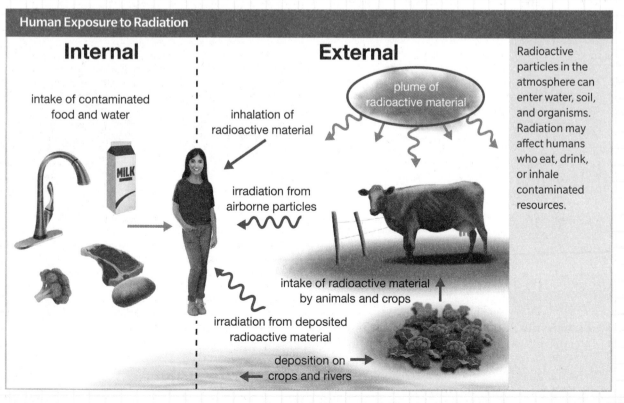

Internal

intake of contaminated food and water

External

inhalation of radioactive material

plume of radioactive material

irradiation from airborne particles

intake of radioactive material by animals and crops

irradiation from deposited radioactive material

deposition on crops and rivers

Radioactive particles in the atmosphere can enter water, soil, and organisms. Radiation may affect humans who eat, drink, or inhale contaminated resources.

Continue Your Exploration

1. Which are some of the effects of radiation poisoning? Select all that apply.

    A. headaches

    B. vomiting

    C. hair loss

    D. death/reduced life span

2. By what process did the radiation spread across such a large area?

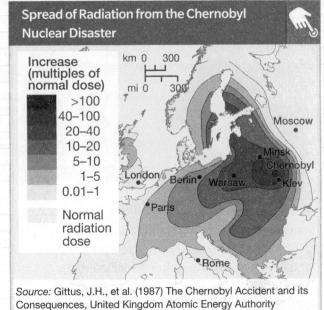

Spread of Radiation from the Chernobyl Nuclear Disaster

Increase (multiples of normal dose)
>100
40–100
20–40
10–20
5–10
1–5
0.01–1

Normal radiation dose

Moscow
Minsk
Chernobyl
London
Berlin
Warsaw
Kiev
Paris
Rome

km 0 300
mi 0 300

Source: Gittus, J.H., et al. (1987) The Chernobyl Accident and its Consequences, United Kingdom Atomic Energy Authority

The map shows the areas affected by the Chernobyl nuclear accident and the amount of radiation contamination.

3. Why are the effects of the Chernobyl disaster so long lasting?

4. What are some possible reasons for the increase in the number of wildlife in the affected areas 25 years after the Chernobyl explosion?

Humans have been out of the affected areas for more than 25 years. In the absence of humans, wildlife numbers have increased, despite some lingering radiation effects.

5. **Collaborate** Research changes made to improve safety of nuclear power plants as a result of the accident at the Chernobyl Nuclear Power Plant.

Can You Explain It?

Name: _____ **Date:** _____

How can farming on land contribute to the growth of algal blooms in the ocean?

 EVIDENCE NOTEBOOK

Refer to the notes in your Evidence Notebook to help you construct an explanation for how farming on land can contribute to the growth of algal blooms in the ocean.

1. State your claim. Make sure your claim fully explains how farming on land can contribute to algal blooms in the ocean.

2. Summarize the evidence you have gathered to support your claim and explain your reasoning.

Checkpoints

Answer the following questions to check your understanding of the lesson.

Use the photo to answer Question 3.

3. Which subsystems of Earth might these wind turbines affect, and how?

   A. the biosphere by endangering birds in flight

   B. the geosphere by disrupting rock and soil when installed

   C. the atmosphere by polluting the air

   D. the hydrosphere by changing ocean currents

Use the photo to answer Questions 4–5.

4. The area in the photo was originally a forested mountain. Building the structures and ski slopes probably affected the environment in a positive / negative way, by fragmenting / preserving natural habitats.

5. The snowmakers shown on the left of the image use a freshwater source to create snow for the resort. Which of the following questions should scientists investigate to determine how these snowmakers impact the environment? Select all that apply.

   A. What is the water source for the snowmakers?

   B. Where do the snowmakers get their power?

   C. Are the snowmakers ugly?

   D. Are the snowmakers a danger to birds in the area?

6. Because a change in one part of the Earth system can / cannot affect other parts, it may be easy / difficult to fully analyze the effects of a human activity. Scientists must collect and analyze data to determine whether a change in the environment is caused by human activity.

7. Creating new roads can alter the biosphere by destroying rocks / habitats. Human actions, such as overfishing, can negatively affect the biosphere by causing some species to become better adapted / extinct.

Interactive Review

Complete this section to review the main concepts of the lesson.

All living things depend on their environment to provide the things they need. A change in the environment may be caused by natural events or human actions, or both.

A. How could natural events and human actions change a coastline?

Human actions can affect all parts of the Earth system, which include the hydrosphere, atmosphere, geosphere, and biosphere.

B. How might a change to the hydrosphere affect the biosphere?

Human impacts on the environment can be positive or negative and vary in scale over time and space.

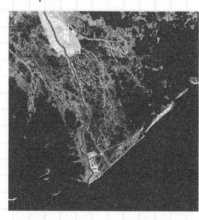

C. Give an example of a human activity that has a greater impact over a longer period of time than it does in the short term.

Human Activities Influence Climate Change

Ice is an important habitat for many seals. When the pack ice breaks up earlier than usual, these seals may starve or drown.

Explore First

Simulating Temperature and Sea Level Fill a graduated flask with 400 mL of water and stopper it. Place a light bulb a few inches from the flask, shining on the flask. Measure the volume of water in the flask every 5 minutes for 20 minutes. How does temperature affect the volume of water in the flask? How can climate change affect sea level?

Go online to view the digital version of the Hands-On Lab for this lesson and to download additional lab resources.

CAN YOU EXPLAIN IT?

What could be causing ice and permafrost to melt in Shishmaref?

The 400-year-old fishing village of Shishmaref, Alaska, used to be surrounded by thick sea ice every winter. Over the last century, less sea ice has been forming and ocean waves have eroded much of the shoreline.

The ground here used to be frozen throughout the year. This *permafrost* has started melting in recent years. The resulting loose soil erodes quickly, damaging buildings and houses in Shishmaref.

1. The amount of sea ice and permafrost have steadily decreased near Shishmaref, Alaska, over the last century. The loss of ice has allowed ocean waves to erode the land and destroy property. What might be causing this melting?

EVIDENCE NOTEBOOK As you explore this lesson, gather evidence to help explain why ice and permafrost are melting in Shishmaref.

Exploring Earth's Climate

Climate

Weather can change from day to day or even several times in one day. *Weather* describes the conditions of the atmosphere over a short period. "A hot, sunny afternoon" or a "cold, snowy day" are descriptions of weather. By contrast, *climate* describes the weather conditions in an area over a long period, such as 30 years. For example, a tropical rain forest climate is warm and rainy throughout the year.

The average climate of Earth can also be described. *Global climate* is often expressed as Earth's average surface temperature, which is currently 16 °C (61°F). Earth's average surface temperature is a combination of the sea surface temperature and the near-surface air temperature.

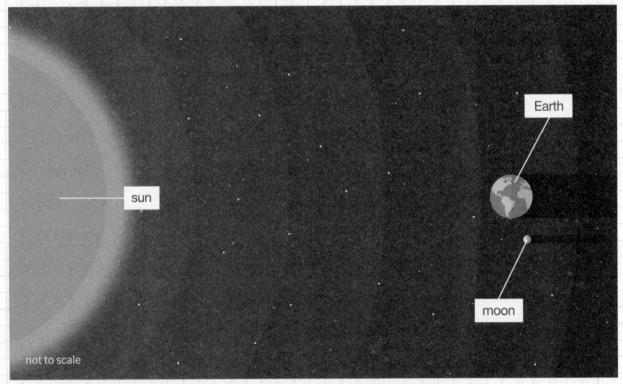

not to scale

Earth and the moon are about the same distance from the sun. Earth's temperatures range from about −88 °C to 58 °C (−126 °F to 136 °F). The moon's temperatures range from about −178 °C to 117 °C (−290 °F to 240 °F).

2. **Discuss** Why do you think the temperature range on Earth is so different from the temperature range on the moon? Make a list of ideas with a partner.

Earth's Climate System

Earth's climate is the result of complex interactions between the biosphere, geosphere, hydrosphere, and atmosphere. These interactions are driven by energy from the sun. Earth's atmosphere and surface absorb and reflect incoming sunlight. Darker surfaces absorb more sunlight than lighter surfaces do. For example, soil and ocean water absorb more sunlight than clouds, ice, and snow do.

The total amount of energy that enters the Earth system almost exactly equals the total amount of energy released by the Earth system into space. However, solar energy can remain in the Earth system for different periods of time. For example, oceans retain solar energy for a longer period of time than land does. This energy is transferred around the globe by ocean currents and is a major influence on weather and climate patterns.

The Greenhouse Effect

A greenhouse regulates temperatures for plants. Similarly, Earth's atmosphere regulates temperatures on Earth. The **greenhouse effect** is the warming of the surface and lower atmosphere of Earth that occurs when greenhouse gases absorb and reradiate energy. Greenhouse gases include carbon dioxide, methane, water vapor, and other gases. The processes that cause the greenhouse effect are shown in the diagram. Solar energy is absorbed and reflected by Earth's atmosphere and surface. The absorbed energy is eventually radiated back out as infrared radiation. Some infrared radiation goes back out to space, and some is absorbed again by greenhouse gases. The infrared radiation absorbed by greenhouse gases is reradiated and some is reabsorbed. As a result, energy stays in the Earth system longer than it would stay if there were no greenhouse gases.

The greenhouse effect keeps the temperature range on Earth suitable for life as we know it. If the concentration of greenhouse gases increases, more radiation is absorbed and reradiated within the Earth system. As a result, Earth's average surface temperature increases. If the concentration of greenhouse gases decreases, Earth's average surface temperature decreases.

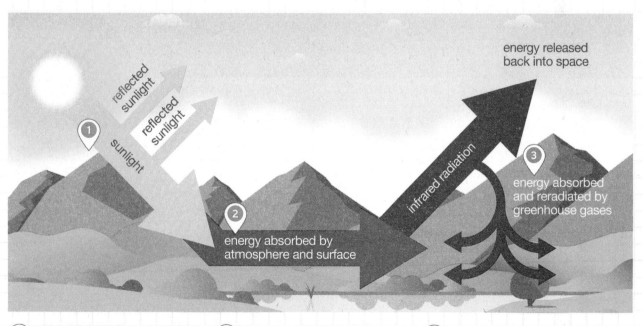

energy released back into space

reflected sunlight

reflected sunlight

sunlight

①

② energy absorbed by atmosphere and surface

infrared radiation

③ energy absorbed and reradiated by greenhouse gases

 1 Sunlight travels through space and reaches Earth. Some solar energy is reflected by the atmosphere and Earth's surface.

 2 Some solar energy is absorbed by the atmosphere and surface. It is transformed into infrared radiation and is reradiated.

 3 Greenhouse gases absorb some of the outgoing infrared radiation and reradiate it back into the Earth system.

Hands-On Lab
Model the Greenhouse Effect

In this experiment, you will construct and use a physical model to explain how greenhouse gases affect Earth's temperature.

Procedure and Analysis

STEP 1 Pour dark soil into both bottles, so the depth of soil is about 5 cm. Why do you think dark soil is used in this model?

STEP 2 Cover the top of one bottle with clear plastic wrap. Tape the plastic wrap to the bottle, so that air cannot escape.

STEP 3 Set up a data table to record the temperature of the air in each bottle every minute for a total of 15 minutes.

STEP 4 Place the two bottles in direct sunlight. Use the temperature probes to measure and record the temperature of each bottle every minute for a total of 15 minutes. Record your data.

MATERIALS

- bottle, plastic, 2L, with the top cut off (2)
- masking tape
- plastic wrap, clear
- ruler
- soil, dark
- temperature probe (2)

Analysis

STEP 5 The bottle with / without the plastic wrap models the greenhouse effect. The air in the bottle with / without plastic wrap became warmer than the bottle with / without the plastic wrap did.

STEP 6 In this model, the bottle represents the Earth system. The atmosphere is represented by the air and the plastic wrap, and the surface is represented by the soil in the bottle. Models are used to represent the real-world, however, no model is perfect. What are some differences between your model and the real-world?

STEP 7 How could you improve your model to better represent the Earth system?

STEP 8 How might you modify your model to show that changes in the concentration of greenhouse gases in the atmosphere affect temperature over time?

Language SmArts

Explain Temperature Ranges on Earth and the Moon

3. Think about the temperature ranges on Earth and the moon. Unlike Earth, the moon has almost no atmosphere. Explain why the range of temperatures on Earth is so different from that on the moon. Cite evidence to support your explanation.

_____

_____

_____

_____

_____

Identifying Global Climate Change Factors

Global Climate Change

Global climate has changed throughout Earth's history, due to both natural processes and human activities. Some climate scientists study how climate has changed in the past and compare that to how the climate is currently changing.

4. One-hundred-million-year-old fossils of tropical ferns have been found in Antarctica. Tropical ferns grow in tropical climates. Therefore, Antarctica's climate was warm and rainy / cold and dry 100 million years ago. Now, Antarctica's climate is warm and rainy / cold and dry.

Climate Data

Systematic measurement of temperatures across Earth's surface began around 1880. Today, satellites and other instruments collect detailed data. But how do we know what the climate was like thousands, or even millions, of years ago? This information comes from paleoclimate data. Look at the photos. *Paleoclimate data* contain clues about past climates and are found in rocks, fossils, tree rings, and ice cores. For example, coal commonly forms from plants that grow in swamps. Finding a 150-million-year-old layer of coal provides evidence that the area was likely a swamp 150 million years ago.

Tables, graphs, and maps are made from paleoclimate data to show trends in climate over time and in different areas on Earth. Both paleoclimate data and recent climate data are used in computer models to explore the causes and effects of climate change. Some climate models are used to predict future climate changes.

An ancient glacier passed over this rock and formed these scratches. This is evidence that the climate was very cold when the glacier existed.

Tree rings form each year as a tree grows. Wider rings form when the tree grows faster due to warmer, wetter conditions.

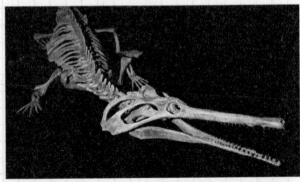

Fossils are the remains of living things from long ago that can give us clues about past climates. This fossil is of an animal that lived in a warm, shallow sea.

Scientists identify different gases trapped in ice that formed thousands of years ago. These data can tell scientists about the levels of greenhouse gases in Earth's past atmosphere.

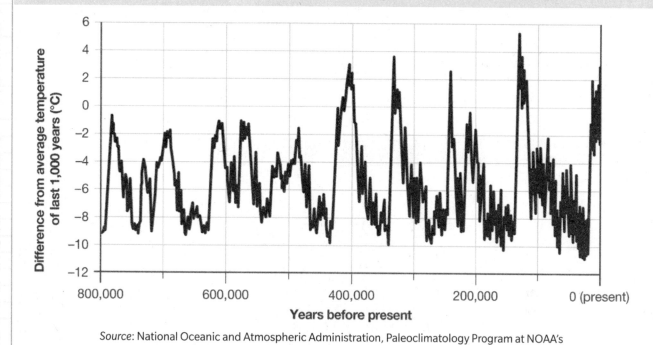

Paleoclimate Temperature Reconstruction from Antarctic Ice Core Data

These data show how temperature in Antarctica changed over the last 800,000 years. Scientists use these data and others to reconstruct Earth's global climate history.

Source: National Oceanic and Atmospheric Administration, Paleoclimatology Program at NOAA's National Centers for Environmental Information

5. The graph shows that the average surface temperature in Antarctica has
   changed / not changed over the last 800,000 years. Scientists think that
   Earth's average temperature has followed a similar pattern. If so, Earth's average
   temperature is currently experiencing a *cooling / warming* trend.

Causes of Global Climate Change

The stability of the global climate can be disturbed. Changes can be caused by many different natural processes. Some changes are caused by short-term or sudden events. For example, explosive volcanic eruptions can temporarily lower Earth's average surface temperature for a period of weeks or for a few years. This temperature drop happens because explosive eruptions send ash particles into the atmosphere. The ash particles reflect a portion of incoming sunlight.

Gradual changes also affect global climate. For example, changes in the shape of Earth's orbit occur over a period of about 100,000 years. These changes affect the amount of incoming solar radiation that reaches Earth and its distribution across Earth's surface, which affect global climate.

Human activities also cause global climate change. For example, daily activities such as driving vehicles and raising livestock emit greenhouse gases. The increased concentration of greenhouse gases in the atmosphere results in an increase in global surface temperatures. How long the temperature remains higher depends on how long the greenhouse gases remain in the atmosphere. If greenhouse gas concentrations continue to increase in the atmosphere, the temperature will continue to rise. If concentrations of greenhouse gases decrease, the temperature will stop rising and will begin to decrease.

Astronomical Changes

The shape of Earth's orbit affects global climate, and so do changes in Earth's tilt on its axis. Earth's tilt varies between about 22 to 25 degrees. These changes take place on cycles of about 41,000 years. When the tilt angle is higher, summers are warmer and winters are colder. Earth also wobbles on its axis as it orbits the sun. Over about 26,000 years, this wobble changes the timing of the seasons relative to Earth's distance from the sun. As a result, the intensity of the seasons changes.

Sunspot activity relates to the amount of solar energy that reaches Earth. Studies show that recent changes in solar energy have had very little impact on global climate when compared to changes in greenhouse gas concentrations in Earth's atmosphere.

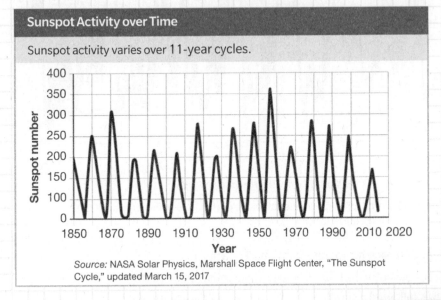

Sunspot Activity over Time

Sunspot activity varies over 11-year cycles.

Source: NASA Solar Physics, Marshall Space Flight Center, "The Sunspot Cycle," updated March 15, 2017

Changes on Earth's Surface

Earth's surface is made up of oceans, forests, deserts, ice sheets, rock, and soil. Changes in the materials exposed at Earth's surface affect global climate. Different Earth materials absorb and reflect different amounts of solar energy, and different materials retain solar energy for different amounts of time. For example, rock absorbs more solar energy than water does, but water retains energy longer than land does. In addition, some materials absorb greenhouse gases from the atmosphere. For example, forests, soils, and oceans absorb carbon dioxide from the atmosphere.

6. As Grinnell Glacier in Montana melts, dark soil and rock are exposed. The soil and rock absorb more / less solar energy than the ice absorbed. The result is an increase / decrease in temperature.

1940

2006

Both natural processes and human activities alter Earth's surface. Human activities generally change Earth's surface more quickly than natural processes do. For example, dark pavement and rooftops in a development could replace forested areas in a matter of months or years.

 Warm water currents carry thermal energy toward the poles. Cold, deep currents carry thermal energy into the deep ocean. This exchange of energy in polar regions affects regional climates and the formation of polar sea ice and ice caps.

 Some surface currents are relatively cold, such as the Antarctic Circumpolar Current. This cold water current keeps temperatures near the pole cold enough to support an ice cap all year round.

 In areas where deep water comes up to the surface, climates of nearby land areas are generally cooler. The cold water also carries nutrients and gases to the surface.

Changes in Ocean Circulation

The circulation of ocean waters transports energy and matter around Earth. Warm surface currents carry thermal energy toward the poles, and cold, deep currents flow toward the equator. The movement of water and thermal energy affects both local and global temperatures. For example, the flow of the Antarctic Circumpolar Current isolates the continent of Antarctica and keeps the climate of the South Pole icy.

The Antarctic polar ice cap formed about 23 million years ago, and the Arctic ice cap formed about 3 million years ago. The formation of the ice caps happened well before the recent trend in rising global temperatures. However, since global temperatures have started to rise, the polar ice caps have started to shrink. Scientists think this is related to the amount of thermal energy being transported toward the poles. This suggests that changes in global ocean circulation and in the size or extent of ice caps are likely effects, rather than causes, of recent rises in global temperature.

7. The movement of ocean water transfers thermal energy around the globe. How might an increase in global average temperatures affect the flow of thermal energy around Earth by surface and deep currents?

El Niño and La Niña

Climate is the long-term weather pattern of a region, and some variation in local climates occur over time. Some of these variations happen in short-term or long-term cycles. Short-term climate cycles that affect weather patterns in California include El Niño and La Niña. Because these patterns are predictable cycles, they are generally referred to as ENSO, or the El Niño–Southern Oscillation.

ENSO cycles are important to California's weather and climates because these cycles affect the air and water temperatures in the Pacific Ocean. Over the course of approximately one to seven years, the trade winds strengthen and weaken, changing the flow of energy in the central and eastern Pacific Ocean.

In California, El Niño events are characterized by weaker winds, warmer temperatures, and wetter weather. During La Niña events, the opposite occurs—trade winds are stronger, which brings cooler, drier weather to California. The graph shows the timing of El Niño and La Niña events for a 30-year period.

El Niño and La Niña Events for a 30-Year Period

ENSO events are classified as weak to very strong, depending on the maximum ocean temperatures.

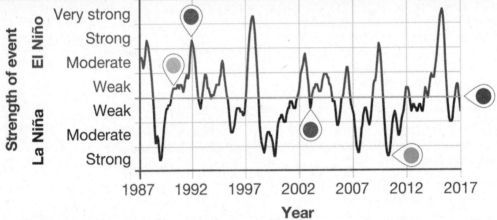

Source: NOAA Climate Prediction Center, Cold & Warm Episodes by Season, 2017

In a weak El Niño event, trade winds weaken slightly, and warmer-than-normal water moves into the central and eastern tropical Pacific Ocean.

In a strong El Niño event, trade winds weaken dramatically and may reverse to blow west-to-east across the tropical Pacific Ocean, drawing warmer-than-normal water into the central and eastern tropical Pacific Ocean.

In a weak La Niña event, trade winds strengthen, blowing strongly from east to west across the topical Pacific Ocean. Warm, moist air and warm surface waters flow to the west, cooling the central and eastern Pacific Ocean.

In a strong La Niña event, trade winds strengthen and carry warm, moist air and waters to the west. The central and eastern Pacific Ocean surface temperatures drop by more than 2 °C.

On average, trade winds blow east to west across the tropical Pacific Ocean. Warm, moist air and warm surface waters flow to the west. The central Pacific Ocean is cool. This is called the "neutral state."

8. Do the patterns in the timing and strength of ENSO events match the timing and trend of recent global temperature change?

Changes in Earth's Atmosphere

Earth's atmosphere plays a large role in global climate. For example, the concentration of greenhouse gases is currently increasing in the atmosphere. The increase in concentration of these gases leads to an increase in the average global temperature.

Greenhouse gases enter the atmosphere from natural and human sources. For example, burning fossil fuels releases greenhouse gases into the atmosphere. Humans burn fossil fuels to power vehicles and to generate electrical energy. Mining, agriculture, and cement production also release greenhouse gases into the atmosphere.

Volcanic eruptions are natural processes that release greenhouse gases into the atmosphere. However, human activities release a larger quantity of greenhouse gases than volcanoes do. Furthermore, explosive eruptions release particles into the atmosphere that reflect sunlight and result in a slight decrease in the global temperature. This effect usually lasts for a period of months or years.

In 1991, Mount Pinatubo erupted in the Philippines. This explosive eruption sent ash into the atmosphere that was spread around the world by global winds. As a result, global temperatures had dropped by about 0.5 °C one year later.

 EVIDENCE NOTEBOOK

9. Which climate change factors might be contributing to phenomena occurring in Shishmaref? Think about how changes can be gradual or sudden and natural or human-caused. Record your evidence.

 Do the Math
Compare Quantities of Carbon Dioxide

10. Use the word bank to complete the statements to compare the amounts of carbon dioxide released by human activities and by volcanoes.

In 2015, human activities added about 40 trillion kilograms of carbon dioxide into the atmosphere. On average, volcanoes release about 600 billion kilograms of carbon dioxide into the atmosphere every year.

40,000,000,000,000 kg / 600,000,000,000 kg is about 67.

Therefore, _____ release about 67 times more carbon dioxide than _____ do.

WORD BANK
- human activities
- volcanoes

Analyzing Recent Climate Change

The maps below show how Earth's surface temperature has changed over time. The colors on each map show how the temperature in a given time period compares to the average temperature during the years 1951 to 1981.

11. The maps show global temperature changes over time. Different locations have warmed and cooled by different amounts, but the overall global temperature has increased / decreased / stayed the same.

Explore Online

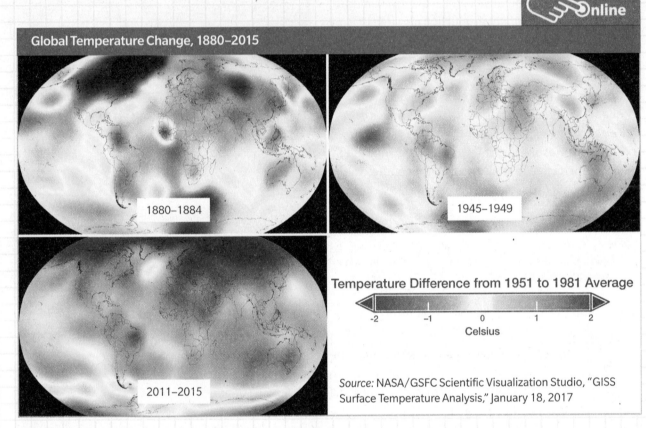

Global Temperature Change, 1880–2015

1880–1884

1945–1949

2011–2015

Temperature Difference from 1951 to 1981 Average

-2   -1   0   1   2

Celsius

Source: NASA/GSFC Scientific Visualization Studio, "GISS Surface Temperature Analysis," January 18, 2017

© Houghton Mifflin Harcourt Publishing Company • (t) Image Credits: (tl, tr, b) ©NASA Goddard Space Flight Center Scientific Visualization Studio

Recent Climate Change

The term *climate change* refers to Earth's increasing global temperature and its effects on natural systems. The recent rise in temperature has been more rapid and has lasted longer than any period of warming over the previous nine centuries. Earth's average global surface temperature has increased over the last century by about 0.6 °C.

This change might seem small, but a change in only a few degrees can completely alter an environment and the things that live there. For example, many organisms in polar regions rely on permafrost. *Permafrost* is a soil that is frozen throughout the year. But small increases in temperatures cause this soil to thaw. When the ice in permafrost melts, the soil becomes more vulnerable to erosion. It no longer supports the trees and other plants that live in the soil. It also releases a greenhouse gas called *methane* into the atmosphere. This gas absorbs solar energy and makes the atmosphere warmer, which thaws more permafrost. These processes form a feedback loop that contributes to the increasing warming of the planet.

12. Look at the diagram. Write the words *increasing* or *decreasing* to tell whether the labeled features are increasing or decreasing as a result of climate change.

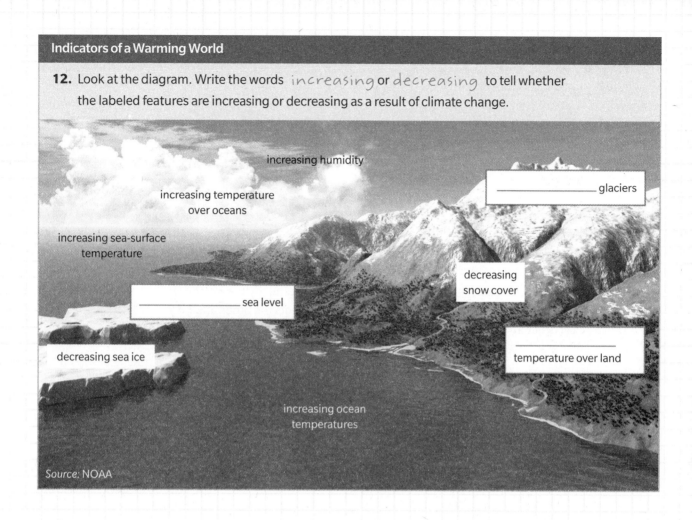

increasing humidity

increasing temperature over oceans

increasing sea-surface temperature

_____ glaciers

decreasing snow cover

_____ sea level

_____ temperature over land

decreasing sea ice

increasing ocean temperatures

Source: NOAA

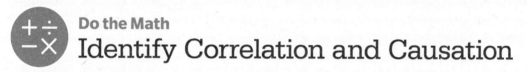
Do the Math
Identify Correlation and Causation

Correlation with Causation Scientists compare trends in global temperature data to trends in other data to identify whether a correlation exists. A *correlation* means that as one variable increases, another variable increases or decreases in a similar pattern. In these graphs, there is a correlation: temperature and ice cream sales decrease in a similar pattern over the same time period. The goal of many climate scientists is to identify all of the factors that contribute to the recent rapid increase in global temperatures. To do this, more than a correlation between variables is needed.

Causation means that one variable causes the other variable to change. It is reasonable to think that more ice cream is sold when the temperatures are warmer because people want a cold treat. A scientist would gather data to test whether this relationship is true.

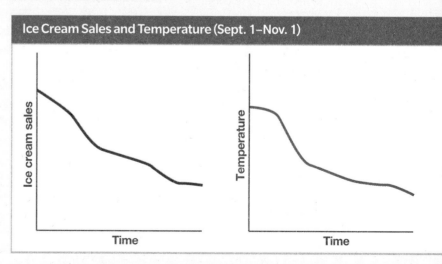

Ice Cream Sales and Temperature (Sept. 1–Nov. 1)

Ice cream sales

Time

Temperature

Time

Correlation Without Causation The graphs of pet adoptions and temperature also show a correlation. They both have in the same pattern in the same time period. However, causation is unlikely as there is no logical explanation of how one factor relates to another. A correlation does not always mean that variables are related.

You can investigate whether there is causation when there is a correlation and it seems likely that one factor could affect the other factor. In order to show causation, you must be able to explain why one factor affects the other. You may find evidence in existing scientific knowledge or by conducting your own investigation.

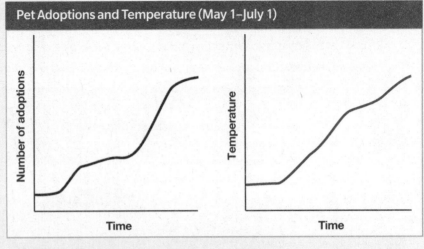

Pet Adoptions and Temperature (May 1–July 1)

These graphs show the levels of carbon dioxide in the atmosphere and the average global temperature over time.

13. Analyze the data shown in each graph. Is there a correlation? Explain.

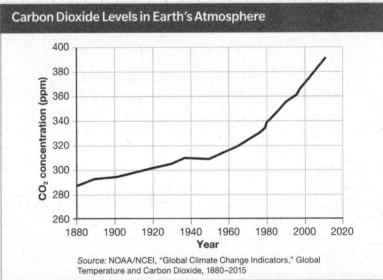

Carbon Dioxide Levels in Earth's Atmosphere

Source: NOAA/NCEI, "Global Climate Change Indicators," Global Temperature and Carbon Dioxide, 1880–2015

14. What questions would you want to investigate to confirm a causal relationship between the concentration of CO_2 in the atmosphere and the average global temperature?

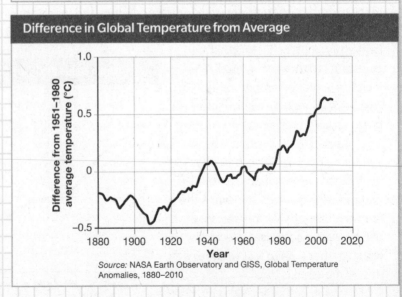

Difference in Global Temperature from Average

Source: NASA Earth Observatory and GISS, Global Temperature Anomalies, 1880–2010

15. **Discuss** With a partner, discuss your answers to questions on the previous page. Create a list of additional questions you could investigate about other factors that might impact climate change. Identify the evidence you would need to answer those questions.

Causes of Recent Climate Change

Most scientists agree that the primary cause of the recent increase in the average global temperature is a rapid increase in greenhouse gas concentrations. Higher greenhouse gas concentrations intensify the greenhouse effect. This is often referred to as the *enhanced greenhouse effect*.

Many human activities produce greenhouse gases. The rates at which humans perform those activities has been steadily rising over the past few centuries as the human population grows and more people use electrical energy, drive cars, fly in planes, and eat commercially farmed food. People can affect the rate and magnitude of climate change by making wise decisions about resource use. People must decide whether and how to modify their behaviors or technologies to reduce their effects on climate.

Most of the carbon dioxide that has entered the atmosphere in the last century is from the burning of fossil fuels for transportation and to generate electrical energy.

EVIDENCE NOTEBOOK

16. How might human decisions and behaviors be contributing to the erosion in Shishmaref, Alaska? Record your evidence.

Describe Cause and Effect

Positive feedback loops are one cause of rapid climate change. A *positive feedback loop* occurs when a change in one quantity changes a second quantity, and the second quantity then amplifies the changes in the first quantity.

17. As temperatures rapidly increase, sea ice is melting. Ocean water is darker / lighter than ice is. Darker surfaces absorb more / less solar energy than light surfaces do. Therefore, ocean water absorbs more / less solar energy than ice does. This warms / cools ocean water over time, which melts more sea ice.

Understanding the Effects of Climate Change

Climate change is more extreme in some places than in others. For example, the average temperatures near Earth's poles have increased at a more rapid rate than temperatures have increased elsewhere.

The environment in North America was quite different 12,000 years ago. Many animals that thrived in that cooler environment, such as woolly mammoths, no longer exist today.

18. Draw During the last "ice age," the average global temperature was about 11 °C (52 °F). Today, it is 16 °C (61 °F). Draw what the area shown might look like now. Describe what it might look like if temperatures were 5 °C (9 °F) warmer than they are today.

Effects of Recent Climate Change

The effects of rapidly changing climate in the past century include sea level rise and changes in habitats. Changes are more extreme in some places. For example, over the past 60 years, the average temperature in Alaska has increased by about 1.5 °C (2.7 °F). That rate of increase is almost twice as fast as that of the rest of the United States.

Changes in the Biosphere

A region's climate affects its organisms. For example, as the climate warms in Alaska, plants begin to grow earlier in the season than they did in the past. This affects any organisms that depend on those plants. As climate changes a habitat, populations of organisms must adapt, move, or die out. In some places, climate is changing so rapidly that some organisms can't adapt or move quickly enough to survive the changes.

Changes in Ice

Earth's ice contains a large volume of water and keeps that water out of the oceans. Recent climate change has caused frozen soil called *permafrost,* continental ice sheets, and glaciers to melt. The meltwater flows into the ocean, and sea level rises. As sea ice melts, animals such as polar bears and seals that rest, breed, and hunt for food on ice lose their habitats. As a result, these organisms may become extinct. Structures built on permafrost can shift and sink into the soil as it thaws.

Changes in the Oceans

Recent climate change has increased ocean temperatures, which affects ocean currents, weather patterns, and sea level. Warmer surface waters generate more powerful tropical storms, hurricanes, and typhoons. Wave action and high winds erode beaches and damage ocean and coastal ecosystems. Rising sea levels flood low-lying coastal areas with ocean water, which kills organisms. Erosion increases as water reaches farther onto shore during storms, often reaching areas that were once protected.

Earth's oceans support a diversity of organisms, many of which are important human food sources. Increasing ocean temperatures affect the kinds of organisms that live in particular locations, the migration and breeding patterns of animals, and sensitive marine ecosystems, such as coral reefs and coastal wetlands. As the amount of carbon dioxide in the atmosphere increases, the amount that dissolves in ocean water also increases. This process makes ocean water more acidic, making it difficult for many marine organisms to form hard skeletons or shells.

Sea ice protects the coastline. When sea ice melts, the coastline can be exposed to erosion from ocean waves.

Thawing permafrost is no longer supported by the solid ice crystals it once contained. As a result, the soil may sink, crack, or collapse. It is also more easily eroded by waves and rain.

Increased ocean temperatures harm coral that live in reefs. In a process called *coral bleaching,* algae that the coral needs for food leave, and the coral turns white.

© Houghton Mifflin Harcourt Publishing Company • Image Credits: (b) ©Ethan Daniels/Stocktrek Images/Getty Images; (t) ©Sven Zacek/Photolibrary/Getty Images; (c) ©Accent Alaska.com/Alamy

EVIDENCE NOTEBOOK

19. Describe how the increase in global temperatures over the last century could be related to the events in Shishmaref. Record your evidence.

Human Vulnerability to Climate Change

Most human populations live in coastal areas that will be threatened as sea level rises. Changing weather and climate patterns affect the availability of resources and the ability of humans to grow crops for food. Higher global temperatures also affect the way diseases can spread, which affects the health of individual people and of communities. Reducing human vulnerability to climate change depends on understanding climate and climate change, on available engineering and technology, and on human behaviors.

Humans and Greenhouse Gases

To reduce the effects of greenhouse gases on global climate, humans must find ways to reduce the amount of greenhouse gases that are being added to the atmosphere. To help in this effort, scientists and engineers are improving technologies that use wind and solar energy to generate electrical energy. These technologies do not produce greenhouse gases as a byproduct of generating electrical energy. Scientists and engineers are also researching ways to absorb and contain greenhouse gases.

Reducing human impacts on climate change and the impacts of climate change on humans takes a commitment from individuals, businesses, and governments. Individuals and businesses can make choices to use energy and other resources more efficiently. People can use resources in a way that limits the emission of greenhouse gases. Governments can work both domestically and internationally to develop laws and programs to reduce greenhouse gas emissions and to keep people safe from the effects of climate change.

20. Identify two ways that people may be affected by climate change. Then suggest a solution for each problem that could be performed by individuals, businesses, or governments.

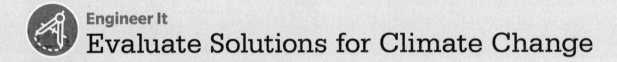

Engineer It
Evaluate Solutions for Climate Change

Engineers solve problems by proposing and evaluating solutions.

Engineering Problem: Carbon dioxide in the atmosphere is causing global temperatures to rise. How can the concentration of carbon dioxide in the atmosphere be reduced?

Solution 1: Remove carbon dioxide from the atmosphere by planting trees in deforested areas.

Solution 2: Add fertilizer to ocean water to encourage the growth of green algae that will remove carbon dioxide from the atmosphere.

21. Evaluate the solutions to find strengths and weaknesses. Think about any unwanted effects. Recommend whether each solution should be considered further.

_____

_____

_____

_____

_____

Continue Your Exploration

Name: _____   Date: _____

Check out the path below or go online to choose one of the other paths shown.

Careers in Science

- **Disappearing Coral Reefs**
- **Hands-On Labs** 🖐
- **Propose Your Own Path**

Go online to choose one of these other paths.

Geeta G. Persad, Postdoctoral Research Scientist

As a freshman in college, Dr. Geeta Persad attended a scientific conference about climate that motivated her to focus on climate science. She believes that one of climate scientists' duties is to inform the public and policymakers about climate research and why it is important.

Scientists like Dr. Persad use computer models to determine how different substances affect the atmosphere and climate. These models include factors such as the amounts of different gases, liquids, and solids in the atmosphere. Scientists change the factors in the climate model to help them understand how each factor may affect climate. Scientists use these models to make predictions about how climate may change in the future.

Dr. Persad's work with climate models has focused on the effects of tiny particles called *aerosols*. These particles affect how clouds form. Dr. Persad has applied what she has learned about aerosols and clouds to computer models so that clouds can be modeled realistically. These data help the computer climate models more accurately recreate the conditions that cause clouds to form and dissipate. These models help scientists understand how clouds, weather, and climate behave and how climate may change in the future.

Dr. Geeta Persad visited the Franz Josef Glacier in New Zealand, which is shrinking as a result of recent climate change.

Continue Your Exploration

1. How does Dr. Persad's work on clouds contribute to our understanding of climate and climate change?

2. Scientists have developed a number of different global climate models. Why do climate scientists use computer models to study changes in climate?

3. A scientist is developing a computer model to study the effects of a certain substance in the atmosphere on climate. Which factors might the scientist need to adjust in the model? Select all that apply.

   A. changes in the sun's output

   B. amount of the substance in the atmosphere

   C. Earth's distance from the sun

   D. whether the substance causes a positive or negative feedback

   E. the source of the substance

4. **Collaborate** With a partner, write at least three questions that you would like to ask Dr. Persad about evidence related to factors that affect climate change.

Can You Explain It?

Name: _____   Date: _____

What could be causing ice and permafrost to melt in Shishmaref?

EVIDENCE NOTEBOOK

Refer to the notes in your Evidence Notebook to help you explain why ice and permafrost are melting in Shishmaref.

1. State your claim. Make sure your claim fully explains why sea ice and permafrost are melting and leading to destructive erosion in Shishmaref.

2. Summarize the evidence you have gathered to support your claim and explain your reasoning.

Checkpoints

Answer the following questions to check your understanding of the lesson.

Use the graph to answer Questions 3–5.

3. Which statement is supported by the data in the graph?

   A. The amount of carbon dioxide in the atmosphere does not change.

   B. Melting sea ice is caused by rising levels of carbon dioxide in the atmosphere.

   C. Adding more carbon dioxide to the atmosphere causes Earth's climate to warm.

   D. Carbon dioxide concentration in the atmosphere is higher now than at any other time in the last 400,000 years.

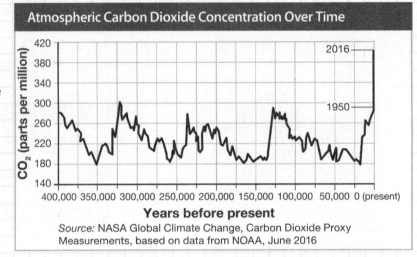

Atmospheric Carbon Dioxide Concentration Over Time

Source: NASA Global Climate Change, Carbon Dioxide Proxy Measurements, based on data from NOAA, June 2016

4. Based on the concentration of carbon dioxide in the atmosphere, Earth's global temperature likely was higher / lower 125,000 years ago than it was 25,000 years ago.

5. The rate at which carbon dioxide is being added to the atmosphere now is higher / lower than ever before.

WORD BANK
- volcanic eruption
- less incoming solar radiation
- more greenhouse gases
- shrinking polar ice caps

6. Complete the table by matching the factors provided in the word bank with the effect they have on global temperature.

Makes Earth Warmer	Makes Earth Cooler

7. When greenhouse gas concentrations in the atmosphere are high, less / more energy is absorbed by the atmosphere. As a result, thermal energy stays in the Earth system for a longer / shorter time, and Earth's average surface temperature rises / drops.

8. Reducing human vulnerability to the effects of climate change requires which of the following? Choose all that apply.

   A. understanding of climate science

   B. improving engineering capabilities

   C. understanding of human behavior

   D. applying knowledge to make wise decisions

Interactive Review

Complete this section to review the main concepts of the lesson.

Climate is driven by energy from the sun and interactions of the Earth system. Greenhouse gases in the atmosphere absorb energy from the sun.

A. How is the temperature range on Earth affected by Earth's atmosphere?

Both natural processes and human activities affect climate. Earth's climate can be changed by sudden events or by gradual changes over time.

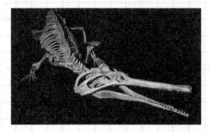

B. Describe how one natural process and one human activity affect climate or cause climate change.

Earth's average global temperature has increased over the last century. The main cause of this increase is carbon dioxide that is released when humans burn fossil fuels as an energy source.

C. How do correlation and causation relate to understanding how natural processes and human activities affect climate or cause climate change?

Minimizing the effects of climate change requires reducing greenhouse gas emissions from human activities and understanding effects of climate change on Earth systems.

D. Give an example of how humans burning fossil fuels affects each of Earth's major systems (atmosphere, biosphere, geosphere, hydrosphere).

Climate Change Affects the Survival of Organisms

When ocean temperatures rise, sea stars, like these ochre sea stars, face a greater risk of contracting diseases. These diseases may cause sea star populations to decline.

Explore First

Modeling Elephant Ears African elephants live on the hot, open savanna. Asian elephants live in cooler, shady jungles. The ears of African elephants are three times larger than the ears of Asian elephants. Model the ears of the two elephants. How does ear size relate to the elephant's environment? How could climate change affect the ears of elephants over many generations?

CAN YOU EXPLAIN IT?

How could climate change affect the survival of koalas?

Koalas are found naturally only in Australia. They have unique adaptations to the cool, moist, eucalyptus forests on that continent. Koalas have thick fur and strong claws, and they eat only eucalyptus tree leaves. In recent years, more and more wild koalas are dying.

1. Koalas spend most of their lives in the branches of eucalyptus trees in cool, coastal and low-elevation forests. What physical and behavioral traits are apparent in the photo and caption that connect the koala to its environment?

2. How do you think climate change might affect the conditions in the koala's environment?

 EVIDENCE NOTEBOOK As you explore this lesson, gather evidence to help you explain how climate change may affect the survival of koalas.

Relating the Adaptations of Organisms to their Environments

Living things depend on resources and services that ecosystems provide. An **ecosystem** is all of the living organisms and their nonliving environment in a specific area. The environment shown in the illustration is a desert ecosystem in southern California. Organisms interact with each other and with their environment on different levels. A *species* is a group of organisms that are closely related and can mate to produce fertile offspring. A *population* is all of the individuals of a given species in an area. All of the different species that live in an ecosystem make up a *community*.

3. Write the answer that describes each level of the ecosystem in the correct box.

WORD LIST
- community
- ~~ecosystem~~
- individual
- population

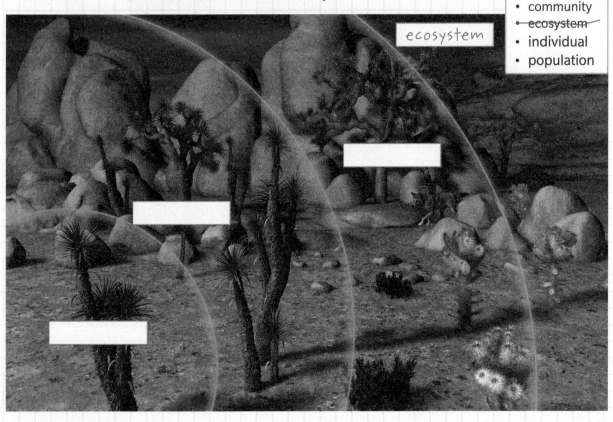

ecosystem

Healthy Ecosystems and Habitats

A *habitat* is the place where an organism lives. The quality of a habitat depends on the local environmental conditions. Local conditions include the availability of food, light, space, and water; air or water temperature; and water or soil acidity. For example, in a desert ecosystem, the air and soil are dry, and there is a lot of open space. Healthy ecosystems provide natural habitats and other important resources and services that organisms, including humans, depend on. These services include producing food, cleaning air and water, decomposing wastes, and regulating climate and disease.

4. An ecosystem that cannot perform essential services is a(n)

healthy / unhealthy ecosystem. Such an ecosystem would

be able to support large / small populations of organisms.

Biodiversity

Biodiversity describes the number, type, and variety of all living organisms in a particular area. It includes the genetic and physical variety of individuals within populations, of populations within species, and of species within communities. It also describes the diversity of ecosystems on Earth.

The reintroduction of gray wolves to Yellowstone National Park has affected the park's biodiversity.

Biodiversity forms the foundation of the ecosystem services that are critically important to human well-being. A higher level of biodiversity generally indicates a stronger, more robust ecosystem that is less likely to be disrupted or destroyed. So, biodiversity can be a measurement of the health of an ecosystem. Wolves are the top predators in the ecosystem of Yellowstone National Park. They affect a number of food webs in the park, including those that include bears, elk, ravens, and even trees and berry-producing shrubs. Because of hunting, there were no wolves in the park area in the early 1900s. The wolves were reintroduced in 1995. By studying the park's ecosystems with and without wolves, scientists have learned about how different species and communities affect the health of the ecosystem.

5. Higher biodiversity generally means that an ecosystem is more / less stable because greater variability in the number of species and in the individuals of each species means the ecosystem is more / less susceptible to environmental changes.

6. Based on the data in the table, how do wolves affect the biodiversity and stability of the ecosystems of Yellowstone National Park?

   A. Wolves don't change the stability of the park ecosystem because mule deer populations didn't change after the wolves were reintroduced.

   B. Wolves make the park ecosystem more stable because biodiversity increased after the wolves were reintroduced.

   C. Wolves make the park ecosystem less stable because after they were reintroduced, populations of elk and coyotes went down.

   D. Wolves make the park ecosystem less stable because after their reintroduction, populations of foxes, bears, beavers, and trees went up.

Estimated Populations of Organisms in Parts of Yellowstone National Park		
Organism	Population before wolf reintroduction	Population after wolf reintroduction
Wolves	0	104
Coyotes	1,560	800
Foxes	175	300
Grizzly bears	150	690
Elk	17,000	7,000
Mule deer	2,100	2,200
Beaver colonies	1	12
Willow-dependent bird species	19	33
Cottonwood trees (>5 cm diameter)	<10	175
Berry-producing shrubs (in one research area)	<5	50

Sources: U.S. National Park Service; Ripple et al., Trophic cascades in Yellowstone, Biological Conservation, 2011; Baril, Lisa. Change in Deciduous Woody Vegetation...in Yellowstone National Park's Northern Range, 2017; Newsome, T.M. and Ripple, W.J., A continental scale trophic cascade from wolves through coyotes to foxes, Journal of Animal Ecology, 2014; Jackson, S.G., Relationships among Birds, Willows, and Native Ungulates in and around Yellowstone National Park, 1992

Adaptations to the Environment

Adaptations help organisms survive and reproduce in specific environmental conditions, such as a dry desert or a shallow ocean. Plant adaptations may include flower colors and odors, hard shells on seeds, and timing of budding and blooming. Physical adaptations of animals include feather or fur color and body size or shape. Animal behaviors include nest or den building, foraging and hunting for food, avoiding predators, mating displays or combat, seasonal behaviors like migration and hibernation, and vocalizations.

Adaptations to the California Chaparral Ecosystem

The California chaparral ecosystem is characterized by shrubs, grasses, trees, and animals that are adapted to relatively hot and dry conditions and occasional wildfires.

Coyote brush has thick bark and waxy leaves and can resprout above the ground, which help it to survive wildfires.

The cholla cactus stores water in its fleshy lobes. Other chaparral plants have long, water-seeking roots.

The tarantula hawk hunts tarantulas to provide food and water for its young.

A jackrabbit's large ears release heat to help keep the animal cool.

The cactus wren nests among the cactus spines for protection.

7. How might eucalyptus trees and koalas be adapted to the local environmental conditions where they live? Record your evidence.

Do the Math

Explore a Kelp Forest

Kelp is seaweed, a plant that thrives where sunlight enters cool, clear water. Many organisms feed on kelp. Kelp also provides shelter for many forms of sea life. Forests of kelp are among the most productive ecosystems on Earth.

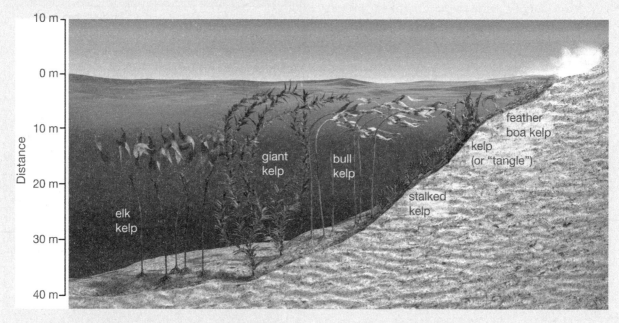

8. How are the different species of kelp adapted to the depths at which each lives?

_____

_____

_____

_____

_____

9. In the space provided, create a number line to plot sea level and the depths at which the different species of kelp live, based on where their roots are.

Analyzing How Organisms Respond to Climate Change

Climate Change Affects the Environment

Climate change disrupts the stability of ecosystems. Climate change affects the nonliving components of ecosystems by changing the temperature of air, water, and soil. Over the past 100 years, average global temperature has risen by 0.6 °C. This increase is primarily a result of the burning of fossil fuels and the raising of livestock for human food. Recent climate change is raising local and regional air, water, and soil temperatures; making water more acidic; and affecting weather patterns.

10. Circle the areas on the maps where the glaciers have changed. Have the lengths of the glaciers shown increased or decreased?

Shrinking Glaciers in New Zealand

Between 1990 and 2017, the Mueller Glacier, Hooker Glacier, and Tasman Glacier in New Zealand shrank significantly due to rising global temperatures.

11. Ice and snow reflect more sunlight than dark rock or soil do. How could the melting of glaciers cause changes in the transfer of energy between Earth's surface and atmosphere?

12. How could the changes in the glaciers affect the local environmental conditions to which organisms are adapted?

Changes to Land Ecosystems

Rising air temperatures affect weather patterns that may lead to heat waves, droughts, and increased wildfire risks. Wildfires can destroy huge areas of habitat and reduce the ability of ecosystems to provide food and clean air and water.

Warming air temperatures also affect the timing of seasonal budding and blooming and of growing seasons. Warmer, drier soil affects the rate of decomposition of organic materials and is also more susceptible to soil erosion. These conditions affect how well plants can grow. Changes in the timing of seasons also affect the migration and reproductive behaviors of animals.

Smoke from a nearby wildfire hangs over the forest in Yosemite National Park.

EVIDENCE NOTEBOOK

13. How could climate change affect the environment in which koalas live? How could koalas respond to that change? Record your evidence.

Changes to Aquatic Ecosystems

As global temperatures rise, ocean and lake water temperatures also rise. Warming waters expand, contributing to sea level rise, which displaces organisms that rely on certain water depths or conditions. Warming oceans also affect weather patterns, which affect regional climates on land. Ocean temperatures are related to severe weather systems, such as hurricanes, and to cyclic climate patterns like El Niño and La Niña. Changes in ocean circulation affect upwelling and cycling of nutrients in the oceans, which affects how and when aquatic organisms get food, migrate, grow, and reproduce.

As carbon dioxide concentration in the atmosphere rises, ocean and lake water absorbs more carbon dioxide from the atmosphere. As a result, the water becomes more acidic. Aquatic organisms are surrounded by the acidic water, which may affect how the organisms grow, move, protect themselves, and reproduce.

14. Climate change *increases / decreases* the acidity of ocean, lake, and river water. Increased acidity *hardens / dissolves* the shells of some marine creatures, *increasing / decreasing* their likelihood of survival or reproduction.

Acidic water dissolves the calcium carbonate shells of some animals. The top photo shows a shell in normal water conditions. The bottom photo shows a shell in acidic water.

Map Monarch Migration

You will map the migration of monarch butterflies between summer breeding and feeding grounds and wintering locations. You will plot data from two different years to model the effects of climate change on the timing of the butterfly migration.

MATERIALS
• colored pencils

Procedure

STEP 1 Color in the key below the maps. Use the same colors for each time interval when plotting the data on both maps.

STEP 2 Look at the table titled "Year 1 Monarch Sightings." Use the location data provided to plot the location for each sighting onto the map for Year 1.

STEP 3 Look at the table titled "Year 2 Monarch Sightings." Use the location data provided to plot the location for each sighting onto the map for Year 2.

Analysis

STEP 4 Year 1 represents an average year, and Year 2 represents a cooler and drier than average year. How did the timing and distance of the migration compare between the two years?

Year 1 Monarch Sightings		
Date	Latitude	Longitude
8/3	38.7	−119.8
8/15	40.5	−122.3
8/16	39.6	−121.8
9/6	36.1	−117.9
9/11	38.6	−121.8
9/12	37.5	−120.7
9/21	37.5	−120.7
9/29	35.4	−120.9
9/30	34.1	−118.8
10/3	34.3	−118.2
10/10	34.1	−117
10/14	34	−117.2
10/18	33.5	−117.7
10/27	33.7	−118
10/29	33.9	−118
11/3	34	−117.2
11/5	33.6	−117.6
12/8	33.9	−118

Year 2 Monarch Sightings		
Date	Latitude	Longitude
8/17	37.8	−122.4
8/18	38.4	−121.8
8/19	38.2	−122.8
8/31	35.1	−120.4
9/1	34.1	−118.1
9/7	34	−117.2
9/16	34	−117.2
9/22	33.7	−117.4
9/25	34.1	−118.1
10/2	33.8	−118.3
10/8	33.7	−118
10/14	33.4	−117.3
10/20	32.7	−117.2
10/24	32.9	−117.2
10/27	32.7	−117.9
11/5	32.8	−116.9
11/10	32.9	−117.2
11/28	32.6	−117.1

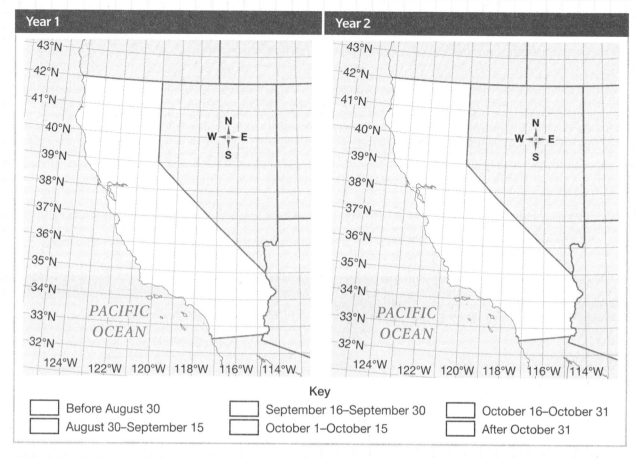

Year 1

43°N
42°N
41°N
40°N
39°N
38°N
37°N
36°N
35°N
34°N
33°N
32°N

124°W 122°W 120°W 118°W 116°W 114°W

PACIFIC OCEAN

N
W—E
S

Year 2

43°N
42°N
41°N
40°N
39°N
38°N
37°N
36°N
35°N
34°N
33°N
32°N

124°W 122°W 120°W 118°W 116°W 114°W

PACIFIC OCEAN

N
W—E
S

Key

| | Before August 30 | | September 16–September 30 | | October 16–October 31 |
| | August 30–September 15 | | October 1–October 15 | | After October 31 |

STEP 5 Which year (Year 1 or Year 2) represents what climates in California will be like if the current trend in climate change continues?

STEP 6 Based on this model, how might monarch butterfly populations respond to recent global climate change?

© Houghton Mifflin Harcourt Publishing Company

Response, Adaptation, and Extinction

Climate changes may also alter an ecosystem's ability to provide important services. The ecosystem may no longer purify air and water, cycle nutrients and wastes, or regulate weather and climate in the same way. These changes can lead to habitat degradation, which is a decrease in the quality, quantity, or range of habitats in an ecosystem. The habitats in which organisms live become less favorable for the survival of organisms that live there. Many organisms or species are adapted to a specific range of air or water temperatures or of soil acidity. When conditions change, organisms and populations may struggle to survive, grow, or reproduce in that environment.

15. Some small animals and most plants *can / cannot* adjust their range quickly when conditions become unfavorable. Native plants that are adapted to extremely *broad / specific* habitats are especially at risk for loss due to climate change.

How Living Things Respond to Climate Change

Individuals Can Respond to Change Some environmental changes happen very quickly. In these cases, individuals must respond in order to survive. Their ability to survive depends on how well the organisms' bodies or behaviors can respond to changes. To find more favorable habitats, organisms may move, or change ranges, into other locations. They may vary the timing or distances of migrations in order to reach better feeding, breeding, or birthing areas. The quino checkerspot butterfly, a native of California, has shifted its range to higher elevations and changed the host plant on which it lays its eggs.

Populations Can Change over Time Changes to environmental conditions can make certain physical or behavioral traits in a population more or less beneficial. Individuals that have beneficial traits then survive and reproduce to pass those traits on to future generations. The frequency of these traits increases in the population over time, and the population is said to be adapted to its new environment. For example, wild thyme populations in France have been slowly changing so that more of the population produces pungent oils that deter animals who would eat the plants. However, the genes that allow the plants to protect themselves from consumers also make the wild thyme less adapted to cold environments.

Species Survive, Evolve, or Become Extinct As populations adapt, they may survive as a species or may evolve into new species that are better adapted to new local conditions. However, if all populations of a species are unable to reproduce or adapt to new environmental conditions, the species may become extinct. Many large mammals, such as the one-horned rhino, that have long life spans and little genetic variability are at risk of becoming extinct due to climate change. Many uniquely adapted organisms are also at risk of extinction.

© Houghton Mifflin Harcourt Publishing Company • Image Credits: (tl) ©Paul Colangelo/National Geographic Creative/Alamy; (r) ©Przemyslaw Muszynski/Shutterstock; (b) ©Robert Pickett/Papilio/Alamy

Climate Change and Biodiversity

Hawaiian honeycreeper birds are unique to the Hawaiian islands. Many honeycreepers are uniquely adapted to eat specific foods. These rare birds are extremely susceptible to avian malaria. This disease is carried and transmitted by mosquitoes when they bite the birds to consume blood. After the introduction of mosquitoes to the Hawaiian Islands in the 1800s, honeycreeper populations declined. The birds survived only at higher elevations where the temperature was too cool for most mosquitoes to survive. As global temperatures rise, the higher elevations become warmer, and mosquitoes can survive there. But the birds cannot move higher up the mountains because the food sources they rely on cannot easily move. The mosquitoes carry deadly diseases to higher elevations as they invade the last refuges for the birds. Today, native Hawaiian birds face one of the highest rates of extinction in the world. Of 41 honeycreeper species and subspecies known since historic times, 17 are probably extinct, 14 are endangered, and only 3 are thriving.

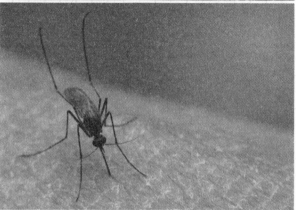

Climate change is expanding the range of mosquitoes, which impacts the scarlet Hawaiian honeycreeper, also known as the i'iwi (ee•EE•vee) in Hawaii.

Do the Math
Evaluate Extinction Probability

The more individuals that are in a population, the more genetically diverse the population is. More diverse populations are more likely to be able to adapt over generations and survive. In a large population, traits that favor the species' survival, such as resistance to disease, could become more common in the population over time. In 2013, the scarlet honeycreeper population was estimated at just over 600,000 birds for all of the islands of Hawaii. However, on some islands, the populations have dropped significantly. On Oahu, for example, scientists estimate that fewer than 50 of the birds remain.

16. Based on the population size and changes to their ecosystems, describe the probability that the scarlet honeycreepers will become extinct in the Hawaiian islands. Does the probability of extinction change if you are looking only at the birds on Oahu? Use scientific reasoning to support your claim.

_____

_____

_____

_____

Monitoring the Effects of Climate Change on Organisms

People and societies can only remain healthy and productive if the surrounding natural ecosystems are healthy and stable. As populations adapt or become extinct, biodiversity changes. In many cases biodiversity decreases, which makes the entire system less able to adapt to future or ongoing changes. Therefore, it is important to monitor and address changes in ecosystems caused by climate change.

17. Coastal wetlands in California are important ecosystems because they stabilize shorelines and *cause / prevent* flooding. These habitats are likely to become *more / less* stable if the populations that live in them move or become extinct in response to climate change.

How Scientists Model Climate Change and Its Effects

Scientists use computer programs to help them model the effects of climate change on different ecosystems and organisms. Scientists use information about the interactions between the atmosphere, land surface, oceans, and biosphere to create computer models that forecast future weather and climate patterns across the globe. Current computer models of climate change project dramatic and rapid environmental changes that are likely to have negative effects on many organisms.

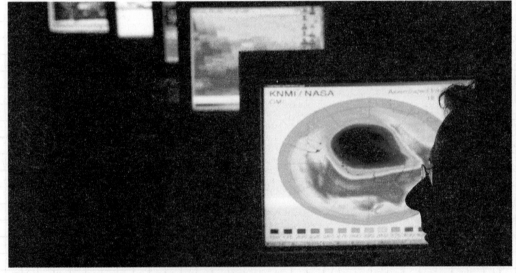

Scientists use several types of computer programs to model the effects of human activity on Earth's atmosphere and oceans. They use computers to analyze data and to predict how changes to Earth's systems will affect humans and other living things.

18. What factors might a computer model need to include for scientists to model the effects of climate change on kelp forest communities off the coast of California?

How Scientists Gather Data about Organisms

Understanding an organism's response to climate change requires *monitoring*. Monitoring involves developing and using technologies and processes to make observations or record data about ecosystem health and biodiversity. Scientists track the responses of individuals, populations, and communities to various nonliving factors and to other organisms in the ecosystem. In some cases, scientists can set up laboratory experiments to investigate ecological changes. But most of the time, scientists have to monitor organisms in their natural environment. How they monitor organisms depends on the particular organism the scientist is studying and the environment in which the organism lives.

Case Study: Using Monitoring Technologies to Study Bats

Large numbers of flying bats may form a crescent shape, shown in pink, on weather radar. Scientists use these data to study bat feeding and migrating behaviors.

Scientists can tag bats with radio or satellite transmitters, which send signals that track and record the travel and migration patterns of the bats over time.

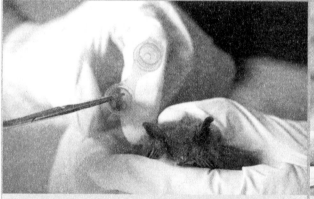

Scientists catch bats to measure their size and weight and to collect hair and blood samples to test the bats' DNA. DNA in bat feces can be tested to find out what the animal has been eating.

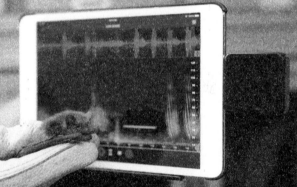

Bats can be tracked by using sound equipment. By recording and analyzing the sounds bats make, scientists can determine whether the bat is traveling, feeding, or mating.

19. How does tracking movements of bats help scientists understand the effects of climate change on bats? Select all that apply.

A. Tracking movements of bats shows whether bats change their range based on where food is available.

B. Tracking movements of bat colonies helps explain how bats fly.

C. Tracking movements of individual bats explains how bats use sound to navigate and communicate.

D. Tracking movements of bats helps explain why bats may change the timing of their migrations in different years.

Language SmArts | Evaluate Text The following passage was written by a student who was researching the use of satellites and other remote sensing equipment to study biodiversity.

Explore Online

Science and Remote Sensing

1 Remote sensing uses special equipment that can capture images of Earth from high in the atmosphere or from space. 2 Remote sensing equipment gathers data by recording visible and invisible light and sound and radio waves. 3 When the satellite data are analyzed, they can show great detail, such as how much coral or sand is in an area or how many different sizes or types of trees are in a section of forest. 4 Remote sensing using satellites and airplanes is better than gathering data by visiting different locations. 5 Remote sensing allows scientists to observe large areas of Earth that would not be easily observed by a scientist on the ground. 6 As more technology is developed, remote sensing equipment will probably provide more detailed data for scientists to analyze. 7 Because it is so useful, most scientists want to include remote sensing when they plan investigations of biodiversity.

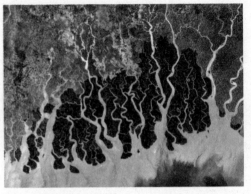

This satellite image shows the extent of the mangrove forest (in black) on the coastlines of Bangladesh and India.

20. Determine whether each numbered sentence is a fact, a reasoned judgment, an opinion, or speculation. Write the number for each sentence in the correct column.

Fact	Reasoned Judgment	Opinion	Speculation

Engineer It

Identify Criteria and Constraints

The Coachella Valley fringe-toed lizard is adapted to life in a dry, hot, sandy environment. The lizards have fringe-like scales on their hind feet that provide traction and enable them to move quickly across sand. They also have adaptations to allow them to burrow quickly into sand.

21. Think about the fringe-toed lizard's lifestyle and environment. What criteria and constraints would apply to a technology that could be used to monitor the fringe-toed lizard's response to climate change?

_____

_____

_____

_____

Continue Your Exploration

Name: _____ Date: _____

Check out the path below or go online to choose one of the other paths shown.

| People in Science | • Superblooms
• Hands-On Labs ✋
• Propose Your Own Path | *Go online to choose one of these other paths.* |

Shayle Matsuda, Marine Biologist

Shayle Matsuda is a marine biologist who identifies as biracial and as a member of the LGBTQ+ community. Matsuda's love of the natural world led him to pursue a double major in both the humanities and the sciences. After college, he spent many years working with young people before learning to SCUBA dive. While diving, Matsuda witnessed first-hand the biodiversity and beauty of coral reefs alongside the undeniable impact humans are having on these fragile marine environments. Matsuda became dedicated to studying the ocean and marine biology. He returned to school to earn his Master's degree in ecology, evolution, and conservation biology. He is currently pursuing his PhD in marine biology.

As part of his work at the University of Hawaii Manoa and the Hawaii Institute of Marine Biology, Matsuda studies how corals respond to rising sea-surface temperatures. In addition to this work, he is investigating how different symbionts, both algae and bacteria, may play a role in coral health under stressful conditions.

Shayle Matsuda transplants coral fragments from Kaneohe Bay in Hawaii into a research tank, where the temperature of the water can be controlled.

Continue Your Exploration

Studying How Corals Respond to Climate Change

While individual coral polyps are small in size, together they form huge colonies. Coral reefs form from calcium carbonate deposits left by corals. Corals form a symbiotic partnership with single-celled algae that live inside the coral's tissues. In exchange for a home, the algae provide the coral with energy in the form of sugars from photosynthesis, other essential nutrients, and even the brilliant colors that healthy corals display.

When ocean water becomes too warm, corals react by expelling the tiny algae that live inside their tissues. This process is called *coral bleaching* because the corals become visibly pale, or white, when the algae are expelled. Corals can survive coral bleaching and regain their algal partners if water temperatures return to normal. If the water temperature gets too high or doesn't return to normal quickly, the corals die.

Matsuda's research examines what makes some corals in Hawaii more resistant to bleaching, a trait known as *thermal resiliency*. He compares different traits, such as the types of algae and bacteria that live within a coral and the size and shape of the coral tissue and skeleton. Matsuda thinks that understanding these differences will give him better insight into what makes some corals survive better under stressful conditions. This information can help scientists develop strategies for protecting, conserving, and managing coral reefs for future generations.

1. Describe a healthy coral-algal symbiosis. What might happen to the coral if environmental stressors cause the partnership to break down?

2. Make a flow chart that describes how corals may respond to changes in the temperature of the water they live in. Use your flow chart to model two scenarios: the water temperature rises and then quickly drops to its original level, and the water temperature rises but does not return to normal for several weeks.

3. **Collaborate** With a partner, discuss whether you think all corals in reefs all over the world would respond in the same way to temperature changes. Then make a list of questions that you would like to ask Shayle Matsuda about how corals and algae respond to climate change.

© Houghton Mifflin Harcourt Publishing Company

Can You Explain It?

Name: _____ **Date:** _____

How could climate change affect the survival of koalas?

EVIDENCE NOTEBOOK
Refer to the notes in your Evidence Notebook to help you construct an explanation for how climate change may affect the survival of koalas.

1. State your claim. Make sure your claim fully explains how climate change could affect the survival of koalas.

2. Summarize the evidence you have gathered to support your claim and explain your reasoning.

Checkpoints

Answer the following questions to check your understanding of the lesson.

Use the maps of the ranges of aspen trees to answer Questions 3–4.

3. What do the maps indicate will likely happen to the range of aspen? Select all that apply.

   A. It will increase.

   B. It will decrease.

   C. It will disappear completely.

   D. It will shift east.

   E. It will shift north.

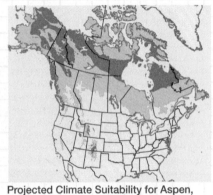

Climate Suitability for Aspen, 1971–2000
Aspen range   Aspen core range

Projected Climate Suitability for Aspen, 2071–2100
Aspen range   Aspen core range

Source: Natural Resources Canada, Canadian Forest Service, Forest Change Indicators, Distribution of tree species, 2017

4. Place the letter I or P next to each statement to indicate whether the response of the aspen trees occurs at the individual (I) or population (P) level.

   _____ Trees that are better adapted to high temperatures reproduce well.

   _____ Young trees do not grow where temperatures have risen but do grow where temperatures remain cooler.

   _____ The boundary of the aspen forest shifts to a new location.

5. When an organism moves into a new environment, it can increase / decrease competition for resources among native organisms, which can cause native organisms to survive / become extinct. Extinctions increase / decrease the biodiversity and stability of an ecosystem.

Use the photos to answer Questions 6–7.

6. Which of the following is an advantage of seasonal changes in fur color?

   A. It makes hares less likely to be eaten by predators.

   B. It makes hares better able to see each other to find mates.

   C. It makes the biodiversity of the ecosystem greater.

   D. It makes hares better able to respond to climate change.

7. As the climate gets warmer, more / less snow is likely to fall in the Arctic, and that snow will melt sooner / later in the spring. Individual Arctic hares that get their white winter coats early in the fall and keep their winter coats later into the spring are more / less likely to survive, and that trait will likely become more / less common in the population.

Interactive Review

Complete this section to review the main concepts of the lesson.

Organisms have physical and behavioral adaptations to the ecosystem in which they live. The diversity of organisms in an ecosystem affects the ecosystem's stability.

A. How is biodiversity related to the ability of an ecosystem to provide essential services?

When climate change affects a habitat, organisms can respond and change, or they may become extinct.

B. Identify two ways that organisms can respond to climate change.

Scientists can monitor changes in ecosystems, organisms, and local and global biodiversity that are caused by climate change.

C. Why do scientists need to understand the interactions of organisms with their environment when studying how climate change affects biodiversity?

Reducing Human Impacts on the Environment

A wildlife overpass allows wildlife to safely move between the parts of their habitat, which has been split by a highway.

Explore First

Comparing Water Quality Gather water samples from one indoor source and one natural source. Place each sample in a clear container and observe them. What criteria would you use to describe the quality of the water in the samples? Which sample do you think humans have affected more?

CAN YOU EXPLAIN IT?

How can human activities be monitored and modified to reduce their effects on salmon?

These Chinook salmon spend most of their life in the ocean, but they swim up freshwater rivers to reproduce. Salmon choose a place to lay eggs based on the depth and temperature of the water and the amount of oxygen in the water.

 Explore Online

1. What human activities might change the quality of the water in which salmon live and reproduce?

2. How might climate change affect the water in which salmon live?

 EVIDENCE NOTEBOOK As you explore this lesson, gather evidence to explain how human activities that affect salmon can be monitored and minimized.

Describing Methods for Monitoring Human Impacts on the Environment

Humans affect the environment in many ways. Sometimes, our actions have unwanted or even catastrophic effects. In order to prevent or correct effects that harm the environment or human health, people gather data. For example, water quality data can be used to find out if water is safe to drink. Some pollutants may not be visible. So, special tools or methods may be needed to determine water safety.

The quality of water varies depending on where it is from.

3. Think about some of the things that might make water unsafe to drink. How can you decide if the water in each beaker in the photo is safe to drink?

Resource Use

The environment provides many resources for humans, such as land, water, and air. Human use of a resource may make that resource unavailable or unsuitable for other purposes. For example, some land uses can destroy or fragment a habitat. This negatively affects the organisms that live there.

There are organizations around the world that record data about the use of land and water. In the United States, much of this data is collected by the United States Geological Survey (USGS). Water or land use may also be regulated and measured by local governments or organizations.

Collection of Resource Use Data

People may take photos or use specialized sensors to measure and record data. Data may be collected locally or remotely. Meters measure the amount of water that is pumped from an aquifer or the amount used at a specific place. Satellite cameras and instruments remotely collect data about larger areas, such as an area the size of a city or larger.

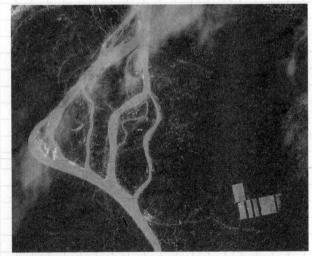

The satellite photo shows how an area of forest near a river has been cleared by humans.

Analysis of Resource Use Data

Once data are collected, the data must be analyzed. Resource use data may be shown in many ways, such as a photo, map, table, or chart. Scientists look at trends when they analyze data. They also use the data to determine correlations. Data are correlated when two data sets have related trends. For example, if one variable increases, another variable increases or decreases at the same time. When data are strongly correlated, scientists look at the data or collect more data to find out if there is a cause-and-effect relationship between the two variables. For a relationship to be cause-and-effect, there must be a mechanism by which one variable causes change in the other.

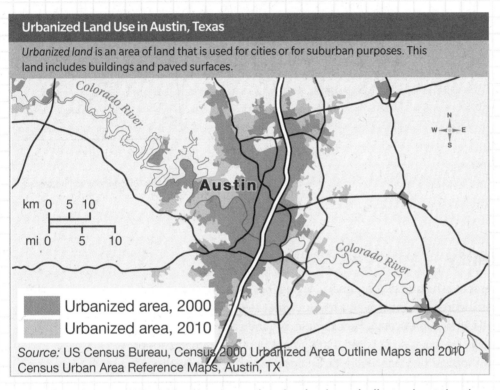

Urbanized Land Use in Austin, Texas

Urbanized land is an area of land that is used for cities or for suburban purposes. This land includes buildings and paved surfaces.

- Urbanized area, 2000
- Urbanized area, 2010

Source: US Census Bureau, Census 2000 Urbanized Area Outline Maps and 2010 Census Urban Area Reference Maps, Austin, TX

4. Analyze the map. What does the change in urbanized area indicate about the change in land use of the city? How might that change affect the environment?

Data about water use are collected so that people can keep track of the amount of water that remains available. Most places on Earth have water beneath the ground in aquifers. People pump this groundwater to the surface for drinking, irrigation, and industrial uses. Groundwater in an aquifer is replaced slowly as water from the surface flows through permeable soil or rock. However, water is not likely to be absorbed if it cannot seep through the land surface or if the land slopes steeply. Impermeable surfaces, such as asphalt, do not allow water to enter soil. Instead, the water runs off the land as surface water, ending up in rivers, lakes, and oceans.

When an aquifer is depleted, it can cause the ground to sink. Another effect of a depleted aquifer is the contamination of the remaining water with salt from nearby oceans or other contaminants. Contaminated or salty groundwater is unusable for most of the purposes for which groundwater is used by humans. People must think about the effects of current resource use and technologies on the long-term health and functioning of societies and ecosystems.

5. Assume the trend of pumping water from the aquifer continues at its current rate. Predict the water level in the aquifer in the years after 2016. Support your claim with evidence and reasoning.

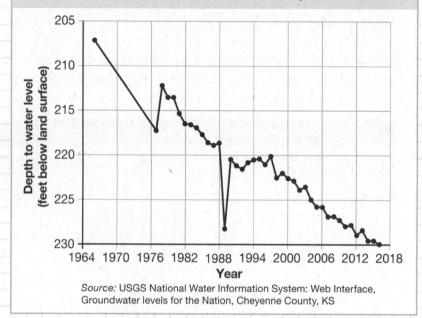

Water Level of a Well in the High Plains Aquifer

This graph shows the water level in a well getting farther from the surface of the ground. This means that the amount of water in the aquifer has decreased.

Source: USGS National Water Information System: Web Interface, Groundwater levels for the Nation, Cheyenne County, KS

Resource Quality

Air, soil, and water are essential resources for humans. When these resources become polluted, their usefulness decreases. Thus, even a resource that seems abundant and is widely distributed can become scarce. For example, groundwater can become nonrenewable if the aquifer becomes so polluted that humans or other animals cannot drink or use the water without getting sick. Pollution and declining resource quality can also affect the ability of the ecosystem to provide essential services, such as the production of food or the availability of habitats.

Do the Math
Compare Concentrations

Pollution levels are usually described in terms of concentration. The concentration of a pollutant is the amount of the polluting substance compared to the total amount of the sample. For example, a concentration of 1% is one unit (gram or mL) of pollutant in 100 units total. However, amounts of pollutants much smaller than 1% can be harmful. Therefore, pollution may be measured in parts per million or parts per billion. One part per million (1 ppm) is one unit of pollutant in one million units total. One part per billion (1 ppb) is one unit per one billion units.

6. A concentration of 1% is 10,000 times *greater / less* than 1 ppm.

A concentration of 1 ppm is 1,000 times *greater / less* than 1 ppb.

A concentration of 1 ppb is 10,000,000 times *greater / less* than 1%.

Collection of Resource Quality Data

There are different ways to collect data about pollution in the environment. Some pollution can be observed directly, like when you smell smoke in the air or see color changes in water. Some pollution can be monitored by observing the effects it has on living things. For example, pollution might cause the leaves of plants to change color. Scientists also use tools that measure substances in air, water, or soil. They can take a sample to a lab or use instruments to analyze data in the field. Some equipment, such as sensors on satellites, can take measurements from far away and send data to computers at remote locations.

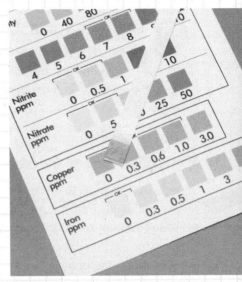

This test result shows the amount of copper in a sample of drinking water.

7. The Environmental Protection Agency (EPA) is a government organization that regulates pollutants. The EPA set the maximum safe amount of copper in drinking water at 1.3 ppm. The test result for a sample of water is shown in the photo. According to this test, the water is / is not safe to drink.

Analysis of Resource Quality Data

The amount of pollution in a resource affects the quality of the resource. Acceptable concentrations of different pollutants are generally set by state or federal agencies, such as the Environmental Protection Agency (EPA). The acceptable concentration of a pollutant depends on the pollutant, its effects on the health of humans or other organisms, and the way the resource is used. For example, drinking water generally has lower acceptable limits for pollutants, metals, and bacteria than water used for irrigating crops does.

Scientists may also measure concentrations of nonpolluting substances to make sure the levels are acceptable. Soil quality measures may include testing for certain nutrients, to make sure the soil can support certain crops.

8. This photo shows water flooding a farm field. How can the effects of runoff from this field be monitored?

Water flows between rows of crops on a farm. As the water flows, it picks up dirt and other substances, including fertilizers or pesticides.

9. What criteria might be useful for determining the quality of water in salmon habitats? What methods could people use to monitor that water quality? Record your evidence.

Propose How to Monitor Human Impacts

Surface and groundwater resources near cities receive pollutants from many different sources. To minimize impacts of urban areas on the environment, city officials must monitor the sources of pollution.

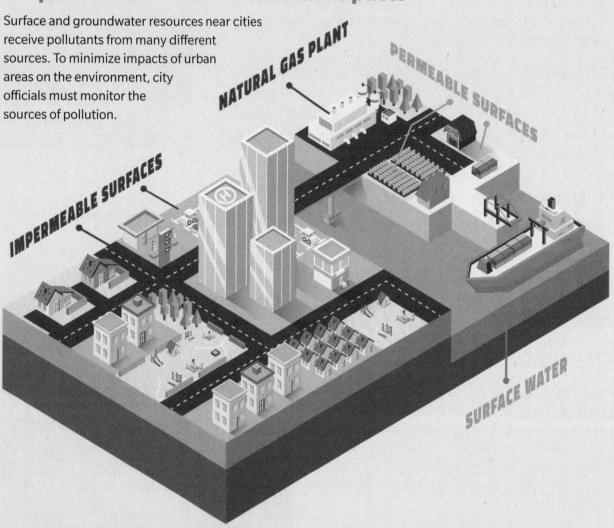

10. The town in the drawing formed a committee to work on ways to detect possible problems with the quality of groundwater and surface water. As a member of the committee, propose what sources of pollution should be monitored and how they should be checked.

_____

_____

_____

_____

_____

Developing a Method to Monitor a Human Impact on the Environment

Once scientists know that a human activity impacts the environment, they can develop methods to monitor the activity and its impact. Monitoring is necessary to determine if changes in human activity affect the impact on the environment.

11. Think about some of the things you disposed of today or in the past week. How could you monitor the solid waste you generate in a week?

Some landfills cover large areas of land. Natural processes break down the solid waste over time, which can cause pollution in the area.

Solid Waste

Solid waste includes organic and inorganic materials. Organic materials, such as paper, are found in or made from living things. Some organic materials decay quickly. Sometimes humans change organic materials in ways that make them take longer to decay. For example, pressure-treated wood is chemically treated so that it is more durable. Inorganic materials, such as glass and metals, may take very long periods of time to break down by natural processes.

Every day, about 2 kilograms (kg) of solid waste per person is generated in the United States. Solid waste is typically taken to a landfill when it is discarded. Most landfills are designed to prevent pollution, but waste can dissolve and pollute groundwater or surface water. Particularly hazardous solid waste goes to specially designed landfills.

About one-third of the solid waste in the United States is either recycled or composted. Organic materials, such as food waste, paper, or yard waste, can be composted. Composted materials can then be used to improve the quality of soil.

When some organic materials decay without oxygen, as they do in a landfill, they produce methane. Methane is a greenhouse gas. When released to the atmosphere, it can contribute to rising global temperatures. But it can also be burned to produce electrical energy.

Under certain conditions, some organic materials, such as plants, decay into compost.

The breakdown of wastes in landfills generates the greenhouse gas methane, which is vented into the atmosphere.

The Engineering Design Process

You can use the engineering design process (EDP) to develop a way to monitor a human activity and determine its environmental impact. The first step of the EDP is identifying the problem, for example "how do we monitor solid waste produced by a school?" Engineering design is an iterative process. That means you might not develop the best solution on the first try. Instead, you assess the results and then adjust your solution. The solution you choose depends on the criteria and constraints. To ensure a solution will solve the problem, you must make sure criteria and constraints are well defined.

The Engineering Design Process Flow Chart

12. Write each step of the engineering design process in the correct location in the flow chart.

WORD BANK
- Define
- Research
- Model
- Test
- Evaluate
- Brainstorm
- ~~Identify~~

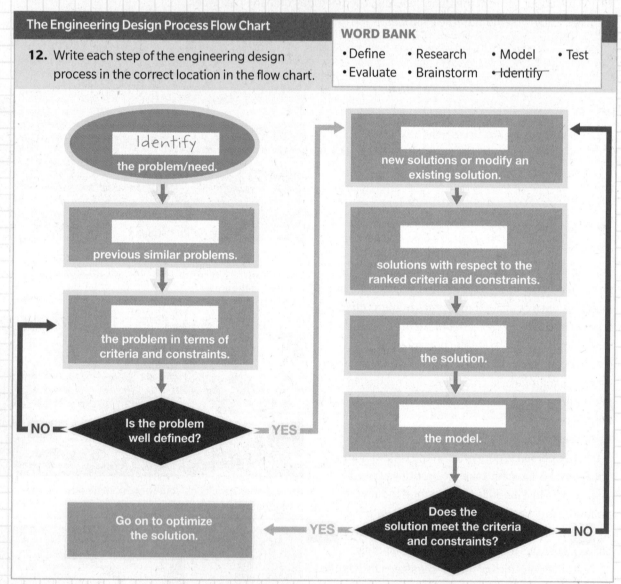

Identify the problem/need.

_____ previous similar problems.

_____ the problem in terms of criteria and constraints.

Is the problem well defined? — NO / YES

_____ new solutions or modify an existing solution.

_____ solutions with respect to the ranked criteria and constraints.

_____ the solution.

_____ the model.

Does the solution meet the criteria and constraints? — YES / NO

Go on to optimize the solution.

13. Each time the EDP is used, steps may be completed in a different sequence. You may return to any previous step in the process at any time, but you may not skip steps. For example, you must always model / optimize the solution before you can test / identify the model. The problem must be well defined / tested before you research / brainstorm possible solutions.

Hands-On Lab

Design a Method to Monitor Solid Waste from a School

You will use the engineering design process to develop a method to monitor the amount and types of solid waste generated by your school.

Scientists know that solid waste in a landfill has a negative impact on the environment. Reducing the amount of solid waste sent to landfills can reduce the negative impact on the environment.

MATERIALS

• computer, for research (optional)

Procedure and Analysis

STEP 1 **Research the Problem** With your group, research the problem of monitoring the amount and types of solid waste and identify existing solutions for similar problems.

STEP 2 **Define the Problem** State the problem related to monitoring your school's waste. Then add at least one constraint to more completely define the problem of monitoring solid waste from your school.

Problem:	
Criterion	Constraint
1. Information is measurable.	1. Students must not handle hazardous waste.
2. Data can be collected by students.	2. All activities must occur during school hours.
3. Waste to be evaluated currently goes to a large trash container outside.	3.

STEP 3 **Brainstorm Solutions** Based on your research, brainstorm possible methods that could be used to monitor the solid waste generated by your school. Record all possible solutions on a separate paper.

STEP 4 **Language SmArts | Evaluate Possible Solutions** On a separate sheet of paper, create a decision matrix for evaluating the possible solutions. Evaluate all of the possible solutions from Step 3 to identify the solution that you think will best satisfy the criteria and constraints of the problem. Be sure to consider any scientific principles and any potential impacts on people or on the natural world that may limit your solutions.

STEP 5 **Choose a Promising Solution to Test** Describe the solution you chose, or draw a diagram of your chosen solution. Explain why you think the solution will work.

STEP 6 **Propose a Test** Before a solution can be implemented, it must be tested. The test results should show whether the solution fully meets the criteria and constraints. In the space below, describe how you would test your solution.

Monitor Solid Waste from a Neighborhood

14. In what ways might the waste from a neighborhood be different from or similar to the waste from a school?

Homes generate many different types of solid waste.

15. Could you use the same method to monitor the waste from your school and the waste from a neighborhood? Explain why or why not.

Describing Methods to Reduce Human Impacts on the Environment

When data show that a human activity impacts the environment in a negative way, scientists and engineers develop ways to reduce these negative impacts. Scientists and engineers rely on their scientific understanding of the problem, as well as on their knowledge of engineering principles and of human behavior. This knowledge allows them to make wise decisions when proposing solutions and deciding whether a change in behavior or a new technology might be needed.

16. You are going on a three-day camping trip with friends. You are able to bring only one gallon of water per person per day. How might you change the way you use water to make sure your supply lasts long enough?

When you are away from a clean water supply, you need to carry drinking water with you. You might also use a tool or process to purify water that you find so that it is safe to drink.

Resource Availability

Using a resource in a sustainable way means that the resource continues to be available. Renewable resources are resources that can, under certain circumstances, be replaced as fast as they are used. For example, new trees can replace a forest when old trees are cut down. In order for these resources to be sustainable, they cannot be used faster than they can be replaced. Other resources, such as metals that are mined or oil that is pumped from the ground, are nonrenewable. It takes millions of years for these materials to form. A nonrenewable resource will eventually be used up. Use of nonrenewable resources must be minimized to make sure the resource is available for as long as possible.

Careful Use of Resources

What are some ways that humans can reduce the rate at which we consume resources and make them more sustainable? It is possible to reduce use by changing the way we behave. For example, you can turn on the faucet only to rinse your mouth and toothbrush. You will use less water this way than if you leave the water running while you brush your teeth. Better technology can also reduce resource use. Modern air conditioning units are more efficient than older ones due to improved technology. They use less energy to cool buildings, so they reduce the use of energy resources. If you monitor how you use resources and are careful to use only the amount you need, you can often reduce your resource use.

17. Do the Math A hotel installs dual-flush toilets to help conserve water. The new toilets use 1.6 gallons for one full flush and 0.9 gallons for one partial flush. Measurements show that in the first week there were 1,190 full flushes and 3,150 partial flushes. How many gallons of water were saved for the week compared to a week in which all the flushes were full flushes?

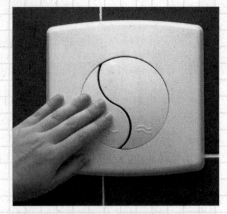

This toilet has two types of flushes. One uses much less water than the other.

Resource Reuse and Recycling

Another way to make resource use more sustainable is to make products last longer by reusing them. A plastic bag or a sturdy canvas bag can be used many times when shopping. Each time you reuse the bag, you reduce the number of new bags that are needed. That saves resources. Things that cannot be reused can often be recycled as materials for new products. Used paper can be recycled to make new paper to reduce the need for harvesting trees. Recycling metal, plastic, or glass containers provides materials for new products. It reduces the use of resources. The diagram shows how recycling aluminum reduces the amount of aluminum that is mined.

Mining bauxite to produce aluminum has a large impact on the environment. Aluminum is made into many products. These products can be recycled over and over, saving the material and energy resources needed to mine bauxite.

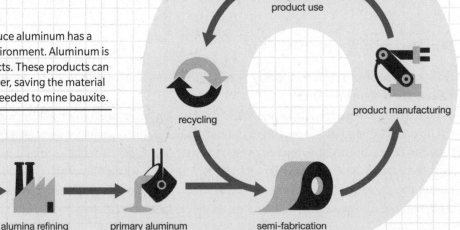

18. How does recycling aluminum reduce the environmental impact of the human use of aluminum?

Resource Quality

The quality of a resource determines its value and usefulness to people and affects the health of people and the environment. Some human activities affect the quality of resources, such as water or soil. The quality of resources can be negatively affected by overuse, by improper use, and by pollution.

Behavior Change

Sometimes the quality of a resource can be maintained or improved if people change their behavior. A person may choose to buy food grown locally rather than food that is shipped from another state or country. This change in behavior may reduce air pollution because foods are often shipped in vehicles or trains that use fossil fuels for energy. Some people leave trash and other items on beaches. These items may then be washed into the ocean, adding to water pollution. By changing their behavior to make sure that these items are disposed of responsibly, people can reduce water pollution.

19. What are some questions you could investigate to determine if a change in behavior would impact resource quality?

Technology Development and Use

New technologies take time and money to develop. Newer technology often costs more than existing technology. Often, without a catastrophic event, people may not see the need to switch to a newer technology. For years, people dumped raw sewage into the same bodies of water from which they drank. It was not until people started getting sick from the polluted water that communities invested in methods to filter and treat drinking water. Since the 1800s, humans have been burning coal to generate electrical energy. Burning coal adds greenhouse gases and other pollutants to the air. Mining coal may also cause air, water, and soil pollution if it is not done carefully. Due to societal needs and regulations, scientists have worked to develop technologies to reduce the pollution produced by mining and burning coal. Scientists have also developed technologies such as wind turbines. Wind turbines generate clean energy because they do not create air pollution when they are running. However, building wind turbines does require resources. Obtaining those resources may impact the environment negatively.

20. **Discuss** With a partner, discuss reasons that humans may continue to use technology that negatively affects the environment when technology with fewer negative effects exists.

Case Study: The Dust Bowl

The Great Plains in the central part of the United States was once a vast grassland. The grasses had deep roots and were adapted to the climate of the plains. Herds of animals lived on these plains and fed on the grasses. In the 1800s, few people used the land to farm crops. In the early 1900s, new technologies made it easier to farm large areas of land. As the price of grain increased, more farmers began plowing the soil and planting grain crops over large areas of land. The grain plants did not have deep roots like the native grasses. When a long drought happened in the 1930s, the fields became dry and crops died. Heavy winds picked up the dry soil and formed giant dust storms. These dust storms caused respiratory problems. Sometimes humans and animals in the area died. Swarms of grasshoppers ate many remaining crops, leading to even less protection for the soil. The loss of fertile topsoil made it more difficult to grow crops.

Since the lessons of the Dust Bowl period, farmers have begun to implement a variety of soil conservation techniques. These methods include contour planting, cover crops, crop rotation, and the planting of windbreaks.

21. Dust storms occurred after humans changed the environment. Which activities contributed to severe dust storms? Select all that apply.

    A. plowing soil for crop planting

    B. overgrazing herds of cattle

    C. removing native grasses

    D. building towns and dirt roads

22. **Write** In the 1950s, a drought similar to the one in the 1930s was predicted. The United States Congress offered farmers money to turn farmland back into grassland to avoid another dust bowl. Farmers had to decide whether to accept the offer or to continue farming their land as they had been doing. Think about the situation from the farmers' point of view. On a separate sheet of paper, write a letter responding to this offer as a farmer in the area at the time. Say whether you would or would not accept the government offer and explain your reasoning.

Native grasses have deep roots that hold soil in place and keep the soil healthy.

Without deep roots to hold the soil in place, the soil was carried away by the wind in massive dust storms.

Farmers can plow the ground and plant crops in straight lines. They can also use contour farming. Contour farming follows the shape of the land when farmers plow and plant.

Analyze the Environmental Impact of a Power Plant

Conventional power plants burn fuel to heat water and make steam. This steam turns a turbine to generate electrical energy. The steam is then cooled, so that the water can be heated again. This heating and cooling repeats in a cycle. The water used to cool the steam is often drawn from nearby surface water. The steam transfers thermal energy to the water, which makes the water hotter and the steam cooler. The hot water is released into a nearby body of water. It causes thermal pollution that may make the body of water too warm for plants and animals living in it. In a combined heat and power (CHP) plant, shown in the diagram, the hot water heats buildings instead of being discharged into the nearby body of water.

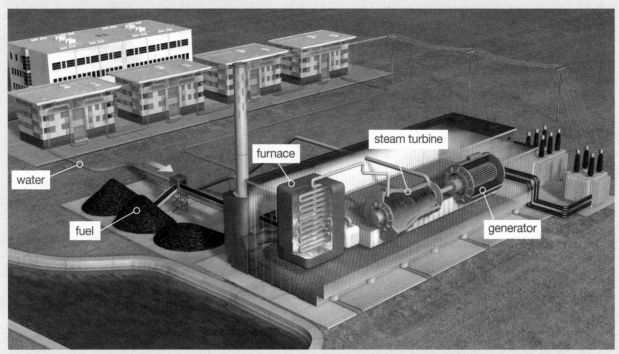

Follow the path of the water through the furnace and steam turbine. Then notice how the hot water passes through the buildings. The water cools down as the buildings are heated. The cool water then returns to the furnace in a continuous cycle.

23. Which of the following are ways in which the CHP plant has a lower impact on the environment than a traditional power plant? Select all that apply.

   A. It uses thermal energy more efficiently than the traditional plant.

   B. It causes less thermal pollution in the nearby body of water.

   C. It uses fuel that causes less pollution than a traditional plant.

   D. It does not produce greenhouse gases when fuels are burned.

> **EVIDENCE NOTEBOOK**
>
> 24. What human activities could have an effect on salmon habitats? How can those activities be modified to reduce their effects on salmon? Record your evidence.

Developing a Method to Reduce a Human Impact on the Environment

Define and Evaluate a Problem Related to Solid Waste

Recall that the engineering design process is a tool that you can use anytime you want to develop a solution for a specific problem. Solutions may be a process or a physical object. The first step of the engineering design process is to identify the problem. An engineering problem must be stated very clearly so that a solution can be developed to address the exact problem. The purpose of the criteria and constraints is to define the problem in a way that makes it possible to measure how well the solution works. Engineers begin with as many ideas as possible, and then they evaluate the ideas to choose a solution they think will be the most successful. A promising solution can then be tested and improved until all of the criteria and constraints are satisfied.

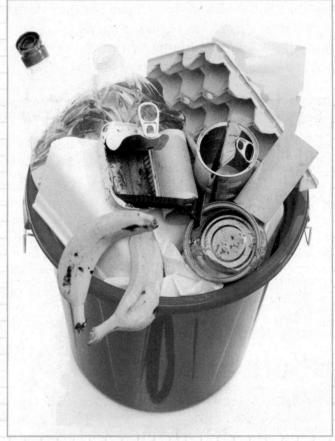

The trash in this can is all going to a landfill. But some of this waste could be disposed of in a different way.

25. Which of the following changes might reduce the impact of your school's solid waste on the environment? Select all that apply.

   A. Start school later in the morning.

   B. Compost food waste to make garden fertilizer.

   C. Reuse the back of worksheets as scratch paper.

   D. Collect plastic bottles for recycling.

26. **Discuss** With a partner or group, discuss the sources and types of solid waste that are generated in your school.

Hands-On Lab
Evaluate a Method to Reduce the Impact of Solid Waste on the Environment

You will use the engineering design process to develop a method for reducing the environmental effects of solid waste generated by your school.

MATERIALS
- camera (optional)
- meterstick (optional)
- scale (optional)

Procedure and Analysis

STEP 1 **Research the Problem** Research the problem and possible solutions for reducing the impact of solid waste.

STEP 2 **Define the Problem** State the engineering problem related to reducing the environmental impact of your school's waste. Then determine criteria and constraints for your problem.

Problem:	
Criterion	Constraint
1. Can be directed by students	1. Does not require any money
2.	2.
3.	3.
4.	4.

STEP 3 **Brainstorm Solutions** Based on your research, brainstorm possible methods that you could use to reduce the amount of solid waste that is generated by your school and goes to a landfill. Record all possible solutions on a separate sheet of paper.

STEP 4 **Choose a Solution** Evaluate the solutions you brainstormed, taking into account any scientific principles and any potential impacts on people or on the natural world that may limit your solution. Choose the most promising solution from your brainstorming step. Describe your solution, and explain how it addresses the engineering problem.

STEP 5 Design and Implement a Test Decide the best method for testing your solution. Perform the test and record your test results on a separate sheet of paper.

STEP 6 Analyze Results Analyze the results to determine whether your solution would work for the whole school. Use evidence and reasoning to support your claim.

STEP 7 Evaluate the Solution Based on your test results, can your chosen solution be used to reduce the environmental impact of solid waste generated by your school? If yes, explain how the solution could be used to reduce the school's environmental impact. If no, how would you change your solution to make it more likely to solve the problem?

Reduce the Energy Use of a School

Schools require electrical energy for many different needs. The environmental impact of the electrical energy used by a school depends on the source of the power.

27. Examine the graph. Brainstorm ways that the school might reduce its energy use. A constraint of this problem is that the recommended change cannot require a lot of money.

_____
_____
_____
_____
_____
_____
_____
_____

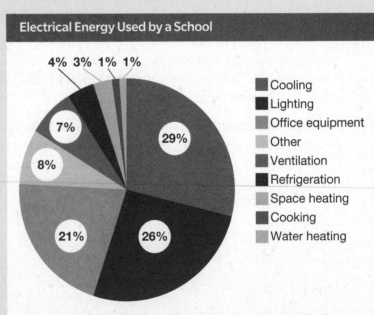

Electrical Energy Used by a School

4% 3% 1% 1%

29%

7%

8%

21%

26%

- Cooling
- Lighting
- Office equipment
- Other
- Ventilation
- Refrigeration
- Space heating
- Cooking
- Water heating

© Houghton Mifflin Harcourt Publishing Company

Continue Your Exploration

Name: _____   Date: _____

Check out the path below or go online to choose one of the other paths shown.

Urban Planning to Reduce Impact

- **Air Pollution Past and Present**
- **Hands-On Labs** ✋
- **Propose Your Own Path**

Go online to choose one of these other paths.

In 2016, about 54% of the world's population lived in cities. A city can have a large impact on the environment, due to the large human population of the city. Urban planners design transportation systems. They also design systems to provide water, electrical energy, and sewage services to all the people in a city. The design of these systems affects the environmental impact of a city. Planned public transportation, such as trains and buses, helps reduce the use of cars. Some cities, such as Copenhagen, Denmark, build infrastructure to make it easier for people to use bicycles instead of cars to get to and from work.

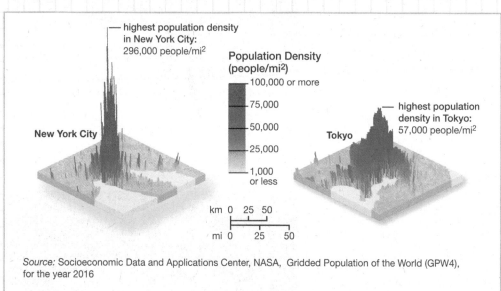

highest population density in New York City: 296,000 people/mi²

Population Density (people/mi²)
- 100,000 or more
- 75,000
- 50,000
- 25,000
- 1,000 or less

New York City

Tokyo

highest population density in Tokyo: 57,000 people/mi²

km 0 25 50
mi 0 25 50

Source: Socioeconomic Data and Applications Center, NASA, Gridded Population of the World (GPW4), for the year 2016

Compare the populations of New York City and Tokyo. How are the people in these cities distributed?

1. The population of Tokyo is a little greater than the population of New York City. Each year, about 1.6 billion people ride the subway in New York City, but about 3.7 billion ride the subway in Tokyo. Can the population distribution for each city be used to explain the large difference in the number of subway riders each year? What other information might you need to explain this difference?

Continue Your Exploration

2. Some urban planners design transportation systems that reduce human impact. How might redesigning a roadway to add a protected bike lane impact the environment?

Riding a bicycle on a busy street is dangerous. Drivers often do not see cyclists, or they drive closer to cyclists than is safe.

3. Urban planners redesign a roadway to encourage people to bike from place to place. How can they monitor or measure environmental impacts related to the new bike lanes?

An unprotected bike lane improves safety. But the cyclist still must deal with vehicles moving in and out of the bike lane.

This protected bike lane is located between parked cars and the sidewalk. The parked cars protect bicyclists from moving vehicles.

4. **Collaborate** With a small group, brainstorm non-transportation-related ways that cities can reduce their environmental impact. Make a brochure to present your ideas to city officials.

Can You Explain It?

Name: _____   Date: _____

How can human activities be monitored and modified to reduce their effects on salmon?

 EVIDENCE NOTEBOOK

Refer to the notes in your Evidence Notebook to help you construct an explanation for how human activities can be monitored and modified to reduce their effects on salmon.

1. State your claim. Make sure your claim fully explains how human activities can be monitored and modified to reduce their effects on salmon.

2. Summarize the evidence you have gathered to support your claim and explain your reasoning.

Checkpoints

Answer the following questions to check your understanding of the lesson.

Use the photo to answer Questions 3–4.

3. Which problem does the storm drain label solve?

   A. It keeps waterways from flooding.

   B. It stops people from overfishing.

   C. It protects groundwater from pollution.

   D. It discourages people from polluting waterways.

4. Which of these criteria appear to be satisfied by the label in the photo? Select all that apply.

   A. It is low cost.

   B. It does not require new technology.

   C. It stops all possible pollution.

   D. It records data on the effectiveness of the solution.

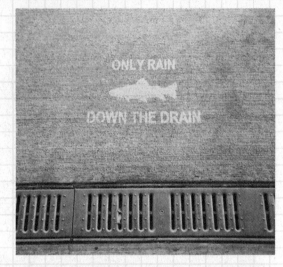

Use the chart to answer Questions 5–6.

5. About how many times more water is needed to produce a pound of beef than a pound of lentils?

   A. 0.5 times

   B. 1.9 times

   C. 13.5 times

   D. 1,450 times

6. A family chooses to eat lentils instead of beef for dinner to reduce the family's impact on the environment. The chart *does / does not* support this reasoning, because raising beef for food requires *less / more* water than lentils. Thus, eating *less / more* beef has a positive impact on the environment, because water is an important and often scarce resource.

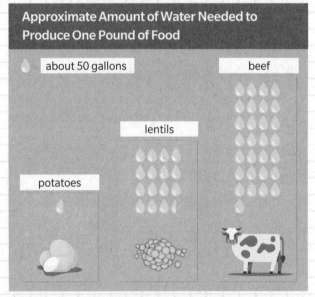

Approximate Amount of Water Needed to Produce One Pound of Food

about 50 gallons

beef

lentils

potatoes

Source: Mekonnen, M.M. and Hoekstra, A.Y. (2010), Value of Water Research Report Series Nos. 47 and 48, UNESCO-IHE, Delft, the Netherlands

7. Which of the following data for monitoring human effects on the environment can be collected by a satellite? Select all that apply.

   A. land use in a rural area

   B. quality of a body of water

   C. air quality around a city

   D. water use per person in a city

8. A new city program encourages people to bike rather than drive a car to work. It is hoped that this program will *monitor / reduce* air pollution in the city and the rate of climate change. The program effectiveness could be *monitored / reduced* by surveying residents to see how they commute.

Interactive Review

Complete this section to review the main concepts of the lesson.

Scientists monitor resource use and quality to determine how humans impact the environment.

A. Give two examples of resources that scientists monitor, and describe how they monitor the quality and use of each resource.

The engineering design process can be used to develop a method for monitoring human impacts on the environment.

B. How can the engineering design process be used to develop a method for monitoring the environmental impact of a human activity?

People can reduce their impact on the environment by changing their behavior or by using new or different technologies.

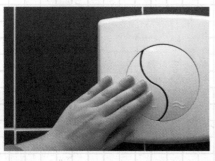

C. How might the effect on the environment of the human activity of traveling be reduced?

The engineering design process can be used to develop ways to reduce human impacts on the environment.

D. Why would a community decide to use the engineering design process as they look for a solution for an environmental problem?

Choose one of the activities to explore how this unit connects to other topics.

☐ People in Science

Dr. Simon Nicholson, International Relations Scholar Dr. Simon Nicholson directs the Global Environmental Politics program in the School of International Service at American University. Dr. Nicholson trained first as a lawyer before becoming a professor. He works to develop laws, policies, and regulations related to climate change technologies that balance the risks of climate engineering technologies and the needs of people affected by climate change.

Research a proposed idea for climate engineering. Create a model that describes the technique, the expected result, potential side effects, and any ethical or regulatory issues.

☐ Music Connection

Songs about Saving Earth Many songwriters and singers have been inspired by human effects on the environment. These artists use music to share information and to encourage action and change regarding issues that are important to them.

Identify a song that was inspired by human impacts on the environment. Read the lyrics. Then write a brief essay explaining how the song is related to natural resources or environmental conservation. Identify Earth systems and natural resources that are mentioned in the song. Then present your findings by playing the song and leading a group discussion.

☐ Social Studies Connection

Science and Activism Some individuals find an environmental cause they feel strongly about and do bold things to raise awareness. Often these people are called "activists." Some activists walk in marches or plan demonstrations to inform others about environmental causes. These activities can raise awareness about environmental issues and motivate people to help make changes.

What else would you like to know about science and activism? Research an environmental activist to find out about the activist's cause and efforts. Create a multimedia presentation to share with the class.

Name: Date:

Complete this review to check your understanding of the unit.

Use the graph to answer Questions 1–2.

1. Which of the following statements describes how rising global temperature affects the caterpillars?

   A. More caterpillars survive and mate each year.

   B. The caterpillars hatch earlier in the season.

   C. The caterpillars move to a new habitat.

   D. The caterpillars change the food they eat.

2. What physical or behavioral adaptations will determine how well the birds survive the change in climate? Select all that apply.

   A. the number of eggs the birds lay

   B. the variety of foods the birds can eat

   C. the timing of the birds' mating and laying seasons

   D. the location and size of the birds' range

Effects of Climate Change on Birds and Caterpillars

Before Climate Change   After Climate Change

— Eggs laid by birds — Birds needing food — Caterpillars hatched

---

Use the decision matrix to answer Questions 3–5

3. Complete the decision matrix by calculating the totals for each product.

Product	Criteria				Totals
	Can be used for at least 3 days (2)	Inexpensive (3)	Produces little waste (5)	Requires little energy to make (5)	
Liquid soap in plastic bottle	2	2	2	2	
Bar soap in paper wrapper	2	3	4	4	

4. Which product would you choose for the guest rooms of an ecologically friendly hotel?

   A. Liquid soap, because it is the least expensive.

   B. Bar soap, because it has the highest total score in my decision matrix.

   C. Liquid soap, because it has the lowest total score in my decision matrix.

   D. Bar soap, because it produces more waste than liquid soap.

5. If the liquid soap in a plastic bottle produced less waste, would it change your decision?

   A. No, it still scores lower in my decision matrix.

   B. No, it still scores higher in my decision matrix.

   C. Yes, less waste outweighs the other categories.

   D. Yes, bar soap is harder to clean up when the guests leave.

6. Complete the table by explaining how the following categories are related to each concept.

Topic Category	Cause and Effect	Patterns	Stability	Change
Climate	A variety of natural processes and human activities cause changes in Earth's climate.			
Human Activities				
Climate Monitoring Methods				
Biodiversity				

Name: _____   Date: _____

Use the plastic usage diagram to answer Questions 7–10.

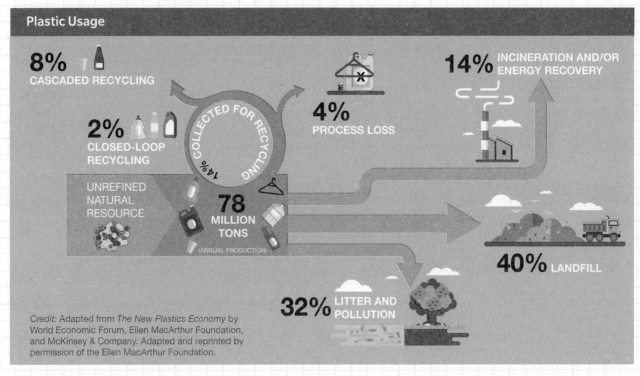

Plastic Usage

8% CASCADED RECYCLING

2% CLOSED-LOOP RECYCLING

14% COLLECTED FOR RECYCLING

UNREFINED NATURAL RESOURCE

78 MILLION TONS (ANNUAL PRODUCTION)

4% PROCESS LOSS

14% INCINERATION AND/OR ENERGY RECOVERY

40% LANDFILL

32% LITTER AND POLLUTION

Credit: Adapted from *The New Plastics Economy* by World Economic Forum, Ellen MacArthur Foundation, and McKinsey & Company. Adapted and reprinted by permission of the Ellen MacArthur Foundation.

7. After a plastic bottle has been discarded, what four outcomes could happen next? List these four outcomes in order from the most likely to the least.

8. Explain why not all of the plastic products that are produced are recycled.

9. Suggest three ways that plastic packaging materials could affect biodiversity in an ocean ecosystem.

10. Suggest at least three ways human behaviors could be changed to minimize the impacts of plastic packaging materials on Earth's systems.

Use the infographic to answer Questions 11–14.

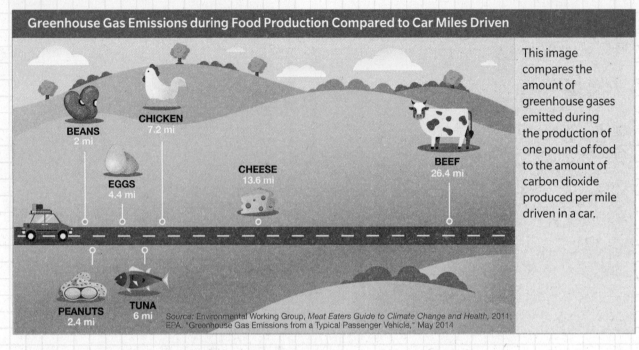

Greenhouse Gas Emissions during Food Production Compared to Car Miles Driven

BEANS
2 mi

CHICKEN
7.2 mi

EGGS
4.4 mi

CHEESE
13.6 mi

BEEF
26.4 mi

PEANUTS
2.4 mi

TUNA
6 mi

This image compares the amount of greenhouse gases emitted during the production of one pound of food to the amount of carbon dioxide produced per mile driven in a car.

Source: Environmental Working Group, *Meat Eaters Guide to Climate Change and Health*, 2011; EPA, "Greenhouse Gas Emissions from a Typical Passenger Vehicle," May 2014

11. Why is the comparison shown in the image useful?

12. If a round-trip distance to the grocery store is 20 miles, which would reduce your greenhouse gas emissions more: making one less trip to the store or eating one less pound of beef? Explain your reasoning.

13. Global Warming Potential (GWP) is a measure of how much heat a greenhouse gas absorbs. Higher GWP means the gas absorbs more heat. The GWP of CO_2 is 1 and the GWP of methane is 21. Producing beef and dairy products releases a lot of methane. Driving a car releases a lot of carbon dioxide. What else would you need to know to determine which action has a greater potential impact on global temperature?

14. If you wanted to reduce your greenhouse gas emissions, how might you change your diet to have the greatest impact? Use evidence and scientific reasoning to support your claim.

Name: _____   Date: _____

How can air travel be improved to reduce impacts on Earth systems?

Air travel is an important part of our global culture and economy. However, it causes significant greenhouse gas emissions and requires large amounts of natural resources. Greener Skies is an initiative that is being implemented to help decrease airport emissions. It improves upon existing area navigation (RNAV) procedures. These new procedures direct aircraft to fly a different course to reduce mileage and, therefore, the amount of fuel burned during the flight. Research Greener Skies procedures that have been put into place at Seattle-Tacoma Airport and other airports. Use what you learn to determine whether any of these procedures would benefit an airport near you.

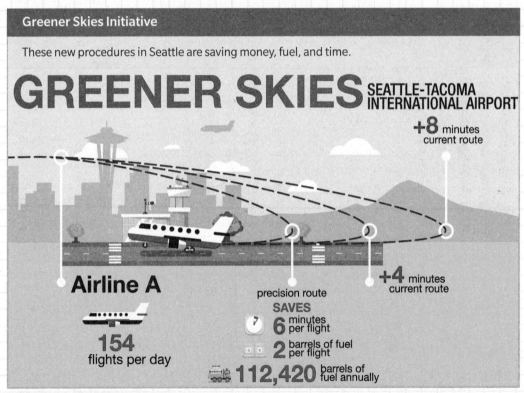

Greener Skies Initiative

These new procedures in Seattle are saving money, fuel, and time.

GREENER SKIES SEATTLE-TACOMA INTERNATIONAL AIRPORT

+8 minutes current route

+4 minutes current route

Airline A

154 flights per day

precision route
SAVES
6 minutes per flight
2 barrels of fuel per flight
112,420 barrels of fuel annually

Source: Federal Aviation Administration, U.S. Department of Transportation, and Alaska Airlines, June 27, 2014

The steps below will help guide your research.

1. **Define the Problem** What questions do you have about the goal of the Greener Skies initiative? Write a statement defining a problem that Greener Skies is trying to solve.

2. **Analyze Data** In a test of the new procedures, a single airline was able to save 87 gallons of fuel per flight and shorten flight times by 9 minutes. As a result, they reduced greenhouse gas emissions by 1 metric ton every time a plane landed at the Seattle-Tacoma Airport. Across all airlines, about 206,085 flights landed at Seattle-Tacoma in 2016. Calculate the amount of fuel and the amount of greenhouse-gas emissions that would be saved using the Greener Skies initiative at Seattle-Tacoma Airport over the course of one year and ten years.

3. **Conduct Research** Research the Greener Skies procedures enacted at the airports in Seattle and other test airports around the country. Consider how the Greener Skies procedures could be implemented at another airport of your choice, taking into consideration the air-traffic patterns at that airport.

4. **Develop a Presentation** Propose strategies that could be used at your chosen airport to improve airport efficiency and reduce impacts on the environment. Use evidence from other airports that have implemented Greener Skies initiatives to support your recommendation.

5. **Communicate** Present your proposal to your class.

✓ **Self-Check**

	I defined the problem that the Greener Skies program is trying to solve.
	I analyzed data about carbon emissions caused by airplane flights and how Greener Skies procedures can reduce them.
	I researched air traffic patterns and procedures at another airport of my choice in order to evaluate which initiatives could be implemented there.
	I developed a presentation that proposed strategies to improve efficiency at my airport and reduce human impacts on the environment.
	My proposal was supported by evidence and clearly communicated.

Go online to access the **Interactive Glossary**. You can use this online tool to look up definitions for all the vocabulary terms in this book.

Pronunciation Key

Sound	Symbol	Example	Respelling	Sound	Symbol	Example	Respelling
ă	a	pat	PAT	ŏ	ah	bottle	BAHT'l
ā	ay	pay	PAY	ō	oh	toe	TOH
âr	air	care	KAIR	ô	aw	caught	KAWT
ä	ah	father	FAH•ther	ôr	ohr	roar	ROHR
är	ar	argue	AR•gyoo	oi	oy	noisy	NOYZ•ee
ch	ch	chase	CHAYS	o͞o	u	book	BUK
ĕ	e	pet	PET	o͞o	oo	boot	BOOT
ĕ (at end of a syllable)	eh	settee lessee	seh•TEE leh•SEE	ou	ow	pound	POWND
ĕr	ehr	merry	MEHR•ee	s	s	center	SEN•ter
ē	ee	beach	BEECH	sh	sh	cache	CASH
g	g	gas	GAS	ŭ	uh	flood	FLUHD
ĭ	i	pit	PIT	ûr	er	bird	BERD
ĭ (at end of a syllable)	ih	guitar	gih•TAR	z	z	xylophone	ZY•luh•fohn
ī	y eye (only for a complete syllable)	pie island	PY EYE•luhnd	z	z	bags	BAGZ
îr	ir	hear	HIR	zh	zh	decision	dih•SIZH•uhn
j	j	germ	JERM	ə	uh	around broken focus	uh•ROWND BROH•kuhn FOH•kuhs
k	k	kick	KIK	ər	er	winner	WIN•er
ng	ng	thing	THING	th	th	thin they	THIN THAY
ngk	ngk	bank	BANGK	w	w	one	WUHN
				wh	hw	whether	HWETH•er

© Houghton Mifflin Harcourt Publishing Company

Index

Page numbers for key terms are in **boldface** type.
Page numbers in *italic* type indicate illustrative material, such as photographs, graphs, charts, and maps.

A

acidic water, 539, *539*
acid rain, 496
Act, 210, 274, 343
adaptation, 391
  in chaparral ecosystem, 536, *536*
  environment affecting, *393*, 394
  of organism, 391, 534–537
  types of, 392
adaptive technologies, 18
adenine, 411
adrenal gland, 171, *171*
advantages, 65
aerodynamics, 8, *8*
aerosols, 527
African cichlid fish, 400, *400*
African elephants, 532
aggregating anemone, 461, *461*
agricultural areas, 387
agriculture
  geosphere affected by, 495
  modeling runoff, 100
  water needs of, 493
air
  atmosphere as, 270
  circulation of, 275–278, 279–282
  currents, 98
  mass of, 319–320, *319*, 326, 331, 359
  as matter, 279
  movement of, 268–287
  particles of, 294, *312*, 314
  quality of, 556–558
air mass, 319
air pollution, 495
air pressure
  element of weather, 314
  formation of, 271–272
  identifying weather associated with, 316–318
  map of, 316
  prevailing wind and, *324*
  system of, 317–318, *317*

  temperature differences causing, 275
  on weather map, *318*
  wind formation caused by, 315
air temperature
  air pressure changes caused by, 275
  clouds effect on, 313
  cricket chirps estimating, 339, *339*
  differences in cause wind, 272
  differences of changing air density, 272
  affecting precipitation, 313
  pressure affected by, 316, *316*
  thermal energy of, 208
  during water changing states, 240, *240*
air travel, 581–582
Akashi Kaikyō Bridge, 62, *62*
Alaska, 384, *384*
Alaskan Inuit Culture, 372, *372*
albedo, 356–357
algae, 90, 101, 425, 489, *489*, 500
allele, 404, 408, *408*
Alpine butterfly, 393, *393*
Alpine wildflower, 350, *350*
alternative energy, 191, 219, *230*, 563
altitude, 360, 361, *361*, 371, 384, *385*, 399
Alturas, California, 366, *366*
alumina refining, 564, *564*
aluminum, 205, 223, 564, *564*
Alvin, 305, *305*
Amazon, 269, *269*, 285, *285*
ambient temperature, 220
American pika, 393, *393*
amoebas, 419
amphibian, 423, *423*, 458, *458*
analysis
  of air mass interaction, 320
  of animal body systems, 146–151
  of board game, 471
  of cells, 113, 115–118, 120–121
  of climate model, 363
  of clouds and rain formation, 243
  of cod population, 502

  of cost-benefit, 45, 65
  of data, 52, 54, 56, 65, 378
  of drought tolerance of plants, 389–390
  of energy transfer, 185
  of factors determining climate, 384–386
  of female mate choice, 465
  of flower parts, 443
  of formation of wind, 271–272
  of greenhouse effect, 512
  of heat, 208–210
  of hibernation, 158
  of honeybee colony loss, 445
  of impact of technology on society, 20
  of insulated container, 229–230
  in investigations, 20
  of model car, 71–72
  of models, 88
  of monarch migration, 540–541
  of pollution, 494
  of processes, 248
  of reaction time, 159
  of relationships between structure and function, 20
  of resource quality data, 557
  of resource use data, 555–556
  of risk-benefit analysis, 49
  of shipping costs, *337*
  of solar water heater, *220*
  of solid waste reduction, 569–570
  of system responses to exercise, 150
  of technological influences, *13*
  of thermal energy loss, 201
  of thermal energy transfer, 222
  of tissue, 94
  of water density, 295
  of water on Earth, 238–240
  of weather forecast map, 343, *343*, 344, *344*
  of wind, 274
Analyze Geothermal Heat Pumps, 230

© Houghton Mifflin Harcourt Publishing Company

Ancient Roman builders, 188

Angus cattle, 468

animal. *See also* **living thing; organism**

adaptation of, 382–394, 421, 468–469

algal bloom affecting, 500

asexual reproduction of, 419–420, 423–424, 426–427, 429, 458, 460

biomimetics, 160

body system of, 146–151

brains of, 155, *155*

cell structure of, 116, *116*

climate influencing, 387–390

environment affecting, 454–473, 477

environment influencing reproduction of, 421

eukaryotic cells of, 116, *116*

extinction of, 495

genetics affecting, 466–467, 477

homeostasis in, 152–153

information processing, 152–156

interaction in systems, 165

memories of, 158

migration of, 161–162

multicellular organism, 110

need for green plants, 99

plants influencing, 388

producing offspring, 418

reproduction passing genetic material in, 418

response to information, 157–160

seed dispersal by, 444, *444*

selective breeding of, 467

sexual reproduction of, 419–420, 424, 425–427, 429, 458, 466

similar environments produce similar adaptation, 394

animal behavior, 157

courtship behavior, 462–463, 477

hibernation, 158

investigating, 86

parenting, 462, 464, 477

reproductive success relating to, 462–465

response to information, 157–160

warming and cooling, 152, *152*

Ansel Adams Wilderness, 393, *393*

Antarctic ice core data, *515*

Antarctic polar ice cap, 517

antennae, 149

anther, 442, *442*, 443, *443*

anthroposphere, 100

Anza-Borrego Desert State Park, 382, *382*

aorta, *151*

aphid, 420

apple trees, 426–427

aquatic ecosystem, 539, *539*

aquatic organism, 539, *539*

aqueduct, 193

aquifer, 555, 556, *556*

Archaean, 110, 115

Arctic tern, 162, *162*

area navigation (RNAV) procedures, 581

argument

engage in argument from evidence, 56

evidence supporting, 96, 136

arid climate, 386, *386*

armadillo, 469, *469*

Art Connection

Landscape Architects, 478

artificial reef, 102

asexual reproduction, 419

of animals, 458

genetic inheritance in, 423, *423*, 455

of plants, 419–420, 423–424, 440

rate of, 424

transfer of DNA through, 423, *423*

aspen, 450, *450*

assembly line, 68

Assessment

Lesson Self-Check, 23–25, 41–43, 59–61, 75–77, 105–107, 125–127, 141–143, 163–165, 195–197, 213–215, 233–235, 255–257, 285–287, 307–309, 329–331, 347–349, 369–371, 397–399, 413–415, 431–433, 453–455, 475–477, 505–507, 529–531, 549–551, 573–575

Unit Performance Task, 83–84, 171–172, 263–264, 377–378, 483–484, 581–582

Unit Review, 79–82, 167–170, 259–262, 373–376, 479–482, 577–580

assistive technologies, 15, 18

astronaut, 70, 139, *139*

astronomical change, 516

Atlantic Ocean, *299*

atmosphere

absorbing sunlight, 354, *354*, 511, *511*

changes in, 519

cycling of matter in, 280

defined, 270, 300

energy flow in, 174, *174*

flow of energy in, 281, *281*, 287

greenhouse effect of, 511

greenhouse gases in, 367–368

human impact on, 495

movement of water in, 241–244

patterns of air movement in, 268–287

reflecting sunlight, 354, *354*, 511, *511*

as subsystem of Earth, 97, *97*, 98

water in, 242–244, 257

atmospheric river, 325, *325*

atrium, *151*

avian malaria, 543, *543*

B

background research, 47

bacteria

asexual reproduction, 424, *424*

binary fission reproducing, 419, *419*

decomposition by, 99

growth of, 225

in hot springs and thermal features, 421, *421*

identifying cell of, 118, *118*

as living thing, 93

prokaryotic cell, 115

unicellular, 110

Baja California, Mexico, 270, *270*

ballpoint pen, 70, *70*

banana crop, 417, *417*, 428, 431, *431*

Banner Peak, 393, *393*

Bañuelos, Gary, 395, 395–396, *396*

basic life function, 93

bat, 462, 545, *545*, 551, *551*

battery, 190, *190*

bauxite, 564, *564*

bear, 392, *392*, 416, *416*, 464, *464*

beaver habitat, 490, *490,* 535
bee, 429, 445
behavior, 157, 158, 165, 392, *392*
Beijing, China, 353, *353*
Bengal tiger, 464, *464*
bighorn sheep, 393, *393*
bigleaf hydrangea, 448, *448*
bike design, 13, *13*
bike lane, 572, *572*
binary fission, 419, *419*
biodiversity, 535
biologist, 123–124
biomedicine, 78
biomimetics, 160
biomimicry, 19, 160
biosphere, 97, *97,* 99, 300, 495, 511, 524
Biosphere 2, 89, *89, 105*
bird
    migration of, 470, *470*
    reproduction of, 458, *458*
    willow dependent, 535
blackbuck antelope, 472, *472*
Black Rock Desert, Nevada, *1*
blood, 146
blood vessel, 95, *95*
bluegill, 420, *420*
blue planet, 238, *238*
blue spruce tree, 436, *436*
board game, 471–472
body temperature, 152, *152*
bone
    connective tissue, 146
    marrow of, 103–104
    in skeletal system, 149
    transplantation of, 103
boundary, 10, 97
bowerbird, 462
bowling ball, 178, *178,* 179, 183, *183,* 186, *186*
brain, 149, 155, *155,* 157, 158
brainstorming, 46, 47, 54, 57, 97, 226, 228, 471, 561, 569, 572
brass, 205
bristlecone, 393, *393*
brittle star, 160, *160*
brown bear, 464, *464*
budding of hydra, 423, *423*
buildings, 100
Butchart Gardens, 478, *478*
butterfly, 111, *111*

C

cactus wren, 536, *536*
calcium carbonate shell, 539, *539*
California
    Alturas, 366, *366*
    Ansel Adams Wilderness, 393, *393*
    Anza-Borrego Desert State Park, 382, *382*
    Banner Peak, 393, *393*
    chaparral ecosystem, 534, 536, *536*
    cities and towns in, 387, *387*
    climates in, 359, *359,* 360, *360,* 366, *366,* 369, *369,* 386, *386*
    coastal wetland, 544
    effects of El Niño and La Niña, 518, *518*
    elevation of, 361, *361*
    fresh water in, 247
    Fresno, 366, *366,* 388, *388*
    Joshua Tree, 387, *387,* 422, *422*
    Joshua Tree National Park, 351, *351,* 365, *365,* 366, *366*
    land cover types in, 387, *387*
    Los Angeles, 357, *357*
    Mojave Desert, 202, *202,* 350, *350,* 369, *369,* 422, *422*
    The Pacific Flyway, 470
    Pacific Ocean effect on effecting weather of, 324
    Point Reyes National Seashore, 268, *268*
    quino checkerspot butterfly, 542, *542*
    redwood tree in, 388, *388*
    regional climates of, 366, *366*
    San Clemente, 352, *352*
    San Diego County, 279, *279*
    San Francisco, 223, *223,* 265, *265,* 352, *352*
    Santa Ana winds, 279, *279,* 282, *282*
    Santa Paula, 270, *270*
    satellite image of, 323
    Sierra Nevada, 323, 350, *350,* 393, *393*
    soil salinity in, 450
    Truckee, 366, *366*
    weather forecast in, 341, *341,* 342, *342*
    weather patterns in, 323–326
    wildfire in, 270, *270,* 279, *279*
    Yosemite National Park, 347, *351,* 360, 369, *369*
California Current, 223, *223,* 292, 324, 325, 331, 359, *359*
camouflage, 391, *391*
cancer cell, 166
canyon, 98
Can You Explain It? 5, 23, 27, 41, 45, 59, 63, 75, 89, 105, 109, 125, 129, 141, 145, 163, 177, 195, 199, 213, 217, 233, 237, 255, 269, 285, 289, 307, 311, 329, 333, 347, 351, 369, 383, 397, 401, 413, 417, 431, 453, 457, 475, 489, 505, 509, 529, 533, 549, 553, 573
capillaries, *151*
capsaicin, 451–452
caracara, 464, *464*
carbon
    cycle of, 304, *304*
    cycling of in atmosphere, 280
    emissions into atmosphere, 101
    in glucose, 112, *112*
carbon arc light, 32
carbon cycle, 304, *304*
carbon dioxide
    in atmosphere, 241
    in Biosphere 2, 89
    from cellular respiration, 280
    comparing quantities of, 519
    concentrations of, 539
    cycling of in atmosphere, 280
    emissions of, 526, *526*
    exchange of, 304, *304*
    from excretory system, 147
    as greenhouse gas, 368, 397, 523
    oceans cycling, 303
    plants converting into oxygen, 133
    from respiratory system, 148
carbon monoxide, 28, 29, *29*
car design, 1, 8–9
cardinal bird, 462, *462*
cardinal flower, 388, *388*
cardiovascular system, 29, 148
Careers in Engineering: Electrical Engineer, 73–74
Careers in Engineering, Energy Conservationist, 235, *235*

Careers in Science: Hydrologist, 253–254

Careers in Science: Physical Oceanographer, 305–306

carnivorous plant, 137, 392, *392*

Carolina Reaper pepper, 451, *451*

Case Study

The Dust Bowl, 566, *566*

Joshua Trees, 422, *422*

The Mississippi River, 498–501

The Pacific Flyway, 470

The Santa Ana Winds, 286

Sierra Nevada, 393, *393*

cat, 197, *197*, 213, *213*

catkins, 436, *436*

causation, 521–522, *521–522*

cause and effect, 523

cause-and-effect relationship, 555

Cavendish banana, 417, *417*, 431, *431*

cell, 93

analyzing systems of, 115–118

division of, 110, *110*

egg, 425

gamete (sex), 425

identifying different systems of, 118, *118*

as living systems, 108–123

living things made of, 110

modeling, 119–121, 127

of nerve, 108, *108*, 149

observing under microscope, 111–113

in organisms, 93

of plants, 131, *131*

size of, 120–122

special junctions connecting, 96

of sperm, 425

structure of, 131, *131*

types and structures of, 115–118, 127

virus particles attacking, 109, *109*

cell membrane, 115, *115*, 116, *116*, 117, *117*

cell nucleus, 123, 405, *405*

cell phone, 72

cell theory, 110

cell wall, 115, *115*, **116**, 117, *117*, 130

Celsius, 240

central collector, 207

ceramic, 221, 224

chameleon, 154, *154*

change, energy flows causing, 176–196

chaparral ecosystem, 534, 536, *536*

Chargaff, Erwin, 411–412, *412*

Checkpoints, 24, 42, 60, 76, 106, 126, 142, 164, 196, 214, 234, 256, 286, 308, 330, 348, 370, 398, 414, 432, 454, 476, 506, 530, 550, 574

chemical change, 211

chemical composition, 221

chemical energy, 181, 182, 190, *190*

chemical reactions, 182, 303

chemical receptor, 154

Chernobyl Nuclear Disaster, 503–504, *504*

cherry tree, 436, *436*

chili pepper, 451–452

Chinon, France, 216, *216*

Chinook salmon, 553, *553*, 573, *573*

chlorofluorocarbon (CFCs), 367–368

chloroplast, 115, *115*, 116, **116**, 117, *117*, 123

cholla cactus, 536, *536*

chromosome, 404, 405, *405*, 408, *408*, 415, 425

cicada, 149, *149*

cilia, 112, 149

circulation

of air, 275–278, 279–282

of oceans, 245–246, 257, 300–305, *302*

of water, 98, 242

circulatory system, 93, 95, 148, *148*, 151

cities, 345–346, 387, *387*

civil engineers, 16

claim

making, 275

stating and supporting, 23, 41, 59, 75, 92, 105, 125, 141, 163, 195, 213, 233, 255, 285, 307, 329, 347, 369, 397, 413, 431, 453, 475, 505, 529, 549, 573

Clark's nutcracker, 483, *483*

climate, 352

albedo and, 356–357

animals affected by, 387–390, 399

in Beijing, China, 353, *353*

classifying, 362

data of, 514–515

description of, 352–353, 510, 531

differences in, 265

on Earth, 510–513

factors determining, 384–386, 399

graphs of, 353, *353*

influences on, 358–361, 371

monitoring effects of, 544–546

ocean energy flows affecting, 303

patterns of, 544

plants affected by, 387–390, 399, 448

problems of, 386

recent changes in, 523, 524–526

regional differences, 350–366

in San Francisco, 352, *352*

sunlight affecting, 354–357, 371, 511, *511*

weather and, 265–383

climate change, 485–582

biodiversity and, 543

monitoring organisms, 545–546, 551

organisms responding to, 538–543, 549

organism's survival affected by, 532–546

response, adaptation, and extinction, 542, 551

climate scientist, 521

climate zones, 362, *362*

climatologist, 345

clone, 419

cloud

absorbing solar energy, 313

element of weather, 313

formation of, 243, 257

on weather map, 318

Coachella Valley fringe-toed lizard, 546

coal, 565

coastal wetland, 544

cold air

in convection cells, 274, *274*, 276, *276*

in global wind patterns, 277, *277*

denser, 272, *272*

cold front, 321
cold ocean current, 223
cold water, density of, 294–296, *294*, 301, *301*, 302
Collaborate, 11, 22, 40, 58, 74, 104, 124, 140, 162, 194, 212, 228, 232, 254, 275, 286, 302, 306, 328, 346, 355, 368, 388, 396, 405, 412, 430, 443, 444, 452, 470, 474, 504, 528, 548, 572
collision, 186–187, 189, 218
colony collapse disorder (CCD), 445
combined heat and power plant, 567, *567*
combustion of fossil fuel, 304, *304*
community in ecosystem, 534, *534*
community project, 486
compact fluorescent lamps (CFLs), 192
compare and contrast
  concentrations, 556
  dog traits, 467
  drought tolerance of plants, 389–390
  hot and cold objects, 200–201
  information, 322
  maps, 387, *387*
  movement of water through stems, 135
  Northern and Southern Hemispheres, 278, *278*
  parents and offspring, 427
  phenotype, 407
  reproduction and growth of organisms, 418
  sexual and asexual reproduction, 428
  temperature, 198
  test data, 228
  thermal conductivity, 210
  thermal energy in objects, 204–205, 206
components
  of Earth systems, 93–98
  of a system, 86, 87
compost solid waste, 559, *559*
computer
  development of, 14
  energy transformation in, 192, *192*
  images generated by, 88

  modeling programs, 544
  raw materials needed for, 14
  weather forecasting on, 341
computer model, 11, 91, 92, 510, 523
conceptual model, 11
concrete reef ball, 102, *102*
condensation, 243, 250
conduction transfer, 209, 215, 219, 281, *281*, 303
cone, 436, *436*, 438, *438*
conifer, 438, *438*, 450, *450*
connective tissue, 95, *95*, 146
conservation efforts, for Florida panther, 496–497
constraints, 33
  best solutions fitting, 45, 61, 232, 560, *560*
  change in, 34, 36, 38, 43
  identifying, 37, 43, 225, 226, 546
  for lighting city streets, 33
  on lunch line design, 21
  making tradeoff, 65
  for model car design, 37–38
  redefining, 34, 43
  for umbrella, 31
construct an explanation, 138, 378
consumer demand, 15
consumer safety laws, 8
continental deflection, 292, 298
contour farming, 566, *566*
convection, 273
  cells of, 274, *274*, 276, *276*
  cycling matter due to different densities, 273, 281, *281*
  modeling, 270–275
  transfers of energy by, 209, 215, 219, 225, 303
convection current, 300–301, *301*
convective thermal energy loss, 225
conventional power plant, 567, *567*
cooling pool, 216, *216*, 219, *219*
Copenhagen, Denmark, 571
copper, 557
coral
  as animals, 146
  bleaching of, 525, *525*
  in coral reef system, 90, *90*
  reproduction of, 420, *420*
coral dahlia flower, 419

coral reef, 90, *90*, 91, 101, *101*
Coriolis effect, 276–278, **276**, *276*, 287, 292, 298
correlation, 521–522, *521–522*
cost-benefit analysis, 45, 65
courtship behavior, 462–463, 477
cover crop, 566, *566*
coyote, *535*
coyote brush, 536, *536*
crabeater seal, 147, *147*
crabs, 90, *90*
crash testing, 12
Crick, Francis, 411–412, *412*
criteria, 32
  best solutions fitting, 45, 48–49, 51, 61, 226, 228, 560, *560*
  change in, 34, 36, 38
  identifying, 38, 43, 65, 225, 546
  for lighting city streets, 32, *32*
  for lunch line design, 21
  for model car design, 37–38
  redefining, 34, 43
  for umbrella, 31
crop rotation, 566, *566*
CTD instrument, 305, *305*
culture, 100
current
  in Mediterranean Sea, 299, *299*
  pattern of, *302*
cryosphere, 98
cytoplasm, 115, *115*, 116, *116*
cytosine, 411

D

dam, 10, *10*, 251, 490, *490*, 491, 499, *499*
damselfish, 459, *459*
damselfly, 462
Darwin's orchid, 390
data
  analyzing, 65, 378, 555, *555*
  on climate, 514–515
  of climate change, 544
  collecting, 217, 545–546, 551, 554, 557
  evaluate and test, 52, 54, 56, 61

for optimizing solutions, 68–70
    scientist gathering, 545–546, 551
    weather prediction using, 341–344, *341*
dead zone, 500
decision-making tool, 48
decision matrix, 48, 50, 54
decomposition, 99, 304, *304*
deep ocean current
    Coriolis effect, 298, 309
    effect of water density on, 298, 309
    formation of, 246, 298–299
    in Mediterranean Sea, 299, *299, 302*
    modeling, 294–299
deer, 462
deforestation, 491, *491*
dehydration, 171, *171*
delta, 498–501
dendrites, 108, *108*
density
    of air, 272
    of air masses, 321
    of hot and cold water, 292–296, *292*
deoxyribonucleic acid (DNA)
    in asexual reproduction, 423, *423*
    of bats, 545, *545*
    in chloroplast, 123
    defined, 404
    in mitochondria, 123
    mutation of, 407
    in sexual reproduction, 423, *423*
    structure of, 405, *405,* 411–412
dependent variable, 158, 424
deposition, 244, 250, *250*
derby car, 36
dermal tissue, 131, *131*
desert
    in California, 202, *202,* 350, *350,* 369, *369,* 387, *387,* 388, *388*
    climate of, 386, *386*
    plants in, 130, *130,* 141, *141*
    Saharan Desert, *384*
    semi-arid desert, 387, *387*
    specific adaptations for, 394, *394*
desert beetle, 392, *392*
design optimization, 64
design problem, 19, 28–30, 37–38
design a video game character, 151

diagram
    of air circulation, *276*
    of carbon cycle, 304, *304*
    of changing seasons, *449*
    of convection current, *301*
    of dam system, *10*
    of deep ocean current, *298, 309*
    of energy transfer, *194*
    of garden bed, *448*
    of heat energy, *200*
    of kitchen fires and simple stoves, *29*
    of latitude, *358*
    of Mediterranean Sea currents, *299*
    of models, *92*
    of ocean circulation, *245*
    of photosynthesis, *133*
    of plant body systems, 131, *131*
    of plant root systems, 134, *134*
    of respiratory system, *151*
    of thermal energy flow, *220*
    of warming world, *521*
    of wind formation, *272*
diatom, *303*
digestive enzyme, 147
digestive system, 90, 147, *147*
digital camera, 72
digital models, 92
digital scale, 7, *7*
dinosaur, 237, *237,* 255
disadvantages, 65
Discuss, 2, 6, 28, 46, 86, 89, 91, 97, 104, 109, 110, 129, 130, 136, 145, 146, 154, 160, 174, 192, 202, 224, 225, 226, 238, 249, 266, 270, 276, *276,* 282, 322, 352, 380, 386, 387, 402, 404, 423, 437, 441, 463, 486, 491, 498, 510, 523, 565, 568
dog, 153, *153,* 467, *467*
doldrums, 277, *277*
dolphin, 86, *86*
dominant allele, 426
dominant gene, 404, 409
dominant trait, 403
Donate Life, 104, *104*
donor, soliciting and identifying, 104
donor tissues and organs, 103
dormant, 449

Do the Math, 11, 38, 40, 102, 121, 150, 328, 339, 564
    Analyze a Cod Population, 502
    Analyze Climate Graphs, 353, *353*
    Analyze Climate Needs, 390
    Analyze Female Mate Choice, 465
    Analyze Hibernation, 158
    Analyze Honeybee Colony Loss, 445
    Analyze Temperatures, 240, *240*
    Analyze Water Density Data, 297
    Calculate Genotype Probability, 410
    Calculate Stomata Percentage, *137*
    Calculate the Rate of Asexual Reproduction, 424
    Compare Concentrations, 556
    Compare Objects' Thermal Energies, 206
    Compare Quantities of Carbon Dioxide, 519
    Compare the Hemisphere, 278
    Compare Thermal Properties of Different Materials, 227
    Describe Relative Humidity, 313
    Energy Efficiency, 192
    Evaluate Extinction Probability, 543
    Evaluate Parachute Designs, 53
    Explore a Kelp Forest, 537
    Identify Correlation and Causation, 521
    Predict Run Times Using a Model, 335, *335*
    Relate Elevation and Precipitation, 361
    Use Math for Design Improvement, 66
double helix, 405, *405*
dragon blood trees, 128, *128*
dragonfly, 458, *458*
Draw, 30, 54, 100, 143, 151, 187, 191, 195, 252, 272, 311, 346, 443, 494, 524
drinking water, 557, *557,* 563
dry burdock, 439, *439*
dry climate, 364–365
Dungeness River, 245, *245*
dust, movement of, 269, *269*
Dust Bowl, 566, *566*
dust storm, 566, *566*
Dutch iris, 446, *446*

E

ear, 149, 153
Earth
  absorbing and reflecting sunlight,
    354, *354*, 511, *511*
  albedo, 356–357
  changes in orbit of, 515, 516
  climates of, 350–366, *362, 364–365,
    371, 384, 384*
  diversity of living things on, 418
  satellites orbiting, 85
  surface changes of, 516
  surface temperature changes, 520,
    520
Earth Science Connection
  Climate and Reproduction, 478
Earth's rotation
  causing winds and air currents, 98
  Coriolis effect, 276, *276*
  effect on gyres patterns, 292–293,
    293
  effect on pressure systems, 317, *317*
  jet streams caused by, 283, *283*
  matter in atmosphere effected by,
    275
Earth System
  air circulation relating to, 279–282
  air movement patterns in
    atmosphere of, 268–287
  air pressure in, 314, *314*
  analyzing water on, 238–240
  carbon cycle on, *304*
  climate system, 511–513
  cycling of matter in, 303
  energy flow in, 174
  ice on surface of, 248, *248*
  interaction in, 89, 310–327, 511
  modeling of, 97–102
  movement of water on, 245–246,
    288–305
  states of water on, 239–240
  subsystems of, 97–102, *97*, 270, 300
Eastern gray squirrel, 458, *458*
E. coli bacteria, 93, *93*
economy, 100

ecosystem, 534
  biodiversity of, 535, 551
  climate change disrupting, 538
  dam system disrupting, 247
  habitat degradation, 542
  health of, 534–535
  importance of, 544
  levels of, 534, *534*
  roads affecting, 16
Eco-Task Force, 483
Edison, Thomas, 44, 57
egg
  of aggregating anemone, 461, *461*
  of birds, 459, *459*, 464
  of dragonflies, 458
  of fish, 420, *420*, 459, *459*, 553, *553*
  of flowering plants, 441
  of octopus, 464
  parents protecting, 464
  of seedless plants, 437, *437*
  of seed plants, 438
elastic potential energy, 181
electrical current, 182
electrical energy
  defined, 181–182
  reducing use of, 570, *570*
  sensory response, 153
  from steam turbines, 567, *567*
  transformation of, 190, *190*
electrical engineer, 73–74
electric circuits in computers, 14
electromagnetic energy, 181, 190,
  190, 219
electromagnetic receptor, 154
electron microscope, 111
elephant, 419, 456, *456*
elephant seal, 462
elevation, 360, 361, *361*, 371, 385,
  385
elk, 463, *463*, 535
Ellesmere Island, Canada, 364, *364*
El Niño, 518, *518*, 539
embryo
  of fish, 118, *118*
  of mollusk, 458
  of plants, 438, 446
Emperor penguin, 383, 397, *397*
endoplasmic reticulum, 116, *116*,
  117, *117*

endoskeleton, 149
endosymbiosis, 123
energy
  causing changes, 178
  clouds absorbing, 313
  collision transferring, 186–187
  convection transferring, 300–301
  Earth balancing, 354, *354*, 511, *511*
  in Earth systems, 97
  flowing and causing change,
    176–196
  flow of in atmosphere, 281, 287
  flow of in oceans, 303, 309
  flow of in systems, 173–264
  flow of water cycle, 251
  forms of, 181–182
  gravitational potential energy,
    180–181
  hydroelectric power station
    transforming, 176
  identifying forms of, 178–183
  kinetic, 178–179
  law of conservation of energy, 180
  loss in systems, 191–192
  mechanical energy, 181–182
  modeling transformation of, 189–
    192
  moving through biosphere, 99
  observing transfer of, 184–188
  from photosynthesis, 90, 130
  potential energy, 180–181
  in radiometer, 218
  stored, 180–181
  from sun, 98, 303
  surface wind and surface current
    transferring, 292
  in systems, 90
  thermal energy, 98, 189
  transfers of within a system, 90, 178
  in water cycle, 98
  from wind, 39–40
energy conservationist, 231–232
energy drive, in water cycle, 236–
  257
energy efficient, 192
energy-efficient appliance, 563
energy-efficient home, 232, *232*

energy transfer, 186
in collisions, 186
conduction, 209
convection, 209
direction of, 200–201
heat as, 208, 215
observing, 184–188
between ocean and atmosphere,
251
radiation, 209
through systems, 218
using thermal energy in systems,
216–235
energy transformation, 189–192, **189**
engineering, 6
careers in, 73–74
defined, 6
looking to nature, 160
problem solving, 1, 6
relationship to science and
technology, 6–9
science and society and, 4–23
solving design problems, 28–30
tools of, 6, 25
Engineering Connection
Building Homes for Different
Climates, 372, *372*
engineering design process
analyze and revise design, 230
analyze data, 84, 582
analyze results, 570
analyze system response, 172
ask questions, 2, 22, 29
background research, 47
begins with a problem, 28
brainstorming solutions, 46, 47
brainstorm solutions, 561, 569
choose best solution, 67, 226, 228,
560, *560*, 562, 569
collaboration, 22
communicate solution, 84, 172,
484, 582
compare solutions, 264
conduct research, 84, 172, 484, 582
consider tradeoff, 70, *70*

define the criteria and constraints,
226, 560, *560*
define the problem, 21, 83, 171,
263, 483, 561, 569, 581
defining problems precisely, 29,
30–34, 41, 225–226
design and implement test, 570
design investigation, 264
design optimization, 64, 70
develop and test models, 228
develop and test solutions, 22
developing and testing solutions,
51, *51*
developing presentations, 582
develop models, 264, 484
evaluate and test solutions, 50–56,
61
evaluate models, 102, 560, *560*
evaluate solutions, 526, 561, 568,
570
examine needs to be met, 21
identify and recommend solution,
84, 264
identifying characteristics of best
solution, 67
identifying problem or need, 102,
560, *560*
identifying the problem, 28–30
identify the problem, 21
improving promising solution,
64–67
making tradeoffs, 65
modeling, 4
open-mindedness and, 47
optimizing solutions, 62–72, 75, 77,
560, *560*
propose a test, 562
propose solutions, 168, 558
recommend solution, 484
research the problem, 561, 569
select solution with decision-
making tool, 48–49
testing many solutions, 57–58, 568
testing prototypes, 51–53
testing solutions, 70, *70*
using data to optimize solutions,
68–70

engineering problems
criteria and constraints of, 32–34,
568
defining precisely, 26–40, 43, 225,
568, 569
developing solutions, 46–49
evaluate test data, 52
identifying problem or need, 102,
560, *560*
improving promising solution,
64–67
making tradeoffs, 65
redefining criteria and constraints,
34, 43
reframing problems, 36–38
research the problem, 35, 561, 569
review data and design, 52
Engineer It, 114, 133, 247, 273, 299,
306, 316, 338, 357, 408
Analyze a Climate Problem, 386
Analyze Applications of Mechanical
Energy, 183
Analyze Evaporative Cooling, 224
Develop a Hybrid, 422
Evaluate a Model, 102
Evaluate Biomimetics, 160
Evaluate Solutions for Climate
Change, 526
Evaluate Tradeoffs, 497
Explain Trait Selection in Dog
Breeds, 467
Explore Plant Hybrids, 447
Explore Thermal Energy Storage,
207
Identify Criteria and Constraints,
546
Unit Performance Task, 83–84,
171–172, 263–264
engineers
careers in, 231–232, 571–572
developing solutions, 225
science practices compared to, 51
studying and solving problems in
natural systems, 91
enhanced greenhouse effect, 523

environment
adaptation of, 536
adjustments for needs of, 39–40
animals affected by, 456–473, 477
animal's response to, 152–156, 165
in changing conditions, 421
climate affects, 385, *385*
communities improving, 486
energy-efficient home, 232
exploring, 490–492
habitat depends on, 534–535
human activity changing, 491, 507
human impact on, 488–502
human impact reduction methods,
  563–567
influencing reproduction, 421, 429
interaction in, 490
living things responding to, 110
monitoring human impact on, 554–
  558, 559–562
natural events changing, 491, 507
organisms adapting to, 382–394,
  534–537
organisms influenced by, 379–484
plants affected by, 137–138, 140,
  434–450, 455
power plant impact on, 567, *567*
reducing human impact on, 552–
  570
reproduction influenced by, 420,
  421, 460
scale of human impact on, 498–502
specific adaptations for, 394, *394*
in stable condition, 421
technology influenced by, 14, 16,
  17, 25
technology's impact on, 17, 20, 29
**Environmental Protection Agency
  (EPA),** 15, 557
Environmental Science Connection
Passive Solar Design, 258
environmental stimulus, 165, 449,
  469
epidermal tissue, 95, *95*
epithelial tissue, 95, *95*, 146
equation, 335. *See also* **formula**
equator
in global wind patterns, 277, *277*
sunlight and, 355, *355*

Erawan National Park, Thailand,
  365, *365*
erosion
humans causing, 495
ocean levels causing, 525
water's role in, 238, *238*
estimate
air temperature with cricket chirps,
  339, *339*
elevation and precipitation, 361,
  361
shipping costs, 338
Etosha National Park, Namibia, 457,
  457
eucalyptus tree, 388, 533, *533*
eukaryotic cell
endosymbiosis of, 123
evolution of, 123
in plants, 130
structure of, 115, 116, *116*
evaporation, 241, 250
evaporative cooling, 224, *224*
evidence
citing, 16, 303, 344, 461, 513
engage in argument from, 56
recording on graphic organizers, 92
supporting arguments, 96, 136
supporting claims, 23, 41, 59, 75,
  92, 105, 125, 141, 163, 195, 213,
  233, 255, 285, 296, 307, 329, 347,
  369, 389, 397, 413, 431, 453, 475,
  505, 529, 549
Evidence Notebook, 5, 12, 16, 18, 23,
  27, 31, 36, 41, 45, 48, 53, 59, 63,
  67, 70, 75, 89, 91, 99, 101, 105,
  109, 112, 118, 122, 125, 129, 132,
  138, 141, 145, 156, 160, 163, 177,
  182, 188, 191, 195, 199, 205, 209,
  213, 217, 218, 222, 224, 233, 237,
  239, 242, 252, 255, 269, 278, 280,
  285, 289, 293, 303, 307, 311, 314,
  317, 322, 329, 333, 341, 342, 347,
  351, 356, 360, 366, 369, 383, 390,
  392, 397, 401, 407, 410, 413, 417,
  419, 428, 431, 435, 439, 444, 453,
  457, 460, 463, 469, 475, 489, 490,
  494, 501, 505, 509, 519, 523, 525,
  529, 533, 537, 539, 549, 553, 558,
  567, 573

excretion, 242
excretory system, 147
exercise, system response to, 150
exoskeleton, 149, *149*
explanation
cell size limits, 122
constructing, 138
Exploration
Analyze Reproductive Success of
  Flowering Plants, 441–445
Analyzing Animal Responses to
  Information, 157–160
Analyzing Animal Body Systems,
  146–151
Analyzing Cell Systems, 115–118
Analyzing Factors that Determine
  Climate, 384–386
Analyzing Heat, 208–210
Analyzing How Organisms Respond
  to Climate Change, 538–543
Analyzing Influences on Technology,
  13–16
Analyzing Recent Climate Change,
  520–523
Analyzing Systems and Models,
  10–12
Analyzing the Scale of Human
  Impact on the Environment,
  498–502
Analyzing Water on Earth, 238–240
Applying the Concepts of Heat
  Transfer, 225–230
Assessing the Impact of Technology
  on Society, 17–20
Comparing Hot and Cold Objects,
  200–201
Connecting Climate Patterns to
  Plant and Animal Life, 387–390
Defining Problems Precisely, 31–34
Defining Systems, 90–92
Describe Weather Patterns in
  California, 323–326
Describing Animal Reproduction,
  458–461
Describing Climate, 352–353
Describing Factors that Affect Plant
  Growth, 446–450
Describing How Plant Systems
  Process Nutrients, 133–136

Describing How Plant Systems Respond to the Environment, 137–138

Describing How Sunlight Affects Climate, 354–357

Describing Information Processing in Animals, 152–156

Describing the Movement of Water in Earth's Atmosphere, 241–244

Describing the Movement of Water on Earth's Surface, 245–248

Describing the Thermal Properties of Materials, 221–224

Describing Types of Reproduction, 418–422

Describing Weather, 312–315

Developing a Method to Monitor a Human Impact on the Environment, 559–562

Developing a Method to Reduce a Human Impact on the Environment, 568–570

Developing Solutions, 46–49

Evaluating Solutions, 50–56

Explaining Factors That Influence Animal Growth, 466–472

Explaining How Adaptations Help Organisms Survive, 391–394

Explaining How Fronts Change Weather, 319–322

Explaining the Accuracy of Weather Prediction, 340–344

Explaining the Circulation of Air, 275–278

Explaining What Influences Climate, 358–361

Exploring Earth's Climate, 510

Exploring Plant Body Systems, 130–132

Exploring the Environment, 490–492

Identifying Cells, 110–114

Identifying Different Forms of Energy, 178–183

Identifying Global Climate Change Factors, 514–519

Identifying Weather Associated with Pressure Systems, 316–318

Improving a Promising Design Solution, 64–67

Investigating How Traits Are Passed from Parent to Offspring, 402–403

Investigating Reproductive Structures of Plants, 436–440

Modeling Deep Currents, 294–299

Modeling Earth Systems, 97–102

Modeling Inheritance of Traits, 408–410

Modeling Living Systems, 93–96

Modeling Surface Currents, 290–293

Modeling the Flow of Thermal Energy through Systems, 218–220

Modeling the Water Cycle, 249–252

Modeling Wind and Convection, 270–275

Monitoring the Effects of Climate Change on Organisms, 544–546

Observing Energy Transfer, 184–188

Relating Air Circulation to the Earth System, 279–282

Relating Animal Behavior to Reproductive Success, 462–465

Relating Genetic Structure to Traits, 404–407

Relating Human Activity to the Environment, 493–498

Relating Ocean Circulation to the Flow of Matter and Energy, 300–305

Relating Reproduction to Genetic Variation, 423–428

Relating Science, Engineering, and Technology, 6–9

Relating Temperature and Thermal Energy, 202–207

Relating the Adaptations of Organisms to their Environment, 534–537

Researching to Define Engineering Problems, 35

Solving a Design Problem, 28–30

Understanding the Effects of Climate Change, 524–526

Using Data to Optimize Solutions, 68–70

Using Mathematical Models to Make Predictions, 334–339

Using Models to Analyze Systems, 101–102

Using Regional Climate Models, 362–367

Explore First, 26, 62, 108, 144, 488

Analyze Historical Weather, 332

Categorizing Traits, 400

Collecting Water, 236

Compare and Contrast Plant Types, 382

Compare Wall Structures, 4

Comparing Solution Designs, 44

Comparing Temperatures, 198

Determining Density, 288

Evaluating Models, 88

Measuring Wind Direction, 310

Modeling Elephant Ears, 532

Modeling Leaves, 128

Modeling the Rate of Warming, 268

Modeling Reproduction, 456

Modeling Seed Dispersal, 434

Modeling Variation, 416

Moving Boxes, 176

Observe Organisms, 350

Observing Thermal Energy, 216

Temperature and Sea-Level, 508

Water Quality, 552

Will It Float? 288

Explore ONLINE! 6, 10, 12, 50, 90, 104, 138, 178, 182, 199, 273, 294, 329, 333, 391, 392, 435, 441, 468, 520, 553

external environment, 152–153

extinct, 495

extinction, 495, 542, 543

eye, 149, 153

F

Fahrenheit, 240

farm

affects algal blooms, 489, *489*, 505

agricultural runoff from, 100, 557

contour farming, 566

feedback, 152–153

feedback loop, 520

© Houghton Mifflin Harcourt Publishing Company

fertilization, 425, 437, *437*, 459

fertilizer, 557

fibrous root, 134, *134*

filament, 57

fire

in homes, 28–30

wildfire, 99, *99*, 270, *270*, 539

winds moving, 279

fireworks, 190, *190*, 197, *197*

fish

in coral reef, 90, *90*

embryo cell of, 118, *118*

reproduction of, 420, 458, *458*

Fisher, Paul, 70

flagella, 115, *115*

flashlight, 178

floating garbage, 289, *289*, 303, 307, *307*, 485, *485*

flood, 491

flood control, 500, *500*

floragraph, 104, *104*

Florida climate, 364, *364*

Florida panther, 496–497, *496–497*

flow chart, *560*

flower, 131, *131*

flowering seed plant, 437, 441–445

fog

formation of, 223, *223*, 324

in San Francisco, 223, *223*, 265, *265*

food

cooking process, 28–29

cooking with solar energy, 173

plants producing, 133

storage of, 9

in systems, 90

food web, 334, *334*, 535

force

of air pressure, 314

kinetic energy started by, 178, *178*

Ford, Henry, 68

forecasters, 333, 341

forest

California land cover, 387

plants in, 130

formation of hail, 244

formula

cricket chirps, 339, *339*

density, 295

relative humidity, 312, 313, *313*

stomatal percentage, *137*

surface area-to-volume ratio, 121

thermal conductivity, 210, 224

trend lines, 336, *336*

fossil, 514, *514*

fossil fuel, 191, *304*, 496, 519, 523, 531, *531*, 538

fox, *535*

Franklin, Rosalind, 411–412, *412*

Franz Josef Glacier, 527, *527*

fresh water, density of, 295

Fresno, California, 366, *366*

frilled lizard, 96, *96*

frog, 148, *148*, 433, *433*, 462

frontal lobe, 155, *155*

front of weather, 319–32

frozen water, 98, *98*

fruit, 436, *436*

full clone, 419

function

of cell structures, 115–118

structure related to, 19–20

of tissue, 94

fungal infection, 417, *417*

fungi

decomposition by, 99

multicellular organism, 110, 430

sexual and asexual reproduction of, 420, 425, 430

on whitebark pine, 483, *483*

furnace, 567, *567*

G

gamete, 425

garbage, oceans cycling, 303

gases

sound energy vibrating particles of, 182

state of water, 239, *239*, 257

thermal energy's relationship to, 221

gas lamp, 32

gene, 404

differences in, 446

location of, 408, *408*

modeling, 406–407

mutation of, 419

passed from parent to offspring, 408–409

traits influenced by, 404–407, 415

generator, 191

genetic, 459

genetic material

in asexual reproduction, 419, 423–424, *424*, 433, 460

in DNA, 405, *405*, 415

information for cell function, 115, *115*

organisms influenced by, 379–484

passed from parent to offspring, 408–409

in plant cells, 130

reproduction passing down, 418

in sexual reproduction, 419, 425, *425*, 433

variation in, 425, 428, 437, 459, *459*

in zygote, 425

genetics

animal growth affected by, 466–467

animals affected by, 456–473, 477

disease caused by, 407, 466

diversity of, 416–428, 455

plants affected by, 434–450, 455

structures of, 404–407

genotype, 406, 409, *409*, 426–427

geosphere, 97, *97*, 98, 300, 495, 511

geothermal heat pumps, 230, *230*

germination, 446

ghost pepper, 451, *451*

giant mirror, 207, *207*

giant sequoia tree, 130

gill, 148

giraffe, 391, *391*

glacier, 98, 248, *248*, 514, *514*, 516, *516*, 538, *538*

glassware, 7

Glen Canyon Dam, 247

global circulation pattern, 301, *301*

global climate, 510, *510*

global climate change, 485–582

biodiversity, 543

causes of, 514–519

monitoring organism, 545–546, 551

organisms responding, 538–543, 549

organism's survival affected, 532–546

response, adaptation, and extinction, 542, 551

global ocean circulation, 302–303, *302*, 309

global temperature changes, 515, 520, *520*, 538, 539

global wind

belt, 276, *276*

influencing climate, 358

pattern of, 277–278

prevailing wind, 324, 331, 352, *352*, 359

spreading volcanic ash, 280

surface wind, 292

glucose, 112, *112*

Golden Gate Bridge, 223, *223*

golden mole, 394, *394*

goldfish, 466, *466*

golf, 488, *488*

Golgi apparatus, 116, *116*, 117, *117*

grain, *566*

grape tomato, 447, *447*

graph

average weight of adult dormice, *158*

of bacteria population, *424*

Beijing, China's climate, *353*

climate in San Francisco, *352*

of climates, *353*

decision matrix, *48*, *49*, *54*

for developing and testing solutions, *51*

of electrical energy used by a school, *570*

elevation and precipitation, *361*

of Northern cod landings, *502*

for optimizing solutions, *69*

of run times, *336*

of water levels, *556*

weather forecast, *341*, *342*

graphic organizer

for key concepts, *3*, *87*, *175*, *267*, *381*, *487*

of systems, *92*

grasshopper, 566, *566*

grassland, 130, 385, *385*, 566

gravitational potential energy, 180–181, 187, 246

gravitropism, 140

gravity

deep ocean current affected by, 298

plants responding to, 138

water cycle affected by, 251

gravity racer car, 35, *35*

gray whale, 161, *161*

gray wolf, 466, *466*, 535, *535*

Great Basin, 360, *360*

Greener Skies, 581, *581*

Green frog and tadpole, 418, *418*

green hermit hummingbird, 442, *442*

greenhouse, 225, *225*

greenhouse effect, 367–368, 511–513, *511*, 512–513

greenhouse gases

atmosphere changed by, 519

emissions of, 515, 531

humans increasing, 526

landfill producing, 559, *559*

melting permafrost releasing, 520

naturally occurring, 367–368, *368*

reducing, 486

green rooftop, 224, *224*

Grinnell Glacier, Montana, 516, *516*

grizzly bear, 416, *416*, 535

ground tissue, 95, *95*, 131, *131*

groundwater, 246, 251, 555

guanine, 411

guitar, 156, *156*

guppy, 465, *465*

gyres, 292–293, *293*

H

habitat, 490, 496–497, 524, 534–535

hail, 244, 313

hailstones, 244

hair, 149

half sphere, 278

hammer, 181, *181*

hand-powered flashlight, 177, *177*

Hands-On Labs

Compare the Drought Tolerance of Plants, 389–390

Compare Thermal Energy in Objects, 204–205

Design a Method to Monitor Solid Waste from a School, 561–562

Design a Model Car, 37–38, 54–55, 71–72

Design and Test an Insulated Container, 229–230

Evaluate a Method to Reduce the Impact of Solid Waste on the Environment, 569–570

Examine the Transfer of Thermal Energy through Radiation, 222

Explore Density of Differences in Water, 295

Investigate a Technology Inspired by Nature, 19–20

Investigate Flower Structures, 443–444

Investigate the Transfer of Energy, 185

Map Monarch Migration, 540–541

Measure Reaction Time, 159

Measure System Response to Exercise, 150

Model an Air Mass Interaction, 320

Model Asexual and Sexual Reproduction, 426–427

Model Genes and Traits, 406–407

Model Ocean Pollution from Land, 494

Model the Formation of Clouds and Rain, 243

Model the Formation of Wind, 271–272

Model the Greenhouse Effect, 512–513

Model the Growth of an Animal, 471–472

Model Tissue Structure and Function, 94

Model Your Climate, 363

Observe Cells with a Microscope, 113

Observe Transport, 135

© Houghton Mifflin Harcourt Publishing Company

Hands-On Labs (continued)

online, 5, 27, 45, 63, 89, 109, 129, 145, 177, 199, 217, 237, 269, 289, 311, 333, 351, 383, 401, 417, 435, 457, 489, 509, 533, 553

Predict Costs Using a Model, 337–338

Use Cell Models to Investigate Cell Size, 120–121

Hawaiian honeycreeper bird, 543, *543*

hawk moth, 441, *441*

Health Connection

Medical Research, 166

heart, 96, *96*, 103–104, *103*, 148, *148*, 151, *151*

heat, 208

energy flow of, 198–215

energy transfer of, 200–201

sensory receptor's response to, 153

heat transfer

applying concepts of, 225–230

designing solutions for, 227–230

heirloom tomato, 447, *447*

heliconia flower, 442, *442*

Hercules beetle, 442, *442*

hibernation, 158, 392, *392*

high elevation, 352, *352*

highland climate, *364–365*, 386, *386*

Highlands of Scotland, 246, *246*

high-pressure air system

affecting weather, 317–318, 331

effect of Earth's rotation on, 276, *276*

in global wind patterns, 277, *277*

Santa Ana winds, 282, *282*

wind formation caused by, 271–272, *272*, 287

high-pressure belt, 358, *358*

homeostasis, 152–153

honeybee colony loss, 445

horse latitudes, 277, *277*

hot air

in convection cells, 274, *274*, 276, *276*

density of, 272, *272*

in global wind patterns, 277, *277*

hot spring, 421, *421*

hot water, density of, 294–296, *294*, 301, *301*

housefly, 145, *145*, 163, *163*

human

analyzing effects of activities of, 90

in anthroposphere, 100

body system of, 146–151

cerebral cortex, 155, *155*

genetic material of, 404

natural system of, 91

organ transplants, 103–104

problems, 28

human activity

atmosphere pollution caused by, 495, 519

climate change influenced by, 525–526, 531

in Earth systems, 492, 507

environmental impact of, 488–502

improving resource use during, 565

influencing climate change, 508–526

Mississippi River Delta impacted by, 498–501

monitoring environmental impact of, 554–558, 559–562, 575

reducing impact of, 552–570, 575

scale of impact of, 498–502

water pollution caused by, 493, 494

human-built river controls, 499

human exposure to radiation, 503

humid continental climate, *364–365*, *386*, *386*

humidity

in air masses, 319

as component of weather, 312, 384

affecting snowflakes, 327–328

relative, 312, 317

on weather map, *318*

humid subtropical climate, *362*, *364–365*

humid tropical climate, *362*, *364–365*

hurricane

in Baja California, Mexico, 270, *270*

climate change affecting, 525

lightning during, 266

hybrid, 422, *422*

hydra, 423, *423*, 433

hydroelectric dam, 191

hydroelectric power station, *176*

hydrogen, 112, *112*

hydrologist, 253–254

hydrosphere, 97, *97*, 98, 300, 493, 511

hypothalamus gland, 171, *171*

I

ice

climate data in, 514, *514*

on Earth's surface, 248, *248*

as habitat, 508, *508*

melting of, 509, 529, *529*

movement of, 251

recent climate change affecting, 525, *525*

state of water, 239, *239*

ice age, 524

iceberg, 248

ice climber, 352, *352*

immune system, 104

impermeable surfaces, 555, 558, *558*

Incan architecture, 4, *4*

incandescent light bulb, 32, 44, *44*, 57–58, 192

independent variable, 158, 424

indicators of a warming world, 521, *521*

individual in ecosystem, 534, *534*, 542, *542*

infection, viruses causing, 109

infiltration, 246, 250

infographic, 166

information

animal's response to, 157–160

processing of, 149, 152–156

transfers of within a system, 90

infrared photography, 199, *199*, 209, 213, *213*

infrared radiation, 154

infrared sensors, 293, *293*

inheritance, 408

in asexual reproduction, 423, *423*

modeling, 408–410

Punnett squares modeling, 409, *409*

of traits, 403

innate behavior, 157

inorganic matter, 559, *559*

input

into atmosphere, 99, *99*

into cell systems, 118

of energy in radiometer, 218

energy transfer, 186

flashlight, 177, *177*

into hydrosphere, 99, *99*

modeling, 218, 363

into photosynthesis, 129, *129*

into systems, 10, 90

insect, 458, *458*

insecticide-treated mosquito net, 5, *5*

insulated coat, 198, *198*

interaction in systems

causing weather, 310–327, 511

computer modeling, 544

digestive and excretory systems, 147

on Earth, 97, 270, 300, 490

of organism, 534

respiratory and circulatory systems, 148, 151

skeletal and muscular systems, 149

Interactive Review, 25, 43, 61, 77, 107, 127, 143, 165, 197, 215, 235, 257, 287, 309, 331, 349, 371, 399, 415, 433, 455, 477, 507, 531, 551, 575

interior vena cava, *151*

internal environment, 152

internal movement, 149

International Space Station, 139–140

investigation method, of Mendel, 403

investigations

animal behavior, 86

performing, 389

iterative design process, 77

iterative testing of prototype, 69

J

jackrabbit, 536, *536*

jellyfish, 420, *420*

jet stream, 283–284, *283*

joey, 459, *459*

Joshua Tree, 388, *388*, 422, *422*

Joshua Tree National Park, 351, *351*, 369, *369*

joule (J), 181, 203

Juliet tomato, 447, *447*

K

kangaroo, 459, *459*

kangaroo rat, 93, *93*

kelp forest, 537, *537*

key concepts, graphic organizer for, 3, *87*, *175*, 267, *381*, 487

kidney, 103–104, 147, 171, *171*

killdeer bird, 464

kinetic energy

of air particles, 312, *312*

defined, 178–179

in energy transfer, 184–188

loss of, *240*

mass proportional to, 179, 197

measuring, 182, 202, 203, *219*, 221

of melting ice cream, 200, *200*

for sublimation, 242

transfer of, 281, 287

transformation of, 189–192, 197

types of, 181

kingfisher bird, 462

kitten, 401, *401*, 413

koala, 388, 533, *533*, 549, *549*

Komodo dragon, 460, *460*

Köppen-Geiger, 362

Kronotsky Reserve, Russia, 270, *270*

Kwan, Garfield, 166, *166*

L

lactococcus lactis, 424, *424*

lake, 98

Lake City, Colorado, 352, *352*

Lake Tahoe, 98, *98*

land ecosystem, 539

landfill, 559, *559*, 568, *568*

landform

affecting weather, 325, 331

influencing climate, 360, 371, 384

landscape architect, 478

Language Development, 3, 87, *175*, 267, *381*, 487

Language SmArts, 185, 205, 230, 252, 275, 282, 301, 344, 363

Compare and Contrast Information, 322

Compare Asexual and Sexual Reproduction, 428

Construct an Argument, 440

Construct an Explanation of Trait Inheritance, 403

Describe Smartphone Requirements, 30

Describe the Problem Precisely, 30

Describe Weather, 315

Discuss, 387

Evaluate Possible Solutions, 561

Evaluate Reproductive Strategies, 461

Evaluate Text, 546

Explain Limits to Cell Size, 122

Explain Sensory Receptor Patterns, 156

Explain Temperature Ranges on Earth and the Moon, 513

Identify Facts, 492

Identify Influences on Technology, 16

Use Evidence to Support an Argument, 96

Use Observations to Develop an Argument, 136

La Niña, 518, *518*, 539

large intestine, 147, *147*

latitude

influencing climate, 358, *358*, 384

of Sierra Nevada, 393, *393*

sunlight and, 355, *355*, 371

lava lamp, 273, *273*

law of conservation of energy, 180, 189, 218

laws of inheritance, 409

leaf, 133

adaptation of, 388

food production of, 129

of plants, 131, *131*

learned behavior, 157, 473–474

leatherback turtles, 155

left atrium, *151*

leopard, 144, 391, *391*

Lesson Self-Check, 23–25, 41–43, 59–61, 75–77, 105–107, 125–127, 141–143, 163–165, 195–197, 213–215, 233–235, 255–257, 285–287, 307–309, 329–331, 347–349, 369–371, 397–399, 413–415, 431–433, 453–455, 475–477, 505–507, 529–531, 549–551, 573–575

levee, 498–501, *499*

lever, 183

Life Science Connection
Biomedicine, 78

light
plants responding to, 138
sensory receptor's response to, 153

light-emitting diode (LED), 32, 192

light energy, 182

light microscope, 7, *7*, 111

lightning, 266

Liles, Kaitlin, 258, *258*

limestone cave, 248, *248*

limitations, 32–34

lion, 157, *157*, 464

liquid
state of water, 239, *239*, 257
thermal energy's relationship to, 221

litter pick up, 486

living donor, 103

living system
cells as, 108–123
modeling, 93–96
organism as, 93
of plants, 128–138

living thing. *See also* animal; organism; plant
in biosphere, 99
cells making, 110, 127
cell theory defining, 110
characteristics of, 110, 127
in Earth systems, 97
needs of, 490
organisms as, 93
responding to environment, 110
water in, 237

local environment
climate affects, 385, *385*
plants affected by, 448

lock-and-dam system, 499, *499*, 500, *500*

long-nosed bat, 442, *442*

long-range weather forecast, 344

Los Angeles, 357, *357*

Lower Mississippi River levee system, 500, *500*

low-pressure air system
affecting weather, 317–318, 331
Earth's rotation affecting, 276, *276*
in global wind patterns, 277, *277*
Santa Ana winds, 282, *282*
wind formation caused by, 271–272, *272*, 287

low-pressure belt, 358, *358*

luna moth and caterpillar, 418, *418*

lunch carrier, 225–230

lung
in respiratory system, 148, *148*, 151
transplantation of, 103–104

lymphatic system, 148

lysosome, 116, *116*

M

magnetic resonance imaging (MRI), 155, *155*

magnification, 113

Maldives, 236, *236*

mammal
nursing young, 464
reproduction of, 458, *458*

manakin bird, 462, *462*

manure, 100

maple tree, 130, *130*

Margulis, Lynn, 123–124, *123*

Mars, 85

mass
of Earth in geosphere, 98
kinetic energy directly proportional to, 179, 184, 197
thermal energy's relationship to, 221

material
cost and availability of, 33
criteria for umbrella, 31
engineers use of, 6
plants moving, 134
thermal conductor, 227
thermal insulator, 227
thermal properties of, 221–224

mathematical models, 11, 92, 334–339, 349

Matsuda, Shayle, 547–548, *547*

matter
constant motion of particles of, 202
convection causing movement of, 300–301
cycling of in atmosphere, 280, 287
cycling of in oceans, 303–304, 309
in Earth systems, 97
energy flow in, 182
moving through biosphere, 99
transfers of within a system, 90

measurement
of average kinetic energy, 202
energy in units of joule (J), 181
of reaction time, 159
of system responses to exercise, 150
of total kinetic energy, 203

measuring devices, 7, *7*

mechanical energy, 181–182, *183*

mechanical receptor, 154

Mediterranean climate, 364, *364*, 386, *386*

Mediterranean Sea, 299

medium-range weather forecast, 344

meerkat, 473, *473*

memory, 152, **158**

Mendel, Gregor, 402–403, *402–403*, 415, *415*

Mendel's Pea Plant Investigation, *402*, *402*, 409, 415, *415*

mental model, 11

meteoroid, 188, *188*

meteorologist, 341, 345

methane, 368, 520, 559

methods for monitoring, 559–562

metric ruler, 114

Michaud-Larivière, Jérôme, 39

microorganisms, 112

microscope, 6, 111–113

microscopic aquatic organism, 419

microwave sensors, 293, *293*

migration, 161–162, 540–541

milkweed seedling, 439, *439*

mining, 495, 496, 565

mirror, 207, *207*

Mississippi River Delta, 498–501, *498*

Mississippi River watershed, 500, *500*, 501, *501*

mitochondria, 116, *116*, 117, *117*, 123

model

of agricultural runoff, 100

cells, 119–120

climate change, 544

of clouds and rain formation, 243

design a model car, 37–38, 54–55

develop and test lunch containers, 228

of Earth systems, 97–102

effects of Earth's rotation on matter in atmosphere, 275

of elephant ears, 532

energy transformation, 189–192

evaluating, 88

of floating garbage, 289, *289*, 307, *307*

of flow of thermal energy, 219

flow of thermal energy through systems, 218–220

of genes and traits, 406–407

global ocean circulation, 302, *302*

of global winds, 277, *277*

of greenhouse effect, 512–513

helping scientists study natural systems, 88–102, 107

of inheritance of traits, 408–410

mathematical models, 334–339

of nautilus, 334, *334*

of oceans' surface currents, 290–293

physical model, 119

prototype, 51, **65**

of Punnett squares, 409, *409*, 415

regional climate, 362–366

science using, 334–339

sexual and asexual reproduction, 426–427

of stems, 128

of systems, 11, 92

to test design solutions, 65

three-dimensional (3D) model, 119

tissue structure and function, 94

of traits, 456

two-dimensional (2D) model, 119

types of, 11, 92

wall structures, 4

of water cycle, 249

weather forecast, 341–343

weather prediction, 178

wind and convection, 270–275

Mojave Desert, 202, *202*, 323, 351, *351*, 388, *388*, 422, *422*

mollusk, 458, *458*

monarch butterfly, 161, *161*

monitoring human impact

describing methods for, 554–558

developing methods for, 559–562

in neighborhood, 562

monitoring organism, 545–546, *545*, 551, *551*

Moscow, Russia, 365, *365*

mosquito, 543, *543*

mosquito netting, 5, *5*, 16, 23

moss, 437, *437*

moss leaf cell, 118, *118*

moth orchid, 434, *434*

moulting, 149, *149*

mountain aspen, 450, *450*

Mount Everest, 314, *314*

Mount Pinatubo, 519, *519*

mouth, 153

movement

of air pressure, 315

of matter through convection, 300–301

muscular system providing, 149

of water on Earth's surface, 245–248, 253–254, 290–305

muffin design, 64–67

mule deer, 535

multicellular organism

animal, 146

cell specialization in, 93

as living thing, 110

plants as, 130

reproduction of, 419, 429–430

multimedia presentation, 363, 372, 396, 452

muscle tissue, 146

muscular system, 149, *149*

Music Connection

Songs about Saving Earth, 576

mutation of DNA, 407

N

Namib desert, 129, *129*, 141, *141*

National Aeronautics and Space Administration (NASA), 73–74, 290

natural gas plant, 558, *558*

naturally radioactive rocks, 98

natural resource, 490

availability of, 14, 563–564

quality of, 556–558, 565

reuse and recycling of, 564, *564*

technology's use of, 14

use of, 490, 554–556, 563–564

natural system

characteristic of, 91

defining, 91

interactions of, 89

models of, 92

properties of, 91

using models to study, 88–102

nautilus, 146, *146*, 334, *334*

nectar, 441

needs, 28, 31–34

negative feedback, 148–149

negatively charged particles, 182

nerve

in animals, 149

impulses in, 108, *108*

nervous system, 149

nervous tissue, 146

neuron, 153, *153*, 155, *155*

New Mexico whiptail lizard, 419

Newton's cradle, 187, *187*, 189, *189*, 197, *197*

New York City, 571, *571*
New Zealand mud snail, 458, *458*
Nicholson, Simon, 576
night blooming plant, 441
nitrogen
  in agricultural runoff, 100
  in atmosphere, 98, 241
  cycling of in atmosphere, 280
  plants need of, 133
nitrous oxide, *368*
nonflowering seed plant, 438, *438*
nonliving thing
  cells lacking in, 110
  in Earth systems, 97
nonpoint-source pollution, 493, 494
nonrenewable resource, 563
nonvascular plant, 131
noria, 193–194
northeast trade winds, 277, *277*
North Equatorial Current, 292
Northern cod, 502, *502*
Northern Hemisphere, 278, *278*
North Pacific Current, 292
nose, 153
nuclear cooling pool, 219, *219*
nuclear energy, 181, 182, 219, 503
nuclear fuel rods, 216, *216*, 219, *219*
nucleotide, 411
nucleus, 116, **116**, *116*, 117, *117*
nutrient
  in agricultural runoff, 102
  in algal bloom, 489
  from animals, 132
  in fertilizer, 501
  ocean cycling, 302, 359, 539
  from plants, 441
  plant systems processing, 131,
    133–136, 417
  respiratory and circulatory system
    transporting, 93, 95, 148
  in soil, 133, 143, 557
  water cycling, 542
nymph, 458

O

obelisk, 183, *183*
observation
  of cells under a microscope,
    111–113
  of energy transfer, 184–188
  of thermal energy, 216
occipital lobe, 155, *155*
occluded front, 322
ocean
  absorbing solar energy, 270
  algal blooms in, 489, *489*
  carbon dioxide in, 303, 304, 539
  changes of salinity in, 297–298
  circulation of, 245–246, 257, 300–
    305, *302*, 517, *517*
  convection currents in, 300–301
  currents of, 245, *245*, 250, *250*, 289,
    290, 300–305, 359, *359*, 371
  cycling of matter in, 303–304, 517,
    517
  density of water in, 297–298
  energy flow in, 174, *174*, 517, *517*
  floating garbage in, *289*
  influencing climate, 359, *359*, 384,
    399
  movement of water in, 288–305
  as part of hydrosphere, 300
  patterns in, 290
  physical oceanographer studying,
    305–306
  pollution from land in, 494
  recent climate change affecting,
    525, *525*
  surface currents of, 290–293, 324
  surface temperatures of, 293, *293*
  temperature rising in, 297–298,
    532, *532*, 539, *539*
  volume of, 238, 300
  wind transferring kinetic energy to,
    281
ocean current, 290
Ochoa, Ellen, 73–74, *73*
ochre sea star, 532, *532*
ocotillo, 382, *382*
octopus, 464

odor memory, 158
offspring, 418
  in asexual reproduction, 419, 421,
    422, *422*, 423–424, *424*, 433
  genetic variation in, 425
  as hybrids, *422*
  organisms producing, 418
  parent passing traits to, 400–410,
    421
  parents protecting, 464
  parents teaching, 473–474, *473*
  of plants, 436, *436*
  reproductive success resulting in,
    462–465
  in sexual reproduction, 419, 421,
    422, *422*, 423, 425, *425*, 433, 459,
    459
  survival of, 420
okapi, 146, *146*
olfactory, 162
one-horned rhino, 542, *542*
online activities
  Hands-On Labs, 19, 37, 54, 71, 94,
    113, 120, 135, 150, 159, 185, 204,
    222, 229, 243, 271, 295, 320, 337,
    363, 389, 406, 426, 443, 471, 494,
    512, 540, 561, 569
  Take It Further, 21, 39, 57, 73, 103,
    123, 139, 161, 193, 211, 231, 253,
    283, 305, 327, 345, 367, 395, 411,
    429, 451, 473, 503, 527, 547, 571
  Unit Project Worksheet, 2, 86, 174,
    266, 380, 486
  You Solve It, 1, 85, 173, 265, 379,
    485
onyanga, 129, *129*
open kitchen fires, 28–29
open-mindedness, 47
orangutan, 474, *474*
organ, 95
  of animals, 146
  brain, 149
  ear, 149
  eye, 149
  of plants, 131, *131*, 133, 143
  sensory organ, 153
  subsystem of different tissue types,
    95

organelle, 115, **115**, *115*, 130
organic matter, 280, 559, *559*
organism, 93. *See also* **animal; plant**
  adaptation of, 391, 421
  binary fission reproducing, 419, *419*
  carbon in, 304, *304*
  cells of, 93
  climate change affecting, 532–546
  climate influencing, 387–390
  decomposition of, 304, *304*
  environmental and genetic
    influences on, 379–484
  environment influencing
    reproduction of, 421
  interaction in systems, 90
  as living systems, 93–96, 107
  multicellular, 93, 110
  needs of, 388
  producing offspring, 418
  responding to climate change,
    538–543
  scientist monitoring and tracking,
    545–546, 551
  subsystems of, 93
  tissues of, 93–94
  unicellular, 93, 110
  water needs of, 238
organ system, 95
  of animals, 146
  of frilled lizard, 96, *96*
  of plants, 131, *131*, 143
  subsystem of group of organs, 95
Origin of Eukaryotic Cells **(Margulis),**
    123
output
  by atmosphere, 99, *99*
  from cell systems, 118
  energy transfer, 186
  flashlight, 177, *177*
  by hydrosphere, 99, *99*
  modeling, 218, 363
  from photosynthesis, 133, *133*
  from systems, 10, 90
ovary, 443, *443*
ovule, 438

oxygen
  during algal bloom, 489, *489*, 500
  in atmosphere, 98, 241
  in Biosphere 2, 89
  in glucose, 112, *112*
  nonliving thing, 110
  oceans cycling, 303
  respiratory system using, 148
  in space station, 139
ozone, *368*

P

Pacific Flyway, 470, *470*
Pacific Ocean
  affecting weather, 324, 325, 331
  surfing in, 352, *352*
Pacific salmon, 458, *458*
paddle boat, 194
paleoclimate data, 514–515, *515*
palm seed, 439, *439*
Panama disease, 417, *417*, 428, 431,
    435
pancreas, 171, *171*
pangolin, 144, *144*
parachute design, 52–53, 56
paramecia
  cilia, 112
  magnification of, 112, *112*
  unicellular, 110
parathyroid, 171, *171*
parent
  in asexual reproduction, 419, 421,
    422, *422*, 423–424, *424*, 433
  behaviors of, 464
  hybrids of, *422*
  passing traits to offspring, 400–410,
    425
  producing offspring, 418
  reproductive success of, 462–465
  in sexual reproduction, 419, 421,
    422, *422*, 423, 425, *425*, 433, 459,
    459
  teaching offspring, 473–474, *473*
parenting behavior, 464
parietal lobe, 155, *155*
parrotfish, 90
patent, 58

pattern
  of air circulation, 275–277
  of air movement in atmosphere,
    268–287
  of deep ocean currents, 298–299
  of global ocean circulation, 302, *302*
  of global winds, 277–278, *277*
  gyres, 292–293, *293*
  in ocean, 290
  of sensory receptors, 156
  of snowflakes, 327–328
  in water density, 296
  of water movement on Earth's
    oceans, 288–305
  on weather map, *318*
  in weather prediction, 332–344
peacock, 463, *463*
pedicel, 443, *443*
pendulum, 180, 186
penguin, 464, *464*
People in Engineering: Liles, Kaitlin,
    283, *283*
People in Engineering: Ochoa, Ellen,
    73–74, *73*
People in Science: Bañuelos, Gary,
    395–396
People in Science: Chargaff, Erwin,
    411–412
People in Science: Crick, Francis,
    411–412
People in Science: Franklin,
    Rosalind, 411–412
People in Science: Kwan, Garfield,
    166, *166*
People in Science: Margulis, Lynn,
    123–124, *123*
People in Science: Matsuda, Shayle,
    547–548, *547*
People in Science: Nicholson,
    Simon, 576
People in Science: Persad, Geeta G.,
    527–528, *527*
People in Science: Puniwai, Noelani,
    372
People in Science: Shepherd,
    J. Marshall, 345–346, *345*
People in Science: Snetsinger,
    Phoebe, 478
People in Science: von Ahn, Luis,
    78, *78*
People in Science: Watson, James,
    411–412

permafrost, 509, 520, 525, *525*, 529, *529*

Peru Current, 292

pesticide, 557

petal, 443, *443*

phenotype, 406, 409, *409*, 426–427

phloem, 134

phosphate, 411

phosphorus
    in agricultural runoff, 100
    in Amazon jungle, 269, *269*
    cycling of in atmosphere, 280
    plants need of, 133

photograph, infrared photography, 199, *199*, 209

photosynthesis
    in biosphere, 99
    in carbon cycle, 304, *304*
    food production of, 133
    of marine organisms, 303
    organ systems performing, 95
    plants performing, 130, 449, *449*
    in space station, 140

phototropism, 138

pH scale, 448, *448*

physical adaptation, 392, *392*

physical disabilities, 15

physical model
    of cities affecting rainfall, 346
    of Earth, 89, *89*, 275
    formation of wind, 271
    of greenhouse effect, 512–513
    prototypes as, 51
    of systems, 92
    three-dimensional (3D) model, 102, 119
    use of, 11

physical oceanographer, 305–306

Physical Science Connection
    transmission electron microscopes, 166

phytoremediation of soil, 395

pineal gland, 171, *171*

Pineapple Express precipitation, 325, *325*

pistil, 442, *442*

pizza, 211–212, *211–212*

pizza stone, 211, *211*

planaria, 460, *460*

plankton, *303*

planned public transportation, 571

plant. *See also* living thing; organism
    adaptation of, 382–394, 421
    algal bloom affecting, 500
    analyze body system of, 132, 143
    animal influence by, 388
    asexual reproduction of, 419–420, 423–424, 440
    body system of, 131–132
    cell structure of, 117, *117*
    cell types of, 131, *131*
    chloroplast in, 116
    climate change affecting, 539
    climate influencing, 387–390
    drought tolerance of, 389–390
    environmental factors affecting, 421, 434–450
    eukaryotic cells of, 116, *116*
    extinction of, 495
    factors affecting, 446–450
    flowering and nonflowering seed plant, 438, *438*
    gravitropism, 140
    growing in space, 139–140
    hybrids of, 447
    as living system, 128–138
    magnification of, 112, *112*
    Mendel's Pea Plant Investigation, 402, *402*
    multicellular organism, 110
    needs of, 388, 446
    organs of, 134
    photosynthesis of, 99
    phototropism, 138
    producing offspring, 418
    reproduction structures in, 436–440, *436*, 442, *442*, 443–444, *443*, 455
    responding to environment, 137–138, 143
    seedless plant, 437, *437*
    sexual reproduction of, 419–420, 425, 437–439, 455

similar environments produce similar adaptation, 394
    specialized cell of, 93
    vascular and nonvascular, 131
    water vapor from, 242

plant breeder, 447

plantlet, 440

Point Reyes National Seashore, 268, *268*

point-source pollution, 493, 494

polar bear, 478, *478*

polar climate, *364–365*

polar easterlies, 277, *277*

polar ice cap, 517

polar jet stream, 283, *283*

pollen, 419, 438, 441, 442

pollination, 438, 441–444, *442*

pollinator, 442, *442*, 445

pollution
    agricultural runoff, 100
    of carbon into atmosphere, 101
    cells affected by, 166
    concentration levels of, 556
    as harmful input, 90
    human activity causing, 491
    modeling of, 494
    nonpoint-source, 493
    plants removal of, 136
    point-source, 493
    testing for, 557, *557*
    in watershed, 501, *501*

polyp, 420, *420*

pomegranate tree, 436, *436*

Ponderosa pine tree, 93, *93*

population
    adaptation of, 542, *542*
    of ecosystem, 534, *534*
    in New York City and Tokyo, 571, *571*
    in Yellowstone Park, 535, *535*

porcupines, 157, *157*

positive feedback, 152–153, 523

postdoctoral research scientist, 527–528

potato, 440, *440*

potential energy
    changes in, 180–181, 197
    in energy transfer, 184–187
    transformation of, 189–192
    types of, 181

power plant, 567, *567*

precipitation, 244
  in California, 361, *361*
  cities affecting, 345
  as component of weather, 312
  formation of, 313
  in fronts, 321–322
  Pineapple Express, 325, *325*
  prediction of, 344, *344*
  in San Francisco, 352, *352*
  in Sierra Nevada, 393, *393*
  in water cycle, 250, *250*, 257
  on weather map, *318*
prediction
  air mass interaction, 320
  with climate graphs, 353
  energy transfer, 184
  of genotype and phenotype,
    426–427
  of growth of blackbuck antelope,
    472
  kinetic energy versus speed, 179
  from models, 334, *334*
  of mutation, 407
  of outcomes, 400
  of shipping costs, 337, *337*
  using mathematical models,
    334–339
  of weather based on patterns,
    332–344
  of weather forecast, 340–344, *340*
pressure, sensory receptor's
  response to, 153
pressure system, types of, 317
pressure-treated wood, 559
prevailing wind, 324, 331, 352, *352*,
  359, 371
prickly pear cactus, 396, *396*, 444,
  444
probability in math, 410, 543
process
  iterative design process, 69–70
  for optimization, 68
processing information, 155–156,
  165
prokaryotic cell, 115, *115*, 123
pronghorn, 468, *468*
property of matter, 210
property of systems, 91
proportions in system models, 11

prosthetics, 18, *18*
protein, 115, **404**
prototype, 51, 65
pulmonary artery, *151*
pulmonary vein, *151*
Puniwai, Noelani, 372
Punnett square, 409, *409*, 410, *410*,
  447, *447*, 484

Q

quality of life, 18
quantities in system models, 11
questions
  asking, 2, 22, 29
  defining engineering problems, 29
  generating, 2
quino checkerspot butterfly, 542,
  542

R

radiant thermal energy, 225
radiation
  Earth emitting, 354, *354*, 511, *511*
  energy transfer by, 209, 210, 215,
    215, 219 ·
  from the sun, 281, *281*
  warming the ocean, 303
radiation sickness, 503
radioactive contamination, 395
radiometer, 218, *218*
rain
  cause of, *310*
  cities affecting, 345
  formation of, 313
raincoat design, 67
rain-shadow effect, 325
rat, 93, *93*
reaction time, 159
reasoning, 23, 41
recent climate change, 520–523
receptacle, 443, *443*
recessive allele, 426
recessive gene, 404
recessive trait, 403
recycling, 139, 493, *493*, 564, *564*,
  579, *579*
red blood cell, 95, *95*

red rock crab, 146, *146*
Red Savina habanero, 451, *451*
red squirrel, 464, *464*
redwood tree, 388, *388*, 420
reef ball, 102, *102*
reef ecosystem, 90, *90*, 91
refrigerator, 258, *258*
regional climate model, 362–366
relationship
  animal behavior and reproductive
    success, 462–465
  between science, engineering, and
    technology, 6–9
  cause and effect, 555
  digestive and excretory systems,
    147
  in ecosystem, 334, *334*
  elevation and precipitation, 361
  models to understand, 11
  organism's adaptations and
    environment, 534–537
  plants and environments, 143
  reproduction and genetic variation,
    423–428
  respiratory and circulatory systems,
    148, 151
  skeletal and muscular systems, 149
  structure and function, 19–20
  surface area-to-volume ratio to
    movement, 121
  temperature and thermal energy,
    202–207
  of traits to genetic structure,
    404–407
  between variables, 297, *297*
relative humidity, 312, 317
renewable energy, 194
renewable resource, 502, 556, 563
reproduction
  animal behaviors affecting, 462–465
  of animals, 458–461
  of cells, 110, *110*
  in changing conditions, 421

reproduction (continued)

environmental influences on, 421

factors influencing, 429–430

genetic diversity in, 416–428

of Joshua Trees, 422, *422*

organs for, 442, *442*

of plants, 434–445

in stable conditions, 421

structures for, 436–440, *436*, 442, *442*, 443–444, *443*, 455

types of, 418–422, 433

reproductive success, 459, 462

reptiles, reproduction of, 420

reservoirs, 247

resource

availability of, 563–564

depletion of, 491

quality of, 556–558, 565

reuse and recycling of, 564, *564*

use of, 490, 554–556, 563–564

respiration, 242, 304, *304*

respiratory system, 92, *92*, 148, 151

review

Interactive Review, 25, 43, 61, 77, 107, 127, 143, 165, 197, 215, 235, 257, 287, 309, 331, 349, 371, 399, 415, 433, 455, 477, 507, 531, 551, 575

Unit Review, 79–82, 167–170, 259–262, 373–376, 479–482, 577–580

ribosome, 115, *115*, 116, *116*, 117, *117*

right atrium, *151*

right ventricle, *151*

Rio Grande, 253, *253*, 254

risk-benefit analysis, 49

river

Mississippi River Delta, 498–501

water and wind shaping, 98

river otter, 474, *474*

roadrunner, 383, 397, *397*

robin, 459, *459*

rock

carbon in, 304, *304*

climate data in, 514, *514*

nonliving thing, 110

rocket car, *1*

rooftop albedo, 357, *357*

root system, 131, *131*, 134, **134**, *134*, 388

roseate spoonbill, 458

rough endoplasmic reticulum, 116, *116*, 117, *117*

Rub'al Khali desert, 365, *365*

rubber tree, 394

runoff, 246, 250

S

sacred lotus flower, 435, *435*

saguaro cactus, 130, *130*

Sahara, 269, *269*, 285, *285*

Saharan Desert, *384*

salivary gland, 147, *147*

salmon, 162, *162*

salt

changes in levels of, 297–298

from excretory system, 147

in soil, 450

salt water

density of, 295

dissolved matter in, 303

large volume of Earth's water, 238, 245

salinity of, 91, 295

San Clemente, 352, *352*

San Diego County, 279, *279*

San Francisco, 352, *352*

San Francisco Bay, 223, *223*, 265, *265*

Santa Ana winds, 279, *279*

Santa Paula, 270, *270*

satellite images

of California, *323*

of deforestation, 554, *554*

ocean surface currents, 288, *288*

scientist using, 334, *334*

of urban heat island, 217, *217*

satellites, 85

scale (on animals), 144, *144*

scale (proportion)

of convection, 274, *274*

drawing to, 114

of health problems, 29

humans' environmental impact, 498–502, 507

under microscope, 113

in system models, 11

of technology, 25

science, 6

careers in, 305–306, 527–528

engineering and society and, 4–23

models in, 334–344

relationship to engineering and technology, 6–9

technology influenced by, 14, 16

scientific models, 11

scientific understanding, 14

scientist

define and study systems, 90–92

engineering practices compared to, 51

gathering data, 545–546, 551, 557

modeling natural systems, 92

monitoring environment, 563, 575

types of microscopes used by, 111

understanding how natural systems function and change, 91

using engineer designed tools, 6

using models to study natural systems, 88–102

Scoville scale, 451

seahorse, 380, *380*

sea ice, 98

seal, 391, *391*, 459, *459*, 462, 508, *508*

sea level, 498, 525

seasons, climate change affecting, 539

sea star, 532, *532*

Seattle, 581, *581*

Seattle-Tacoma Airport, 581, *581*

seed, 438, 444, *444*, 446

seedless plant, 437

selenium, 395

Self-Check, 84, 172, 264, 378, 484, 582

semiarid climate, 386, *386*

semidesert, 387, *387*

sensory information, 153, *153*, 155–156

sensory organ, 153

sensory receptor, 153, *153*, 154, 156

sepal, 443, *443*

serval, 154, *154*

sex cell, 425

sexual reproduction, 419
of animals, 458, 459, *459*, 477
asexual reproduction compared
with, 428
defined, 419–420
environmental influences on,
421–422
genetic variation in, 423, 425, *425*
modeling, 426–427
of plants, 437–439, 455
shake table, 4, 11, *11*
sharks, 90
shelter, 90
Shepherd, J. Marshall, 345–346, *345*
Shishmaref, Alaska, 509, *509*
shoot system, 95, 131, *131*
short-range weather forecast, 344
short-term climate cycle, 518, *518*
shrub, 387, *535*
Sierra Nevada, 323, 350, *350*, 393,
393
silkworm, 154, *154*
simulation
crash testing, 12
of engineered systems, 10, 11
of natural systems, 11
types of, 11
Sinopoda, 394, *394*
skeletal system, 149, *149*
skin
epithelial tissue, 146
part of nervous system, 149
as sensory organ, 153
transplantation of, 103
sleet, 313
small intestine, 147, *147*
smooth endoplasmic reticulum,
116, *116*, 117, *117*
smooth muscle tissue, 95, *95*
Snetsinger, Phoebe, 478
snow, 98, *98*, 244, *311*
snowflakes, 327–328, *327*
snowy tree cricket, 339, *339*
soapbox car racing, *35*
social awareness, 15
Social Studies Connection
Alaskan Inuit Culture, 372, *372*
Chilling Out, 258
Epic Failures, 78
Science and Activism, 576

society
adjustments for needs of, 39–40
engineering and science and, 4–23
technology influenced by, 15, 16,
25, 32
technology's impact on, 17–20, 25
soil
acidity of, 448
carbon in, 304, *304*
conservation techniques, 566, *566*
during Dust Bowl, 566, *566*
matter from organisms in, 99
quality of, 556–558
salinity of, *450*
soil fungus, 417
soil scientist, 395
solar energy
for cooking food, 173
Earth system's use of, 511, *511*
improving use of, 526
in space station, 139
storing energy of, 207
solar oven, 210, *210*, 215
solar panel, 139, 191
solar power plant, 207
solar system, 90
solar water heater, 220, *220*
solid
sound energy vibrating particles of,
182
state of water, 239, *239*, 257
thermal energy's relationship to,
221
solid waste, 559, 561–562, 568–570
solution
brainstorming, 46, 47, 54, 57, 227,
228
combining best parts of, 72
decision-making tool, 48–49, 50
developing and testing, 44, 46–49,
51–53, *51*
evaluate advantages and
disadvantages, 65
evaluating and testing, 50–56, 59
identifying characteristics of, 67,
228
improving, 64–67
making tradeoff, 65
open-mindedness and, 47

optimizing, 62–72, 69, 75, 77
risk-benefit analysis, 49
selecting promising, 49
selecting with decision-making tool,
48–49
tradeoff, 49
using data to optimize, 68–70
song sparrow, 421, *421*
Sonoran Desert, 469
Sonoran pronghorn, 468–469, *468*,
469
sound energy, 181, 182, 190, *190*, 191
sound wave, 154
southeast trade winds, 277, *277*
Southern Hemisphere, 278, *278*
space pen, 70, *70*
Space Shuttle Discovery, 73
specialized cell, 93, 94, 112, *112*
special junctions in heart, 96
species, 534, *534*, 542, *542*, 543, *543*
**speed, kinetic energy proportional
to,** 179
sperm
of aggregating anemone, 461, *461*
of flowering plants, 441
of seedless plants, 437, *437*
of seed plants, 438
in sexual reproduction, 425, *425*
spider, 154, *154*, 463, *463*
spider plant, 440
sponge, 146, 460, *460*
spore, 437, *437*
squirrel, 444, 464, *464*
stamen, 442, *442*
state of matter, 221
stationary front, 322
steam turbine, 567, *567*
steel, 223
stem, 134
of plants, 131, *131*
water movement through, 135
stigma, 443, *443*
stimuli, 153, 157
stoma, 136, *136*, 137, *137*, 143, *143*
stomach, 147, *147*
stored energy, 180–181
storm, causes of, *311*
St. Peter's Square, 183, *183*,
Strait of Gibraltar, 299
Strait of Juan de Fuca, 245, *245*

strawberry plant, 430

street lighting, 32, *32*

structure
  of coral reefs, 90, *90*
  of *E. coli* bacteria, 93, *93*
  function related to, 19–20
  of nerve cells, 108, *108*
  of tissue, 94

style (of flower), 443, *443*

sublimation, 241, **242**, *242*, 250, *250*

subsystem
  of circulatory system, 148
  circulatory system, 93, 95
  of Earth, 97–102, 107
  immune system, 104
  organs as, 95
  respiratory system, 93
  smallest subsystem of organism, 93–94
  tissue, 93–94

subtropical jet stream, 283, *283*

sugar
  in DNA, 411
  movement of through plants, 134
  from photosynthesis, 133

sun
  atmosphere receives energy from, 98
  Earth and climate powered by, 354
  energy from, 182, *182*, 281, *281*
  energy from for wind formation, 270

sundew, 132, *132*

Sun Gold tomato, 447, *447*

sunlight
  absorption of, 354, *354*, 511, *511*
  affecting climate, 354–357, 371, 511, *511*
  hitting Earth's surface, 355, *355*, 511, *511*
  latitude and, 355, *355*, 371
  plant cells absorbing, *112*, 130
  reflection of, 354, *354*, 511, *511*
  in temperate rain forest, 385, *385*
  water cycle affected by, 251

sunspot activity, 516

superior vena cava, *151*

surface area, calculating, 120–121

surface area-to-volume ratio, 120–121

surface current
  continent's effect on, 292, 309
  Coriolis effect, 309
  Coriolis effect on, 292
  defined, 246
  formation of, 290–291
  gyres patterns of, 292–293, *293*
  modeling, 290–293, *291*
  satellite images of, 288, *288*
  surface wind transferring energy to, 292

surface water, 251, 558, *558*

surface wind
  direction of, 276, *276*
  modeling, *291*
  transferring energy to surface currents, 292

suspension bridge, 62, *62*

system, **10**, **90**, **218**
  of animals, 146–151
  boundaries of, 91, 218
  of cells, 115–118
  components of, 10
  defining, 90–92
  digestive, 147
  energy flow in, 173–264
  energy loss in, 191–192
  engineered systems, 10, 25
  excretory, 147
  interaction in, 107
  living, 93–96
  modeling, 92
  models of, 11
  muscular, 149, *149*
  natural systems, 10, 25
  nervous system, 149
  nonvascular, 131
  optimizing solutions, 68
  of plants, 128–138
  properties of, 91
  radiometer as, 218
  skeletal, 149, *149*
  using thermal energy transfer in, 216–235
  vascular, 131

T

table
  of adaptations, 392, *392*
  of calculations, 66

of cause and effect, *470*

of criteria and constraints, *34*, *42*, *46*, *569*

of data, *296*, *337*, *465*

decision matrix, *48*, *386*

of dispersal method, *439*

energy used by light bulbs, *192*

of estimates, *361*

of facts and opinions, *546*

of monarch migration, *540–541*

of natural system, *91*

of observations, *294*

for order of importance of criteria, *33*

of paleoclimate data, 515, *515*

of population in Yellowstone National Park, *535*

of precisely stated problems, *30*

of questions, *35*

relative humidity, *313*

of reproduction, *422*, *426*, *427*, *440*, *458*

of run times, *335*

snowflake types, *328*

of test data, *54*, *56*

thermal conductivity, *224*, *227*

of traits, *426*

Take It Further
  Capsaicin Levels in Peppers, 451–452
  Careers in Science: Physical Oceanographer, 305–306
  Careers in Science: Postdoctoral Research Scientist, 527–528
  Chernobyl Nuclear Disaster, 503–504
  Design of the Incandescent Light Bulb, 57–58
  Designing an Efficient Lunch Line, 21–22
  Ellen Ochoa, Electrical Engineer, 73–74
  Energy Conservationist, 231–232
  Exploring the Greenhouse Effect, 367–368
  Factors That Influence Reproduction, 429–430
  Growing Plants in Space, 139–140
  Harnessing Wind Energy, 39–40

Heat and Cooking, 211–212

Hydrologist, 253–254

Jet Streams, 283–284

Lynn Margulis, Biologist, 123–124

Migration, 161–162

Moving Water Uphill, 193–194

People in Science: Bañuelos, Gary, 395–396

People in Science: Chargaff, Erwin, 411–412

People in Science: Crick, Francis, 411–412

People in Science: Franklin, Rosalind, 411–412

People in Science: Shepherd, J. Marshall, 345–346

People in Science: Watson, James, 411–412

Snowflake Sizes and Patterns, 327–328

Teaching Offspring, 473–474

Transplantation, 103–104

Urban Planning to Reduce Impact, 571–572

taproot, 134, *134*

tarantula, 536, *536*

technology, 6

  development and use of, 565

  influences on, 13–16, 25

  as part of anthroposphere, 100

  reducing human impact with, 563

  relationship to science and engineering, 6–9

  scientific tools, 6–7, 111

  society affected by, 17–20

Teddy bear cactus and clone, 418, *418*

teeth, 147

telescope, 6

temperate rain forest, 385, *385*

temperature, 202

  affecting energy transfer, 200–201, 208, 220, 223

  in air masses, 319, 321

  animal response to, 152, *152*

  average kinetic energy, 202, 215

  in California, 324

  causing movement, 270

changing water density, 294–299, *294*

  comparing, 198

  as component of weather, 312, 384

  for cooking food, 211

  differences in, 208, 215

  on Earth, 513

  affecting snowflakes, 327–328

  of global air and water, 101

  in global climate change, 515, 520, *520*, 538, 539

  greenhouse effect, 367–368

  greenhouse effect regulating, 511

  influencing climate, 358

  infrared photography capturing, 199

  in nuclear cooling pool, 219

  of oceans' surface, 293

  ranges of on moon and Earth, 513

  in San Francisco, 352, *352*

  systematic measurement of, 514

  thermal energy's relationship to, 202–207, 221

  in urban heat island, 217

  on weather map, *318*

temporal lobe, 155, *155*

tensile strength testing, 50, *50*

thermal battery, 207

thermal conductivity, 210, 224, *224*, 227, *227*

thermal conductor, 227, 235

thermal energy, 203

  ambient temperature, 220

  analyze loss of, 201

  applying concepts of transfer of, 225–230

  changes in, 223

  comparing amounts of, 204–205, 206

  conduction transfer, 209

  convection transfer, 209

  for cooking food, 211

  energy form of, 181

  energy transfer of, 208, 224

  for evaporating water, 241

  factors affecting, 205, 235

  flow of, 219, 235

  in geosphere, 98

modeling flow of, 218–220

  of objects, 221–223

  ocean currents affected by, 303

  radiation transfer, 209

  state of water changed by, 239–240, *240*

  temperature's relationship to, 202–207

  total kinetic energy, 203, 215, *219*, 221

  transfer of, 567, *567*

  transfer of in atmosphere, 281, *281*, 287

  uses of, 190, *190*

  using energy transfer in systems, 216–235

  in water cycle, 251

thermal insulator, 227, 235

thermal mass, 225, 235

thermal properties

  of materials, 221–224

  of substances, 223–224

thornback ray, 418, *418*

three-dimensional (3D) model, 119, *119*

3D-printed coral skeletons, 102

Three Gorges Dam hydroelectric power station, 176, *176*, 492

thunderstorm, 266

thymine, 411

thymus, 171, *171*

thyroid gland, 171, *171*

tidal energy, 191

tiger shark, 147, *147*

tissue, 93

  in heart, 96, *96*

  model structure and function of, 94

  of plants, 131, *131*, 134, 143

  subsystems of an organism, 93

  types of, 95, *95*, 146

toilet, 564, *564*

Tokyo, 571, *571*

tomato, 447, *447*

tool

  for decision making, 48–49

  engineers developing, 28

  for mechanical energy, 183, *183*

  metric ruler, 114

  microscope, 19, 111–114

tools, 6
Tottori sand dune, 352, *352*
touchscreens, 72
tradeoff, 49, 497
trait, 402
  of animals, 466–467
  inheriting from parent, 400–410, 413
  modeling, 406–407
  modeling inheritance of, 408–410
  of pea plants, 402, *402*
  relating to genetic structure, 404–407, 415
  reproduction passing down, 391
  selective breeding of, 467
transformation of energy, 189–192
transmission electron microscopes, 166
transpiration, 241, **242**, *242*, 250, *250*
transplantation of organ and organ systems, 103–104
transportation system, 16
trebuchet, 26, *26*
tree
  dragon blood tree, 128, *128*
  as living thing, 93
  maple tree, 130, *130*
  rings of, 514, *514*
tree frog, 458
treehouse design, 27, *27*, 41
trend, 555, *555*, 556, *556*
Truckee, California, 341, *341*, 342, *342*, 366, *366*
tuber, 440, *440*
tufa pinnacles, 98, *98*
tundra, *394*
Tunguska, Siberia, 188, *188*
two-dimensional (2D) model, 119, *119*
typhoon, 525

U

ultraviolet light, 154
umbrella design, 31, *31*, 34
unicellular
  asexual reproduction of, 419
  as living thing, 110
unicellular organism, 93
United States Geological Survey (USGS), 554

Unit Performance Task
  How can air travel be improved to reduce impacts on Earth systems? 581–582
  How can dehydration be prevented? 171–172
  How can you cool water faster? 263–264
  Save the Whitebark Pines! 483–484
  What Influences Marine Layers in California? 377–378
  What is the best feature for a new pool entry ramp? 83–84
Unit Project Worksheet
  Community Climate Change, 486
  Energy Flow in the Earth System, 174
  Investigate an Animal Behavior, 86
  Investigate Severe Weather, 266
  Optimize a Race Track, 2
  Unique Reproductive Behaviors, 380
Unit Review, 79–82, 167–170, 259–262, 373–376, 479–482, 577–580
urban heat island, 217, *217*, 224, *224*, 233, *233*
urbanized land use in Austin, Texas, *555*
urban planners, 571–572
urchin, 90, *90*
ureter, 171, *171*
urethra, 171, *171*
urinary bladder, 171, *171*
U.S. Clean Air Act, 15
U.S. Clean Water Act, 15

V

vacuole, 117, *117*, 130
variable, 158, 424, 555, *555*
vascular plant, 131
vascular system, 131
vascular tissue, 93, 95, *95*, 131, *131*
Vatican Obelisk, 183, *183*
velocity, 179
Venn diagram, *134*, 394, 428
Venus flytrap, 137
video game character, 151
video game system, 90
virus particle, 109, *109*, 125
visible light, 199
visual memory, 158

volcano
  ash from in atmosphere, 280, 519, *519*
  in carbon cycle, 304, *304*
  scientists studying, 6, *6*
volcanologist, 6, *6*
volume, calculating, 120–121
von Ahn, Luis, 78, *78*

W

walking stick insect, 458, *458*
wall structures, 4
warm front, 321
waste
  from human activities, 559–562, 568–570
  plants removal of, 133, 136
water
  algal bloom affecting, 489, 500
  analyzing, 238–240
  carbon dioxide in, 539
  changing states of, 239–240, *239*
  circulation of, 98, 245
  condensation of, 243
  conservation of, 563
  copper in, 557
  cycling of in atmosphere, 280
  density of, 294–299, *294*, *297*, 301, *301*, 303
  energy flows through, 208, 303
  energy transferring from, 187, 303
  erosion by, 98
  evaporation of, 241
  global warming of, 101
  gravitational potential energy of, 181, 187
  in hydrosphere, 98, *98*
  importance of, 238
  movement of, 98, *98*, 193, 241–244, 246–247, *247*, 257, 288–304, *302*
  nonliving thing, 110
  organism needing, 238
  in plants, 133, 135, 137
  pollution of, 493, *493*
  in power plants, 567, *567*
  as precipitation, 244
  quality of, 556–558
  role on Earth, 238, *238*
  runoff and infiltration of, 246
  in space station, 139
  states of, 239–240, 257

water cycle, 249
changes in energy drive in, 236–257
cycling matter in, 251
flow of energy in, 251
hydrologist's study of, 253–254
model of, 249–252
solar energy driving, 98
sunlight and gravity driving, 251
water level in High Plains aquifer,
556, *556*
water lily, 130, *130*
water molecule
kinetic energy of, 242
recycling of, 237, 255
in water cycle, 257
water pressure, in plants, 138
water quality data, 554, *554*
watershed, 500, *500*, 501, *501*
water supply infrastructure, 17, *17*
water vapor
in atmosphere, 98, 241, 280, 312
in cloud formation, 240, *240*, 243,
358
in fog formation, 223
as greenhouse gas, 367, *368*, 511,
511
humidity, 312
humidity measuring, 312–313, *313*
in lungs, 147
as precipitation, 244, 322, *322*
in Space Station, 139
state of water, 239, *239*
in water cycle, 240, *240*, 242, 249–
250, *249*, *250*
water wheel, 187, *187*, 193–194,
193–194
Watson, James, 411–412, *412*
watts (W), 192
weather, 312
in California, 323–326
climate and, 265–282, 544
elements of, 312–315, 331

global climate change affecting, 539
interactions causing, 310–326
ocean energy flows affecting, 303
prediction accuracy of, 340–344
predictions based on patterns,
332–344
pressure systems associated with,
316–318
sun's role in, 182, *182*
water's influence on, 238, 303
weather forecast, 178, 340–344,
340, *343*, *349*, 544
weather forecaster, 333, *333*, 341
weather forecast map, 343, *343*, 349,
349
weather forecast model, 341–343,
349, *349*
weathering, 238, *238*
weather map, 316, *316*, 318, *318*,
343, *343*
weather prediction model, 178,
340–344, *341*
westerlies, 277, *277*, 359, *359*
whale, 462
wheat, 20, *20*
whitebark pine, 483–484, *483*
white-tailed ptarmigan, 469, *469*
wildfire, 99, *99*, 270, *270*, 539
wildlife overpass, 552, *552*
wild thyme population, 542, *542*
willow tree, 436, *436*
wind
as air movement, 270
air pressure forming, 316
analyzing, 274
assisting plant reproduction, 441
as component of weather, 315, 384
Coriolis effect, 276–278, *276*, 287
creation of, 98
erosion by, 98
fire moved by, 279
formation of, 271–272

harnessing energy of, 39–40
kinetic energy transferred from, 281
modeling, 270–274
prevailing, 324
sediment moved by, 280
seed dispersal by, 444
on weather map, *318*
windbreak, 566
windmill, 191
Wind Tree, 39–40
wind turbines, 39, 565
Witch Fire, 279, *279*
wolf, 535, *535*
woolly mammoth, 524, *524*
worm, 99, 146
Wright brothers, 78, *78*
Write, 14, 360, 566

X

x-ray crystallographer, 411–412, *412*
x-ray diffraction, 411
xylem, 134

Y

Yellowstone National Park, 483, *483*,
535, *535*
Yosemite National Park, 351, *351*,
360, *369*, 539, *539*
You Solve It, 1, 85, 173, 265, 379, 485
yucca, 388, *388*

Z

zebra, 457, *457*, 469, 475, *475*
zygote, 425